Understanding Torture

Contemporary Ethical Debates

General Editor: Brenda Almond, Emeritus Professor of Moral and Social Philosophy, University of Hull

Contemporary Ethical Debates looks at the most pressing ethical concerns confronting human beings at the beginning of the twenty-first century.

Books in the series:
- Focus on important topical issues
- Are written by ethical thinkers from philosophy and other disciplines
- Are polemical in approach but fair in presenting controversial views
- Emphasise collective moral issues and matters of public policy

Published

New Terror/New Wars
Paul Gilbert

Euthanasia – Choice and Death
Gail Tulloch

Understanding Torture
J. Jeremy Wisnewski

Understanding Torture

J. Jeremy Wisnewski

Edinburgh University Press

© J. Jeremy Wisnewski, 2010

Edinburgh University Press Ltd
22 George Square, Edinburgh

www.euppublishing.com

Typeset in 10/12pt Sabon
by Servis Filmsetting Ltd, Stockport, Cheshire and
printed and bound in Great Britain by
CPI Antony Rowe, Chippenham and Eastbourne

A CIP record for this book is available
from the British Library

ISBN 978 0 7486 3537 5 (hardback)
ISBN 978 9 7486 3538 2 (paperback)

The right of J. Jeremy Wisnewski
to be identified as author of this work
has been asserted in accordance with
the Copyright, Designs and Patents Act 1988.

Contents

Series Preface

Changing views of what should engage the attention of social philosophers and students of ethics make this an appropriate time for a book series which aims to make a reasoned contribution to debate about ethical decision-making in many areas of practical policy where the moral map seems unclear and opinion is frequently divided.

To some extent, this is always to be expected, but the start of the third millennium was greeted in the Western world with particular hope and optimism. It was a world eager to put behind it the twentieth century, the first half of which had seen two world wars, the second a period in which the two ideologies of communism and free democracy had remained precariously poised on the brink of mutually assured destruction. The apparent removal of that threat produced a millennial mood of new hope for the future that was reflected in public celebration and a widespread welcome for change; the new, the novel, the innovatory, the modern and the modernising, were key words reflecting these aspirations. And indeed the world *did* change, although it took another year or two to reveal that this was not to be in the benevolent way people had hoped. The events in New York of September 11th 2001 and subsequent developments elsewhere in the world produced a seismic shift in the way the world would be viewed, reversing the complacency that had followed the ending of the cold war. A new religious divide was opening up between a secularised West with its origins in Judaeo-Christian values and an observant Islam; at the same time, religious divisions attached compulsory labels even to the religiously uncommitted.

One consequence of all this is that it has become clear how far Western values, public and private, shifted in the second half of the twentieth century. Even the first half of that century would not have produced such contrasts in values, expectations and behaviour amongst the main cultural divisions of the world. Dress, customs, marriage traditions, women's role, entertainment – in all these areas, a certain commonality would have prevailed, capable of oiling the wheels of cultural contact and exchange. Currently, though, a widening gulf is to be found in views about what is decent or permissible in the private sphere; and this difference in viewpoint expresses itself publicly in the media, in sexual behaviour, in family policy. At the same time, on the broader stage of states, nations and communities, other differences emerge. Old assumptions about the nature, conditions and justifications of war no longer fit the contemporary world while, for some, terrorism has become the weapon of choice. And, as concepts of ethnic and national identity have become less defined, individuals and groups in a globalised world have voluntarily uprooted themselves, ignoring traditional territorial boundaries and jurisdictions, and facing the residents of coveted destinations in wealthier parts of the world with contentious questions concerning refugees, immigration and control of borders.

In another sphere again, the world of scientific research and the pursuit of knowledge, Western science – now a world science – has produced advances on many fronts. One of these is in the technology of war and weaponry; another, discoveries in biomedical areas, especially genetics. The first of these generates new fears and a sense of individual helplessness in the face of threats; the second, new ethical questions concerning the margins of life – questions about how to deal with the extending human life-span, and how to regulate the possibilities that have arisen for controlling new human life at the embryonic stage. Science and technology have also dramatically changed methods of communication and expanded the scope of media influence, and are certain to go on doing so.

Again, while wars rage between peoples, there are those who predict that a war-front of a different kind will open up between humans and other forms of life, perhaps even at the bacterial level. The brief period of human dominance of the planet may be coming to an end, aided and precipitated by our careless treatment of the natural environment. On the one hand, then, some would paint a Malthusian picture of the new era, ending in planetary destruction, possibly precipitated by a self-destructive Armageddon. On the other hand, however, there remains the inestimable gift of human reason which, if supported by longstanding values that still command widespread respect, may yet lead us out of the current darkness into a second Enlightenment. The questions remain, however, uneasily unanswerable. Will we use scientific and medical advance for good? Will we be able to take a thoughtful and restrained approach to the world environment? Will we choose to embrace the best rather than the worst aspects of the world's religious heritages? Will we be able to retain and indeed reassert the ethical values, public and private, with which these are linked: the private values of love, trust, faithfulness, duty, modesty, unselfishness, respect for one another; the public values of non-licentious freedom, regard for the rights of the human individual, and the pursuit of the common good?

A thin strand of optimism suggests that open thought and honest reflection may at least contribute towards finding the right answers to these questions. It is this thin strand of optimism that provides a background and a justification for a series of books such as this, which address the ethical dimensions of some key controversies of our time. In this careful and broad-ranging discussion of one of the most contentious of these controversies, the use of torture, J. Jeremy Wisnewski forces the reader to confront the paradox that, while the right not to be tortured stands as an unconditional and unqualified right, yet there is no chapter of human history, including our own, that has been without it.

Brenda Almond
February, 2010

For all those lives undone

Acknowledgments

This book has benefited from the feedback and criticism of a great many people, and several institutions that provided me with an opportunity to voice some of the arguments here in a public setting. I am also grateful for permission to use some previously published material in this book.

The following people offered valuable feedback in various ways – some by reading the manuscript in its entirety, some by reading parts of it, and some through conversation concerning some of the ideas in it. I list them alphabetically: Fritz Allhoff, Brenda Almond, Janet Donohoe, Ralph Ellis, Dillon Emerick, Maurice Hamington, Gordon Hull, Bill Irwin, Joe Jones, Lani Roberts, Pete Res, Bob Stolorow, George Teschner, Jackie Seamon, and Peter Wallace. Thanks also go to Meg Lonergan and Dom Thomas for help with research and bibliographic matters. Finally, I would like to thank the staff at Edinburgh University Press, and in particular Carol MacDonald, for their assistance as I wrote this book.

I have used material in Chapter 5 that first appeared as "Hearing the Still-Ticking-Bomb: A Reply," in the *Journal of Applied Philosophy*, 2009, Volume 26, Number 2. I am grateful for permission to use this material. I have also drawn selectively on three book reviews published over the past two years. These reviews appeared in *Philosophy in Review* (April 2009, Volume 29, Number 2) and in *Metapsychology: Online Reviews*, October 9, 2007, Volume 11, No. 41, and in February 5, 2008, Volume 12, Issue 6. My thanks go to the publishers for allowing me to draw from this material.

A shorter version of Chapter 8 was presented as part of the *Ideas Matter* series at Oregon State University in February, 2009 under the title "Human Rights and Linguistic Subterfuge in the Bush League". I am grateful to members of the Philosophy Department there for the invitation. I am also grateful to the participants of the 16th-Annual Conference for the *Society for Philosophy in the Contemporary World*, which was held in July, 2009, at the Pine Lake Environmental Campus of Hartwick College in upstate New York. I was graciously allowed to present some of the ideas in this book under the title "Racism and Sexism as Weapons in the Defense of Torture: A Cautionary Note." I received feedback that was critical to correcting a number of mistakes I had made in thinking through the limitations of argument.

I would also like to thank other audiences who helped me to clarify a number of issues. While the material I presented to these audiences has not been used in this book, the conversation and criticism was crucial to my sorting out some of the complexities of torture. I would thus like to thank the Department of Philosophy at the University of Colorado, Denver, the faculty at Hartwick College, and the Athens Research Institute.

Last but not least, I want to extend my gratitude to Dorothy, my wife, as well as to my children, Audrey and Lucian, for providing an emotionally supportive environment where it is safe to think through the darker aspects of our world.

Chapter 1

The Persistence of Torture: An Affliction That Won't Go Away

Introduction

One morning, as I was finishing this book, the following story broke:

> PUERTO LAS OLLAS, Mexico – The Mexican army has carried out forced disappearances, acts of torture and illegal raids in pursuit of drug traffickers, according to documents and interviews with victims, their families, political leaders and human rights monitors.[1]

The day before, a similar story had been released about another corner of the world:

> (New York) – The Iranian authorities are using prolonged harsh interrogations, beatings, sleep deprivation, and threats of torture to extract false confessions from detainees arrested since the disputed June 12 presidential election, Human Rights Watch said today. The confessions appear designed to support unsubstantiated allegations by senior government officials that Iran's post-election protests, in which at least 20 people were killed, were supported by foreign powers and aimed at overthrowing the government.[2]

These stories broke in the wake of decisive evidence that the US had engaged in torture. The US President had even admitted as much (though he had not called the techniques 'torture'). Former President Bush told reporters: "I told the country we did that [water-boarding]. And I told them it was legal. We had legal opinions that enabled us to do that . . . I didn't have any problems at all trying to find out what Khalid Sheikh Mohammed knew."[3] Even after George W. Bush left office for the greener pastures of Texas, his former Vice President continued to defend techniques that constitute torture. As Cheney told reporters, "I think those programs were absolutely essential to the success we enjoyed of being able to collect the intelligence that let us defeat all further attempts to launch attacks against the United States since 9/11. I think that's a great success story."[4]

So, the news from Iran and from Mexico came as no surprise – but I wish it had.

I wish that these stories were the only news stories that dealt with torture as I finished my manuscript. They were not: there were reports of torture victims testifying against the former chief of the Khmer Rouge's Tuol Sleng torture facility;[5] reports dealing with attempts on the part of the US government to destroy evidence relating to torture;[6] reports of the long-term effects of torture on persons detained at Guantanamo Bay,[7] and the list goes on.

We have grown up in a world that tortures. It is the same world that our parents, grandparents, great grandparents, and the generations before them grew up in. While I have been mercifully removed from this torture, it has nevertheless at times gone on under my nose, and in my name. In 2004, the torture of persons at Abu Ghraib was made public. It seemed that many were surprised that such a thing could happen under the watch of the United States – but they should *not* have been surprised. After all, the CIA had been experimenting extensively with torture since its inception, most notoriously and famously in the MKUltra program – a program that involved soldiers and civilians alike, along with extensive sensory deprivation, electro-shock, forced drug use, and more. These techniques were codified in a manual (the KUBARK manual, presumably named after a codename for the CIA), and this manual was then used to train interrogators in various parts of the world.[8]

But the US was not alone in its abuses – far from it. Elsewhere in the world, regimes were torturing with impunity, and some nations had been doing so for decades (just like the US): the countries of the former Soviet Union, the UK, China, Germany, Iran, Greece, Brazil, Argentina, Iraq, France, Israel, Egypt, Cambodia, Canada, Syria, Mexico, Lebanon, and more besides. Again, the list goes on. As I write, people are also seeking redress from their torturers:

A man who claims his torture was effectively arranged by British intelligence officers and police is planning legal action aimed at forcing the home secretary, Alan Johnson, to agree to an independent inquiry into his mistreatment.

Rangzieb Ahmed had three fingernails ripped out after he was allowed to travel to Pakistan while under surveillance, and after MI5 and Manchester detectives drew up a list of questions for a Pakistani intelligence agency that had detained him at the suggestion of MI6.

Lawyers for Ahmed and a second British man, Salahuddin Amin, who also says he was tortured after being detained by the same Pakistani agency at the request of the British authorities, have written to Johnson asking he "establish a public inquiry to investigate the complicity of government employees in the illegal detention and torture" of both men, and several others. If Johnson refuses, Ahmed's lawyers are expected to seek a judicial review.[9]

A slow murmur has been building in various parts of the world, demanding that those who have permitted torture be brought to justice. This murmur is audible in the midst of continuing evidence that leaders of the UK and the USA had extensive knowledge of the torturous techniques being employed – that they had, in fact, ordered the use of these techniques.[10]

These reports are against a background that has become horribly familiar. We are a world of torment, populated by the only animal that tortures. Meet yourself, *homo torquere, homo tormentum.*

Confessions of an anti-torture absolutist

The news I read is undeserving of its name – there is nothing new about it. It is nonetheless distressing. As someone unconditionally opposed to torture, no matter the circumstances, the sheer *persistence* of torture baffles and troubles me. Each day brings more word of how unlikely we are ever to eliminate torture. As an 'absolutist,' to use a standard term employed in the torture literature, I find the very *fact* of torture an ominous question mark above humanity.

I confess my position at the outset from a sense of professional responsibility – every reader deserves to know the rough terrain of the world she is about to enter. My charge in this work is to demonstrate that there is good reason to be an anti-torture absolutist – that, once we understand in gruesome detail what torture is and what it does, once we have assessed those arguments for and against it, we will be prepared to fight against it.

I use the term 'we' cautiously. I do not presume to speak for everyone, or to think such a thing even possible. But I do possess the same vulnerability that we all possess – a vulnerability that, as Judith Butler argues, unites us in at least a minimal way.[11] In our vulnerability – one which is physical, emotional, psychological, and political – torture is of interest to everyone. We are both those who torture and those who can fall prey to it. This simple fact unites us, and the *fact* and *persistence* of torture demands our attention. It is something done by us and against us, sometimes in our names, and sometimes as a means of destroying our ability to *be* named – our ability to be agents in the world.

My aim in writing this book is to understand torture – why it is done, who does it, and how it leaves its mark on the world. I want to understand torture because I am *homo torquere, homo tormentum* – the animal that tortures and is tortured.

Some perplexities of torture

There has never been a time when the world was without torture. It has emerged in many ways, and has been supported in many institutional venues, but it has never been far from civilization – waiting within it, plain to all, or on its outskirts, hidden but no less operative. Our changing relations to torture are one of the most interesting features of its history. We have at once thought torture absolutely necessary to secure a just trial, and thought it utterly incompatible with any kind of justice. We have both abhorred it and demanded it. Surprisingly, the two attitudes are often much closer to one another in time than any account of the humanistic view of the moral progression of civilization would like to admit.

Unfortunately, torture doesn't seem to be going anywhere. This painful and lamentable fact – that torture is both in our past and on our horizon – demands our scrutiny. As with so many inquiries, the place to begin a discussion of torture is in its definition. Such a beginning, after all, often serves to set the domain of discourse – to insure that we know what it is that we are talking about. But part of the problem, as we will see, is that we really often *don't* know what we're talking about. The term 'torture' is as debatable as its practice.

Of course, standard definitions exist. The definition found in the 1984 United Nations Convention against Torture is considered customary.

UN Convention against Torture
The term "torture" means any act by which severe pain or suffering, whether physical or mental, is intentionally inflicted on a person for such purposes as obtaining from him or a third person information or a confession, punishing him for an act he or a third person has committed or is suspected of having committed, or intimidating or coercing him or a third person, or for any reason based on discrimination of any kind, when such pain or suffering is inflicted by or at the instigation of or with the consent or acquiescence of a public official or other person acting in an official capacity. It does not include pain or suffering arising only from, inherent in or incidental to lawful sanctions.

There are many more besides this one, and these are often in response to particular problems associated with this definition. International humanitarian law, for example, does not require that a person engaging in torture act in an official capacity of a state. The International Committee of the Red Cross, similarly, offers a much broader definition of torture and related terms:

Torture: existence of a specific purpose plus intentional infliction of severe suffering or pain;
Cruel or inhuman treatment: no specific purpose, significant level of suffering or pain inflicted;
Outrages upon personal dignity: no specific purpose, significant level of humiliation or degradation.[12]

The World Medical Association defined torture as follows in its 1975 Tokyo Declaration (revised in 2006):

> For the purpose of this Declaration, torture is defined as the deliberate, systematic or wanton infliction of physical or mental suffering by one or more persons acting alone or on the orders of any authority, to force another person to yield information, to make a confession, or for any other reason.[13]

Some definitions of torture duplicate the UN definition in domestic statutes. This allows torture to be prosecuted under domestic laws within a country rather than through recourse to international statutes, many of which are not recognized by individual countries as binding. The United States Code, Title 18, 2340, defines torture as follows:

> [Torture is an] act committed by a person acting under the color of law specifically intended to inflict severe physical or mental pain or suffering (other than pain or suffering incidental to lawful sanctions) upon another person within his custody or physical control.

There is no dearth of definitions, some more permissive than others. The limitations of these definitions are understandable. Each definition aims to address particular issues. It is thus no surprise to find the UN definition confining 'torture' to those acting on the authority of the state. The treaty is meant to cover *nations*, not merely individuals. It would thus make little legal sense to have a definition that covered, for example, the Marquis de Sade. The treaty would have no bearing on his particular actions, regardless of whether or not these were torture. Likewise, the World Medical Association is concerned with what kinds of medical assistance might either count as torture or count as making a medical doctor complicit in torture. In this respect, it matters little whether or not such actions are carried out by an official of the state.

From the philosopher's and the historian's points of view, however, all of these definitions are inadequate to the phenomenon. For the historian, as we will see, torture has functioned in too many divergent ways, and in too many wildly different contexts, for any of these definitions to capture its overwhelming range of application. For the philosopher, on the other hand, the account that covers all cases (and only cases) of what is to be analyzed is traditionally the gold standard of explanation. A failure to achieve this kind of account, for many philosophers, is simply the failure to provide any worthwhile account at all.

To see why a philosopher might not approve of the above definitions, one need only consider some thought experiments that would meet the definitions provided above, but which would not count as torture to anyone familiar with the term. Such thought experiments are easy enough to produce for anyone trained in the discipline. Consider first the broader definitions offered above. These definitions require only that a person is intentionally inflicting pain (physical or psychological) on another person against that person's will. This can be to acquire information, to dehumanize the person, or "for any other reason." One need only consider the boxer or the bully to see why this definition is inadequate: a boxer willfully inflicts pain on his opponent in an attempt to get the opponent to *lose the boxing match*.[14] The bully inflicts psychological and physical pain on those he bullies on the playground in order to dominate them, or to express his importance, or for fun, or for whatever other reason. While these activities might have certain similarities to torturous practices, they are certainly a far cry from water-boarding and the rack.

It is only slightly more difficult to produce counter-examples to the stricter definitions offered above (as in the UN Convention). These definitions require only one additional feature – namely, that the person engaged in torture is acting in an official capacity as an agent of the state. To construct a counter example here only involves imagining some agent of the state (a police officer, a prison guard, a soldier in the military, a schoolteacher, a fireman) engaging in intentional violence that is not part of 'lawful sanctions' (this clause serves to eliminate imprisonment and the death penalty from inclusion in countries where such things are lawfully employed).[15]

To see the ease with which a counter-example can be constructed, consider a case involving a school teacher in a district where corporal punishment has only recently been made illegal. This teacher has been teaching for 30 years, and has, in the past, routinely employed paddling as a means of disciplining the unruly children in her class. A child (who has been paddled before for unruly behavior) continues to bully other children. In consequence, the teacher decides to paddle the child again, despite the current illegality of such an action.

In this case, we have all of those things required to call this event 'torture' under the above definition, despite the fact that it looks very little like the cases of torture with which we are familiar. The teacher is acting in an official capacity as an agent of the state (it is a public school, and the teacher is carrying out a regular duty – namely, discipline). The teacher is intentionally inflicting physical pain for the purpose of altering the behavior of the child (or perhaps punishing the child – the actual explanation is immaterial). The action taking place is not part of the "pain or suffering arising only from, inherent in or incidental to lawful sanctions" (corporal punishment is no longer legal).

It might well be the case that the teacher is wrong to use corporal punishment against the child. This, however, hardly makes the action torture. Does it matter that the action in question used to be legal? Certainly not. As we will see, torture used to be an essential part of court proceedings in capital cases, and this alone hardly makes it excusable. We thus have a counter-example to the definition offered by the UN cited above: the definition would demand that we call this action torture, although it clearly is not an instance of torture. For the philosopher of a traditional ilk, then, these definitions of torture are entirely inadequate.[16]

The historian's love of particularity, and a reluctance to engage in reductive analyses of complex, changing phenomena, however, offers an important lesson to the philosopher (admittedly somewhat of a caricature here). The complexity and diversity of torture does not mean that torture cannot be adequately analyzed. It means, rather, that our analysis must be careful to respect the historical record, not allowing ourselves to be sucked in by the desire for a *single* account of the thing under investigation. Following Wittgenstein, we should regard such concepts as displaying a family resemblance: the practice of torture is as diverse as the types of games there are.[17] There are similarities across the diversity, but no single, unifying account will be able to capture all of this diversity under a single definition.[18]

The following taxonomy of types of torture, based largely on Henry Shue's seminal article "Torture," is a useful place to begin appreciating the complexity that characterizes torture.[19]

Kinds of torture

- Judicial: this form of torture exists as part of judicial proceedings. It is used to obtain evidence that will allow a court to convict. This kind of torture was prevalent until the seventeenth century, at which time its existence began to wane (this is discussed in detail in the following chapter).
- Punitive: this is torture inflicted as punishment. An astonishing example of this is found in Foucault's *Discipline and Punish*, where a man convicted of regicide is drawn and quartered (described in more detail in Chapter 2).
- Interrogational: this is torture aimed at acquiring information, such as that which might be useful to law enforcement. When members of the US military defend torture, it is almost always this *kind* of torture that is under discussion: torture aimed at information, *not at* evidence for criminal proceedings.
- Dehumanizing: this is torture aimed primarily at 'breaking' a subject. The aim of such torture is "to bring about a change in the victim's self-conception" (351).[20] As we will see, in some respects *all* modern torture aims at this (see Chapter 4).
- Terroristic/Deterrent: this is torture which aims to deter future incidents of certain sorts (for example, future military operations, insurgencies, etc). This type of torture obviously can and does overlap with some of the other categories. One aim of punitive torture, after all, might well be to deter future crimes. Likewise, engaging in torture as a means of de-humanizing

a person might well have a deterrent effect. Christopher Tindale usefully characterizes this form of torture as follows: "Its aim is to discourage or encourage certain activities on the part of the victim or other people, or perhaps both. Unlike interrogational torture, the victims of deterrent torture may be chosen at random" (351).

- Sadistic: this is torture undertaken for the sheer joy of it, as seen in some of the fictional work of the Marquis de Sade.

This preliminary account of the range of types of torture serves to better illustrate the difficulty of any single definition. In certain respects, the only way to come to grips with what torture *is* involves diving into its history, the psychology behind its use, the effects it has on its victims, the arguments employed for and against it, and the way it has functioned in the operations of governments.

Many analyses begin with a definition of the thing to be analyzed. As I suggested above, this is not possible in our case: torture is too diverse, too multifaceted for any easy definition to capture its range and barbarity. So, unlike other accounts, my aim will be to articulate and analyze the aspects of torture adumbrated above. It is only through such an approach, I contend, that we will be in a position to know what we're talking about. In this respect, this book, in its entirety, is *itself* a definition of torture, though one that embraces the particularity and complexity rightfully sought by historians. It is at the end of this analysis that one will be able, not to define torture in some universal definition, but to participate in a meaningful conversation about it.

Physical and psychological torture

In the wide-ranging literature on torture, a distinction is often made between psychological torture, on the one hand, and physical torture, on the other. This distinction is meant to cut across the kinds of torture specified above. In other words, one can engage in terroristic torture or interrogational torture either physically or psychologically. This distinction is employed in various ways in the literature on torture, but it usually comes to this: physical torture involves the use of violence against the body of the most overt kind; psychological torture involves the manipulation of an agent's inner world, usually by manipulating the body in various ways.

Not surprisingly, the distinction between physical and psychological torture comes in many guises. Some utilize the distinction between torture and so-called 'torture lite' to mark this distinction, while others deny that this distinction is equivalent.[21] Some deny that psychological torture even *counts* as torture. The most notable example of this position is to be found in the Bush administration's continued insistence that they used 'enhanced interrogation techniques' rather than any kind of torture, despite the fact that these techniques have for many years been counted as torture, even by the United States. This position has also been advocated in the legal and philosophical literature. Seumas Miller, for example, claims that "non-physical mental torture is not really torture as such."[22]

The claim that there is no such thing as 'psychological torture' can be read in two ways, one very dangerous, the other not. The sense in which it is *true* that there is no such thing as psychological torture is rather straightforward: *all* torture leaves its mark on the body, and it almost all involves a manipulation of the body, even if only indirectly. Standard forms of psychological torture, such as the use of stress positions (forcing a person to stand in a position for several hours, often repeatedly) involves the direct manipulation of the body to sap the resistance of the person being subjected to it. The same is true of sleep deprivation. But even those methods that do not use the body in any direct way (such as the threat of execution, the use of threats against one's family, or simulated torture of one's family) leave their mark on the victim – marks that are *measurable*, even if difficult to quantify. The stress induced by torture of any sort can be detected in the brain of the victim, through altered EEGs, for example.[23]

But the distinction between psychological torture and physical torture is sometimes criticized for far more pernicious purposes. In the Bush administration's denial that psychological torture *even counts* as torture, the aim was clearly to justify its own use of torture, despite the fact that every major international statute counts psychological torture as a real category. This kind of semantic legerdemain risks obscuring all that is objectionable about torture, as well as the reality that so-called 'psychological torture' can be *worse* than so-called 'physical torture' (though it certainly isn't always worse). Accepting the distinction thus may well come at a cost. It might, for example, lead to the systematic underestimation of what is wrong with particular kinds of torture; it may also make it easier for practitioners to engage in torture by providing what some may regard as excusing conditions. As Jessica Wolfendale has remarked, distinctions such as this make it even easier to engage in self-deception about what one is *in fact* doing: "favorable comparison enables torturers (and states that use torture) to believe that they, at least, are not as brutal and cruel as others, and that their motivation for using torture is different from, and morally preferable to, the motivations of other torturers" (54).[24] This same view has led some clinicians to reject the distinction as irrelevant.

> From the perspective of a clinical psychologist, the physical and psychological damage to human beings resulting from torture is often so devastating, with

such a profound impact, that it cannot be viewed as an acceptable practice in any scenario. Recovery from the serious trauma resulting from torture can be a long and arduous path, fraught with life-long vulnerabilities. (121)[25]

What, then, is the basis of the distinction? It appears that so-called 'psychological methods' emerged, at least in part, because of the need to hide what was taking place from the public at large.[26] The birth of 'no-touch torture' nevertheless involved, and continues to involve, brutality of the most ignoble sort: the victim of torture is subjected to a technique "designed to persist long after the moment of its application" (14).[27] Rather than being inflicted on the body, torture comes to be directed first and foremost at the *agency* of its victim.[28] This is evidenced in the interrogation manuals of the twentieth century.[29]

There are, in fact, different kinds of methods of torture that match up with the distinction between 'psychological' and 'physical.'

> The paradigm of psychological torture follows a different paradigm, namely the disruption of behavior that would allow an appropriate response of the individual to the organismic need states and to stimuli from the environment. Psychological torture thus prevents the maintenance of balance, or homeostasis. (166)[30]

The mapping of effects to paradigms, however, is sloppy at best. In most cases of torture, these techniques tend to be combined. Beatings are mixed with sleep deprivation; waterboarding is carried out alongside threats to one's family. Moreover, physical torture often leaves psychological scars that are as intense as those left by the application of psychological torture. The use of methods as the crucial distinguishing feature of these kinds of torture, then, tends to obscure some of the relevant similarities in the *effects* these methods have, as well as in the brutality of both methods. An alternative strategy for distinguishing psychological and physical torture involves thinking about what kinds of *effects* torture has rather than what methods are employed. As Hernan Reyes argues,

> The term 'psychological torture' can relate to two different aspects of the same entity. On the one hand, it can designate *methods* – that is in this case the use of non-physical methods. While 'physical methods' of torture can be more or less self-evident, such as thumbscrews, flogging, application of electric current to the body and similar techniques, 'non-physical' means a method that does not hurt, maim, or even touch the body, but touches the mind instead. Just as readily recognizable as methods of torture in this category are prolonged sleep deprivation, total sensory deprivation, or having to witness the torture of family members, to cite only three examples. On the other hand, the term 'psychological torture' can also be taken to designate the psychological *effects* (as

opposed to physical ones) of torture in general – torture 'in general' meaning the use of either physical of psychological methods, or both. (594–595)[31]

When we conceptualize psychological torture in this way – as concerned with the *kinds* of *effects* techniques can have, the distinction between physical and psychological torture becomes a rather different one – but still one with its own sets of problems. As we will see, much torture results in physical affliction (such as chronic pain) for which there is no obvious physical cause.[32] In this respect, the distinction between physical and psychological effects can be a rather artificial one.

Distinctions are always the products of particular interests. In many instances, distinguishing one thing from another can yield fruitful results. In others, such distinctions only serve to obfuscate the issues at hand. Uwe Jacobs argues that "the notion of psychological torture is itself artificial, and . . . it is of interest mainly to those who hope to conceal and deny the practice of torture" (163). In the case of torture, the distinction between psychological torture and physical torture often does more harm then good. We should take this distinction with a grain of proverbial salt. As one way of picking out a range of methods for torture, it seems to me, there is nothing particularly objectionable about it. I thus part company with the rather categorical rejection of the distinction offered by Jacobs – but I embrace the warning he offers us. We may distinguish these kinds of torture in particular contexts if it is of heuristic value, provided that we always keep in mind precisely how dangerous any hard and fast distinction can be.

In this book, then, there will be the occasional reference to 'psychological torture.' This is to be understood as a reference to a set of methods largely developed in the twentieth century. In my view, as we will see, these methods are not any more moral than physical torture. In fact, both kinds of torture produce certain kinds of psychological effects (construed very loosely) that constitute the essential barbarity of torture.

Throughout the book, we will also have to keep in mind what we might call 'the problem of degree.' The 'psychological' tortures are not as obvious as the 'physical' ones, nor are they as immediate. Psychological techniques include sleep deprivation, environmental manipulation, threats of abuse and execution, the systematic manipulation of phobias, sexual humiliation, forced nudity, and so on. Many also include forced standing in stress positions as among the psychological tortures. The effects of such techniques are not nearly so immediate as being beaten, having one's fingernails removed with pliers, being water-boarded, or being electrocuted. This raises the perplexing issue of *how much* of a given technique is required for, say, forced standing in a stress position to count as torture. Two hours? Twenty hours?[33]

There is no obvious answer to this question; nor, I think, is there a universal one. What matters in identifying torture, it seems to me, is not a specific amount of time during which abuse occurs. What matters is the intention of the practice itself, and the effects on the agent. In this respect, some more recent definitions of torture come closer to capturing the nature of torture. In 2005, for example, Physicians for Human Rights defined torture in terms of the use or threat of "procedures calculated to disrupt profoundly the senses and personality."[34]

Rather than getting bogged down in the problem of degree – trying to pinpoint the precise amount of time required to make something torture – we would do well to focus on the intent of torture, as well as on the subjective responses to this intent. By doing this, we can keep the notion of torture within our reach without being distracted by what amount to academic questions. Rather than asking "how long can we make someone stand in a painful position without it being torture?", we can ask "what is this procedure *aimed at?* What is the effect on the person being subjected to it?"[35]

A roadmap to the book

The previous sections have aimed to present an understanding of what torture is *as a problem* – and show that it is one that needs to be addressed. My aim in this book is to address *homo torquere, homo tormentum* for what it is – the animal that twists, turns, and torments its fellow travelers. To accomplish this, we'll cover a good deal of terrain in a few pages. Given this, a few guidelines should be given on how to approach this book.

Each chapter takes up a particular aspect of torture: Chapter 2 gives a condensed history of torture, while Chapter 3 focuses on what is uniquely wrong about torture. Chapter 4 provides an account of the effects of torture. Chapters 5 and 6 concentrate on the arguments for and against the use of torture in exceptional circumstances, whether as a policy or as a one-time event. Chapter 7 offers an account of the psychology of the torturer. Chapter 8 examines the use of torture under President Bush, and Chapter 9 explores some reasons for pessimism regarding the prospects of ending torture.

The chapters have been cross-referenced. Thus, references to other sections of the book that discuss a given topic are given within chapters also dealing with that topic. In this respect, one can read the book in varying orders. It is my hope, however, that most readers will read the book in the order it is presented. The reason to have such a hope is straightforward: I believe that it is only by correcting the chronic misperception of torture that we can fully address the moral issues surrounding it. We need to understand what it is, what it does, and why it's wrong. Chapters 2 through 4 aim to correct that.

One cannot appreciate the complexities of torture without knowing some of its history. Some of this difficulty and perplexity can be seen in our discussion of the distinction between physical and psychological methods and effects of torture. In what follows, however, we must face more complexity rather than less of it. Obviously, it is impossible to do justice to this vast and complex history in a short chapter of a book; my aim in Chapter 2 is not to provide any sort of definitive account. Rather, in sketching a brief account, I have had to take a stand on some controversial issues. I have also advocated some positions over others. My aim is not to settle these debates; it is rather to sketch some of the dimensions of the complexities we face, with the understanding that this is *only* a sketch, and that understanding the history of torture – even in a rudimentary way – has significant benefits for understanding this recurrent feature of our world.

Notes

1. "Mexico Accused of Torture in Drug War: Army Using Brutality To Fight Trafficking, Rights Groups Say," July 9, 2009, *Washington Post*. Complete bibliographic information is available in the Selected Bibliography for all of the material cited in this book.
2. "Iran: Detainees Describe Beatings, Pressure to Confess," July 8, 2009, Human Rights Watch.
3. Helen Thomas, "Bush Admits he Approved Torture," *Seattle Post, Intelligences*. This was widely reported.
4. "Interview with Dick Cheney," *State of the Union with John King*, CNN, March 15, 2009.
5. "Cambodia's torture prison survivors testify at tribunal," July 3, 2009, ABC Radio Australia.
6. "Alleged Torture Photos Slated for Destruction" *The Washington Independent*, July 7, 2009.
7. "The Lingering Effects of Torture: After Guantanamo, Scientists and Advocates Study Detainees," July 3, 2009, ABC News.
8. See Alfred W. McCoy, *A Question of Torture*.
9. One example of this is from this morning's news, though there are many that could be employed. "Pakistan torture victims plan legal action to force inquiry," July 8, 2009, *The Guardian*. For the evidence against the Bush administration, see Mayer, *The Dark Side*, and Sands, *Torture Team*, for starters.
10. "Tony Blair knew of secret policy on terror interrogations," June 18, 2009, *The Guardian*; meanwhile, the Attorney General of the US is contemplating (as of this writing) appointing a special prosecutor to investigate torture under the Bush administration: "Attorney general leaning toward torture inquiry," July 16, 2006, *The Baltimore Sun*.
11. See Judith Butler, *Precarious Life*.

12. http://www.icrc.org/Web/Eng/siteengo.nsf/html/69MJXC
13. http://www.wma.net/e/policy/c18.htm
14. Of course, the boxer's opponent has presumably consented to enter the match. This question is actually more difficult than it initially appears: many of those who enter into sports such as boxing do so out of the sense that there are no other viable ways to become successful, given their poverty. So, while they do consent in some sense of that term, the consent cannot be regarded as complete. If it *is* complete, we run the risk of a parallel argument: soldiers who willingly enter the military are *consenting* to torture, as they *know* that torture can result if they are captured (much like the boxer knows that he will be hit if he is not fast enough to avoid his opponent's punches).

    The parallel might not be strong enough to make the argument work; the boxing case and the torture case certainly are different in many respects. My point here is just that determining what counts as 'consent,' and when it is relevant, is an incredibly tricky question. My thanks to Gordon Hull for pushing me on this point.
15. In this respect, the proviso is unacceptably question-begging. We should be open to the possibility that some of our sanctions – like solitary confinement – are in fact torture. Claudia Card makes this point in "Ticking Bombs and Interrogations."
16. There is another substantial problem with any definition that requires a torturer be an agent of the state – namely, such a definition automatically excludes certain cases of rape and domestic violence that seem to have all the characteristics of torture. To exclude these cases automatically is to beg the question about the nature of torture. Trusting our intuitions that domestic violence and rape (or, more carefully, certain instances of them) are not torture, moreover, might well represent a subtle form of sexism in the torture literature. I will not take up this issue in the current context, but it is an issue of considerable interest. To what extent are our presuppositions about gender played out in our analysis of torture, and what does this reveal about our thinking about political violence, on the one hand, and gender, on the other? For some interesting analyses of some of these issues, see Copelon, "Intimate Terror" in *The Phenomenon of Torture*, Cherie Booth "Sexual Violence, Torture, and International Justice," in *Torture: Does It Make Us Safer? Is It Ever OK?*, Lisa M. Kois, "Dance, Sister, Dance!" in *An End to Torture: Strategies for Its Eradication*, Claudia Card, "Torture in Ordinary Circumstances," in *Moral Psychology: Feminist Ethics and Social Theory*. For book length treatments, see, for example, *One of the Boys*, edited by Tara McKelvey, Susan Brownmiller, *Against our Will*, Laura J. Shephard, *Gender, Violence & Security*, and Judith Butler, *Frames of War*. Complete bibliographic information for all sources can be found in the bibliography.
17. See Ludwig Wittgenstein, *Philosophical Investigations*.
18. R.D. Emerick and I make a similar point in *The Ethics of Torture*, Continuum, 2009. The indebtedness to Wittgenstein should be clear.

19. This taxonomy is adopted from *The Ethics of Torture*, pp. 6–7. In distinguishing types of torture here, I am not offering necessary and sufficient conditions for particular types of torture. My aim here is only to distinguish each category from the others in a provisional way. It is thus no objection to my view that there are things that are not torture which might also be 'interrogational' or 'dehumanizing.'
20. Tindale, Christopher W. "The Logic of Torture: A Critical Examination."
21. See, for example, David Sussman, "'Torture Lite': A Response."
22. Seumas Miller, "Is Torture Ever Morally Justifiable?" See also Davis, "The Moral Justifiability of Torture and other Cruel, Inhuman, or Degrading Treatment."
23. Chapter 3 will explore this in some detail. See, in particular, the section 'Torture's effects on the body'.
24. Jessica Wolfendale, "The Myth of 'Torture Lite'."
25. Fabri, "Treating Torture Victims," in *Torture*.
26. See Alfred McCoy, *A Question of Torture*.
27. Rejali, *Torture and Modernity: Self, Society, and State in Modern Iran*.
28. We will consider this in much more detail below, as well as in Chapters 2 and 3.
29. We will have occasion to discuss these manuals in detail below. See, in particular, Chapter 3.
30. Uwe Jacobs, "Documenting the Neurobiology of Psychological Torture: Conceptual and Nueropsychological Observations." in *The Trauma of Psychological Torture*.
31. "The worst scars are in the mind: psychological torture" *International Review of the Red Cross*, Volume 89 Number 867, September 2007.
32. See Chapter 4.
33. On one of the many Bush administration memos on torture, Rumsfeld scrawled sarcastically that he stood eight hours a day, so he didn't see why standing was limited to only four hours.
34. *Break Them Down*, Report by Physicians for Human Rights, Washington, D.C., 2005, cited in Reyes, p. 595.
35. I will return to these issues in Chapter 4.

Chapter 2

The History of Torture: A Sketch

Introduction

My aim in this chapter is to begin to explore the complexities and nuances of torture as a historical phenomenon. Because torture has always been with humanity, the history of torture is as long as our own. Thus, my account will be incomplete, as perhaps any historical account must be; this is a sketch of some of the broad features of torture as they have presented themselves in various historical venues. There will be significant instantiations of torture that I do not discuss, or which I discuss only very briefly. My aim, then, is certainly not to be exhaustive – it is, rather, simply to be *informative*. By better understanding the history of torture, I maintain, we'll be better equipped to deal with its serious moral and political implications.

The beginnings of torture: ancient and medieval law

In ancient Greece, the citizens of Athens were regarded, by default, as a people with a love and capacity for truth-telling. When they had to testify before a court, the fact that they were citizens was regarded as a sufficient reason to take seriously what they said. Slaves and foreigners, however, did not have it so easy. The xenophobic law courts didn't have an immediate trust of non-Greek testimony. In fact, quite the opposite was true: *nothing* could be trusted from the non-Greek. Truth had to be generated and tested in any instance where a non-Greek provided testimony to the courts. To 'guarantee' the testimony of slaves, they needed to be subjected to some procedure that would secure the veracity of their testimony: that procedure was torture. As Edward Peters remarks,

> The honour of the citizen lent great importance to his sworn word . . . one possessing no such citizen status could not provide 'evidence' as the Greeks understood that term . . . those without legal privilege had to be coerced into a special status in which their testimony became acceptable. *Their testimony became equal to that of citizens by means of physical coercion . . .* originally,

then, the importance of the honour of a citizen created a classification of evidence that distinguished between a 'natural' kind of evidence that might be obtained readily from the word of a citizen and a coerced kind of evidence that had to be extracted by force from everyone else. (Peters, *Torture*, 13, my italics)

But the Greeks were not naïve about their fellow citizens, even if some were naïve about torture. As Demosthenes remarks, addressing the Athenians who constituted the juries of the ancient Greek world,

Wherever slaves and free men are present and facts have to be found, you do not use the statements of the free witnesses, but you seek to discover the truth by applying torture [*basanos*] to the slaves. Quite properly, men of the jury, since witnesses have sometimes been found not to have given true evidence, whereas no statements made as a result of torture have ever been proved untrue.[1]

The truth-telling proclivities of the ancient Greeks were made possible by the very thing that *also* made their testimony unreliable: namely, the capacity to reason. 'Slaves by nature,' as Aristotle called them, could *comprehend* but not employ reason. The free citizen had no such limitation. He could determine that *hiding* the truth would best protect his interests. Thus, despite the worth of a citizen's testimony (grounded in the capacity to reason), it was tainted by this very ability: reason itself could lead one *away* from the truth. "The testimony of a free citizen was considered to be tainted by his capacity to reason, which could produce truth or lies" (4).[2] Because torturing the citizen was not an option in the Greek legal system, the testimony of the 'natural' slave, carried out under torture, became worth more in Greek court proceedings. "The evidence derived from the slave's body and reported to the court, evidence from the past, is considered superior to that given freely in the court, before the jury, in the presence of the litigants" (14).[3] Indeed, such evidence was regarded as "the highest form of truth" (5).[4]

The Greek term for torture (*basanos)* reflects its epistemological significance. The term connotes putting metal against a touchstone to verify its quality. Torture, then, was a way to verify the truth of the testimony of those who could not be trusted (i.e. non-citizens). Despite its prevalence in court proceedings, though, torture was widely recognized as problematic (Aristotle, for instance, expresses reservations in his *Rhetoric*). Roman law had more rules surrounding the when, where, and who of torture, but it was used in largely the same capacity.

In the earliest Roman law, as in Greek law, only slaves might be tortured, and then only when they have been accused of a crime. Later, they might be tortured as witnesses . . . Freemen, originally preserved from torture, come under its shadow in cases of treason under the Empire, and then in a broader and broader spectrum of cases determined by imperial order. (Peters, 18)

Roman slaves, however, could only be tortured in criminal cases, *not* (as in Greece) in civil cases. Moreover, slaves could not be made to testify against their masters. As Rome ventured into an imperial government, rather than a republic, the basis of torture legislation moved away from the rights of Roman citizens to the emperor. Whereas the basis of torture legislation had been the majesty of the citizens of Rome, it came to be more a representation of the power of the emperor. As Ross puts it,

> With the expansion of Roman authority under the Empire, the neat distinction between free citizen and slave blurred, as there developed after the second century C.E. a class of freed slaves and non-Romans with partial rights of citizenship. During the late Empire, judicial torture was extended to include this very large group of second class citizens. (5)

Two terms gradually merge into one in the history of torture: '*quaestio*' referred both to the court and to the investigative procedure; '*tormentum*' referred to punishment. When these two things were brought together, we get, essentially, an evidentiary and interrogational torture. To be subjected to '*quaestio per tormenta*' was to be subjected to torture. As the commonality of this practice increased, '*quaestio*' and '*tormentum*' came to be synonymous (Peters, 28). To be put to the question was, in essence, to be tortured.

The roots of the use of torture in law can thus be found in antiquity. The presence of torture in the medieval courts was not very far from this basic model, although it was much more extensive. "[T]he use of torture during the middle ages went well beyond anything that the Roman law would have sanctioned" (3).[5] This extension was part of an interesting shift in the use and role of torture that emerged in the late middle ages, where torture became, not a supplementary way to pursue a truth residing in the body of the slave, but a *necessary* part of attaining adequate evidence. Interestingly, the body remained a vessel for the revelation of *political* and *religious* truth (as we will see), but in radically different contexts. This can be seen, in particular, in punitive torture, on the one hand, and inquisitorial religious prosecutions, on the other.[6]

What does it mean to say that torture became *necessary* for adequate evidence? It certainly should *not* be taken to mean that torture actually produced solid proof. Even in the middle ages, many jurists were far from convinced that this was the case.[7] Torture was regarded as necessary to the acquisition of evidence because the rules of evidence in capital cases were exceptionally stringent in these times. To be convicted of a capital case required either 1) a confession, or 2) two eye witnesses. Without a way of extracting a confession, clandestine crime would go unpunished – a result that the masses (let alone the government) were simply unwilling to tolerate. When there was no confession, or only one witness, something additional needed to be done.

This is not to say that chaos reigned in the criminal courts. Quite the opposite. The rules surrounding who could be tortured, and by whom, as well as rules regarding the admissibility of evidence obtained through torture, the lines of questioning that would be permitted, and so on, were put in place to safeguard what was already regarded as a questionable practice. It *was not* the case that medieval courts were convinced of the worth of torture. Rather, knowing that the practice of torture might get someone to say virtually anything, the law of continental Europe attempted to establish safeguards against what would eventually be seen as the inevitable abuses of such a system of interrogation.[8]

This of course raises some serious and difficult questions: why would medieval courts employ a practice that they knew to be faulty? Why did a system of torture re-emerge in the courts in the 13th century, rather than earlier or later? Why did the same system disappear from the courts a few centuries later? While the later role of torture in medieval courts resembles, in certain ways, torture as it was practiced in ancient Greek and Roman courts, earlier medieval courts did not follow this particular model. What explains this difference?

Some preliminary answers to these questions will help us understand the complexity of torture as it has existed in the history of the west. There is no doubt that the re-discovery of Roman law played a crucial role in the re-emergence of torture. The (Germanic) law employed in Europe had been primarily *accusatorial* rather than *inquisitorial*. Charges were brought by persons against one another; the state simply played no part. Answering charges typically involved the use of oaths. When these were not regarded as trustworthy, charges could no longer be settled by the judgment of (mere) human beings. The matter was put in the hands of God. We should not claim, however, that the accusatorial trial was unconcerned with evidence. This is an oversimplification, and one that does little to dispel the idea that the medieval period was one of ignorance and barbarity. There *was* a concern with evidence – as seen by the fact that insufficient evidence required appeal to something more, namely, the divine. But the problems with this were widely recognized. What was lacking was an *alternative* jurisprudence, one that was ultimately supplied by an appropriation of Roman law. The move to torture, in many ways, was a *rational* move motivated by a desire for an enhanced judicial epistemology. Seeing why this is the case – seeing how torture could constitute an increase in the rationality of jurisprudence, however counter-intuitive this might seem, can be accomplished by a more nuanced look at the system it replaced: the ordeal.

The traditional notion of the 'trial by ordeal' is of course an oversimplification, but it is nevertheless an adequate way of characterizing how the ordeal functioned in the early middle ages. The 'trial by ordeal' was largely regarded as a way for God to enact a just conclusion to a criminal case. The accused would be subjected to some type of physical injury or mortal danger (such as a hot iron applied to the hand, or repeated dunking in water). This exposure was intended to inflict a wound on the accused (a burnt hand, for example). Given the belief that God's justness would never permit an innocent person to be found guilty of a crime he or she did not commit, God would intervene in the case of any innocent person: the hand would (miraculously) be unburned by the hot iron, the feet would be unharmed by the hot coals, and so on. God was thus part of those criminal cases involving the use of the ordeal: his justice would be guaranteed by his intervention in the case of the innocent.

It is extraordinarily easy to make fun of the idea of a 'trial by ordeal,' at least as it is described above. As noted, though, this initial story is an oversimplification. Robert Bartlett points out that although "envisaged as a regular part of judicial activity, [the ordeals] were employed only in certain specified circumstances and only against certain kinds of criminals" (26).[9] More importantly, "the absence of evidence, or witnesses, or even accusers [was] a necessary precondition for the use of the ordeal" (30). In other words, the ordeal was not applied willy-nilly, irrespective of other evidence that might be available to the courts. Indeed, the Medieval court recognized a variety of forms of admissible evidence in the courts. In cases where said evidence was insufficient, however, and in which the stakes were very high (the sentence for a crime might well be death), something else was needed. The forms of this 'something else' were many and varied. Different ordeals were suited to different occasions. Here are descriptions of two such ordeals:

The judgment of the glowing iron

After the accusation has been lawfully made, and three days have been passed in fasting and prayer, the priest, clad in his sacred vestments with the exception of his outside garment, shall take with a tongs the iron placed before the altar; and, singing the hymn of the three youths, namely, "Bless him all his works," he shall bear it to the fire, and shall say this prayer over the place where the fire is to carry out the judgment: "Bless, o Lord God, this place, that there may be for us in it sanctity, chastity, virtue and victory, and sanctimony, humility, goodness, gentleness and plentitude of law, and obedience to God the Father and the Son and the Holy Ghost." After this, the iron shall be placed in the fire and shall be sprinkled with holy water; and while it is heating, he shall celebrate mass. But when the priest shall have taken the Eucharist, he shall adjure the man who is to be tried . . . and shall cause him to take the communion. Then the priest shall sprinkle holy water above the iron and shall say: "The blessing of God the Father, the Son, and the Holy Ghost descend upon this iron for the discerning of the right judgment of God." And straightaway the accused shall carry the iron to a distance of nine feet. Finally his hand shall be covered under seal for three days, and if festering blood be found in the track of the iron, he shall be judged guilty. But if, however, he shall go forth uninjured, praise shall be rendered to God.

Test of the cold water

Consecration to Be Said over the Man. May omnipotent God, who did order baptism to be made by water, and did grant remission of sins to men through baptism: may He, through His mercy, decree a right judgment through that water. If, namely, thou art guilty in that matter, may the water which received thee in baptism not receive thee now; if however, thou art innocent, may the water which received thee in baptism receive thee now. Through Christ our Lord. *Afterwards He Shall Exorcise the Water Thus*: I adjure thee, water, in name of the Father Almighty, who did create thee in the beginning, who also did order thee to be separated from the waters above, . . . that in no manner thou receive this man, if he be in any way guilty of the charge that is brought against him; by deed, namely, or by consent, or by knowledge, or in any way: but make him to swim above thee. And may no process be employed against thee, and no magic which may be able to conceal that (fact of his guilt).[10]

If the results had always found those accused to be guilty, the ordeal would not long have survived in the criminal courts. In fact, however, there was much variability in the outcome of any of the ordeals. Even grabbing a hot iron does not guarantee 'festering blood.' The amount of holy water 'sprinkled' on the iron, the length of time the iron was allowed to heat, and other variables certainly played a role in God's verdict of justice.

But the abuses of the ordeal – for example, people repeatedly calling for others to prove their piety through such ordeals – was too much for the system to bear. And here we see the emergence (or, more truthfully, the re-emergence) of organized torture into the courts. In order to replace a justice that is coming down from God, standards of proof must be exceptionally high. If mere mortals are to judge one another in cases where the accused might face death or maiming as a consequence of his purported crimes, judgments of guilt had best be supported by evidence to the point of near certainty. And how might such certainty be achieved?

Leaving aside the question of torture for the moment, the answer provided by the Medieval courts seems to be a plausible one, given the context and the absence of a forensic science: if one can produce two eye-witnesses for a given crime, both of whom are of reputable character, we have approached as near as we can to certainty regarding the guilt of the accused. This is not to say that witnesses are always to be trusted. They obviously are not (hence the restriction on who could *be* a witness).[11] Having two witnesses, though, approaches a level of certainty that was unavailable under the ordeal system. In fact, only one other means of proof rivaled it: a confession. It is here, in concerns about the strength of this evidence, that the 'two rule' system is born. A person can be convicted of capital crimes only if there are either 1) two eye witnesses to the crime, or 2) the person confesses to the crime. When our standards of evidence demand near certainty, and absent any forensic science, it is hardly surprising that this system was adopted.

It is easy for anyone to see how plausible the above criteria are for evidence of guilt; it is equally easy to see what sorts of problems these criteria might pose in practice. Crimes like murder are not typically carried out amidst eye-witnesses, and those facing death are not likely to admit their crimes. The system that favors certainty in criminal convictions also seems to favor the criminal. From a recognition of these difficulties, the Medieval courts operated with notions of the 'half-proof,' the 'quarter-proof,' and so on. If there was ample circumstantial evidence, or one eye-witness, a court could license the use of torture to acquire 'full proof': namely, a confession.

The Medieval courts utilized Roman law to develop their two rule system for proofs, but the courts were incredibly careful to build into the law as many safeguards against abuse as possible. If torture was to be used, it could not be used on just anyone at any time and for any reason. Everyone recognized that torture could be abused, that innocent people could be convicted, and that evidence might be unreliable. Thus, there needed to be a system that could enable the punishment of clandestine crime but preserve criteria of conviction that were as good as God's. The following rules were meant to govern the use of torture in the courts:

(1) Torture could occur only when half-proof was obtained.
(2) Torture could not employ leading questioning.
(3) Torture had to be supervised by the judge who ordered it.
(4) Confessions of the crime were insufficient evidence for conviction. Defendants had to produce evidence that could be corroborated by the court, and which only the guilty ought to know.
(5) Any confession acquired through coercion was not admissible in court. For a confession to count, it had to be given in the court, and could not take place before 24 hours had passed.

Torture was thus, in theory at least, anything but haphazard. Only when sufficient evidence (*indicia*) was available could torture be

ordered, and only in order to obtain a confession which could be verified by further investigation (the location of a body, a weapon, and so
on). Once a confession was obtained, it was not admissible in court,
as it had been obtained under duress. Thus, a confession had to be
repeated in the court to be admissible (if it was not repeated, of course,
one could be subjected to additional torture). Not just anyone could be
tortured: persons below and above certain ages, for example, as well
as pregnant women and persons of high status, were immune from the
practice.

The system of safeguards was anything but immune to abuse. The
extent of this abuse cannot be known, but it must have been rather
significant: judges could determine at their own discretion whether or
not there was sufficient evidence to warrant torture; interrogators could
violate rules about questioning. In addition, as had been known by critics
of judicial torture, the innocent sometimes confessed, and the guilty
sometimes did not.

It is easy to criticize such abuse as demonstrative of the unworkability
of any system of legalized torture. This sort of criticism is unfair for two
reasons. First, abuses of the torture system were *not* simply ignored. In
fact, criticisms of abuse were common, as were suggestions for how to
deal with these abuses. Johannes Voet, for example, a Dutch legal scholar
of the 17th century, thought of torture as "a natural method of obtaining
evidence by which criminals would convict themselves." He nevertheless
recognized that the system was imperfect, and that abuses were common.
"For him simply because torture was at times misused or abused did not
invalidate its practice within the criminal justice system" (9).[12] This, in
fact, was the primary kind of criticism leveled against torture. For many,
such as Antonius Matthaeus II, who catalogued problems with torture in
1644, "the problem was not torture per se but the danger that it could be
used against the innocent" (10).[13]

The second reason it is unfair to criticize torture as 'unworkable' can be
seen by simply considering our own criminal justice system in the United
States. The jury system, to take one example, is anything but immune to
criticism. Lay persons are frequently incompetent to assess complicated
genetic evidence, psychological neuroses, and so on, and yet we allow
them to do just this when acting as jurors. Despite this obvious problem,
we continue to utilize the jury system. Another example – and one that is
directly analogous to the torture case – concerns our own criminal justice
system's abuses: prisons in the United States are notoriously racist, and
house incredible violence of all sorts (including, most infamously, rape).
This has led very few, if any, to advocate the abolition of the prison.[14]
Likewise, innocent persons are incarcerated, and sometimes put to death,
in the current legal system. This is not, however, regarded as an obvious
indication that there should simply be *no* incarceration. The ease with

which the institution of judicial torture is criticized, it seems, is facilitated only by a willing blindness concerning the failings of the US system of criminal justice.

In one respect, the system of torture was an improvement over the earlier trials by ordeal. In re-discovering Roman law (the most complete system of law available at the time), Medieval courts were able to introduce stricter standards of evidence, even if the means of obtaining this evidence were questionable. The logic of evidence had taken a great leap forward, even if the notion of human rights needing to be protected under the rule of law was nowhere to be found.

And it is here that the use of torture in Medieval courts was anything but an improvement. As Ruthven has put it, the fusion of secular Roman law with church canon law led to the worst of both worlds.[15] Summing up this point, Evans and Morgan remark:

> In the canonical tradition a confession was required – indeed heresy could not be proven without it – but torture was forbidden. In the secular tradition torture could be used, but only if lack of proof required it. Now confessions were almost demanded and torture, or the threat of torture, became the means of obtaining them. (4)

It was neither sadism nor stupidity which led to the re-emergence of torture in the displacement of the ordeals. Rather, it was at least in part a desire to produce a more *rational* system of criminal justice, where verdicts were the result of the evaluation of evidence and the production of *proof* – the highest of which was the confession, so-called 'Queen of Proofs' – which led to the near inevitability of torture. This, however, should not be exaggerated. For whatever improvements a return to Roman law offered, it still bore a nasty resemblance to the very thing it aimed to make obsolete: the ordeal. As Foucault remarks,

> Beneath an apparently determined, impatient search for truth, one finds in classical torture the regulated mechanisms of an ordeal: a physical challenge that must define the truth . . . in the practice of torture, pain, confrontations and truth were bound together: they worked together on the patient's body. The search for truth through judicial torture was certainly a way of obtaining evidence, the most serious of all – the confession of the guilty person; but it was also the battle, and this victory of one adversary over the other, that 'produced' truth according to a ritual. (41)[16]

The abolition of torture: Langbein's thesis

There are four prominent explanations for the disappearance of torture from the courts of Europe.

Political: the rise of Enlightenment rulers (like Frederick the Great) devoted to science, reason, and the principles of humanistic politics.

Humanistic: torture was condemned by some of the finest writers and thinkers of the day. These critics included Beccaria and Voltaire.

Juridical: changing notions of proof required for conviction in capital cases, less stringent criteria for the admission of acceptable evidence, and shifting conceptions of possible punishment. (Langbein)

Socio-Anthropological: a shifting conception of the nature of humanity led to new views about what sorts of punishments (and, indeed, what ways of acquiring evidence) were acceptable. (Foucault)

Before examining some of these explanations in detail, two words of caution are in order. First, the disappearance of torture from the European courts of the late Medieval period was *not* an elimination of torture *tout court*. In addition to judiciary torture, torture was used on those who were *convicted*. Such torture was called '*torture preable*' (preliminary torture). It was preliminary "in the sense of being preliminary to the execution of the capital sentence. The safeguards of the ordinary law of torture, such as the requirement of probable cause, did not exist" (17).[17] Even *Voltaire*, a staunch advocate of the abolition of torture, defended *torture preable*. Likewise, torture occurred elsewhere on the political horizon – and continues to do so even today – despite its flight from the evidentiary and punitive procedures of criminal justice. It also existed in other parts of the world – particularly in the colonies of Europe.

Second, the explanations offered above of torture's disappearance are not mutually exclusive. The juridical and socio-anthropological views, for example, can easily be seen as complimentary. Indeed, Foucault (the primary advocate of the socio-anthropological view) is primarily interested in *punitive* torture, Langbein (the primary advocate of the juridical view) with *juridical* torture. As such, the explanations offered by these thinkers may well work in tandem to explain shifts in both criminal procedures and criminal sanctions that emerge in the 18th and 19th centuries. These accounts, in turn, may well explain why some political leaders and thinkers advocated reform of criminal courts. In this respect, it would be wrong to say that the humanist and political explanations for the abolition of torture played *no part* in an account of changes in legal processes. The point would be to say that the driving forces in judicial reformation were not to be found in the manifestos of humanists, but rather in changing conceptions of proof. This is a far cry from saying that such manifestos were completely inconsequential.

The most popular view of the so-called disappearance of torture is certainly the humanistic one. It consists of the claim that the end of torture was a result of the humanitarian publicity campaigns of 18th-century authors like Voltaire and Beccaria. On this view, the story of the abolition of torture is a story of moral progress, attributable, in large part, to the efforts of those few persons who saw what morality demands more clearly than their immediate peers. This view is well-captured in Daniel P. Mannix's *The History of Torture*:

> If a single man can be said to have started the moral crusade that finally abolished the legal use of torture, that man was Cesare Beccaria . . . [he] lived to see torture abolished, as a result of his book, in France, Germany and the Netherlands. (136)

There is no doubt that Beccaria's criticisms of torture are very powerful, even if they weren't novel.[18] To see the force of Beccaria's condemnation of torture as it existed in the courts, one need only consider his powerful either/or:

> No man may be called guilty before the judge has reached his verdict; nor may society withdraw its protection from him until it has been determined that he has broken the terms of the compact by which that protection was extended to him. By what right, then, except that of force, does the judge have the authority to inflict punishment on a citizen while there is doubt about whether he is guilty? (Beccaria, *Of Crimes and Punishments*)

Beccaria here presents a devastating dilemma: either proof of guilt has been provided, in which case torture is not needed, or such proof *has not* been provided, in which case torture is unjustified. Thus, torture is either unjustified or unnecessary. Moreover, Beccaria colorfully articulated one of the well-worn criticisms of the use of torture powerfully and succinctly: "[Torture] is a sure route for the acquittal of robust ruffians and the conviction of weak innocents" (ibid.).

Can a book single-handedly change a well-entrenched legal system? That seems doubtful. Of course, Mannix offers only a hypothetical: *if* one person can be credited with the abolition of torture, *then* that person is Beccaria. But there are some significant problems with attributing such power to Beccaria even *hypothetically.*

As Langbein notes, "the 18th-century writers were advancing arguments that had been known for centuries" (11). The claim that torture was unreliable was news to no one. Indeed, Aristotle had said this quite explicitly over 2000 years before Beccaria.

> We must say that evidence under torture is not trustworthy, the fact being that many men whether thick-witted, tough-skinned, or stout of heart endure their ordeal nobly, while cowards and timid men are full of boldness till they see the ordeal of these others: so that no trust can be placed in evidence under torture. (Aristotle, *Rhetoric*, 1:15)

If Beccaria can be given credit for the abolition of torture, it could not have been due to the arguments he used. These same arguments had been articulated many times before, in many different contexts, and by many different authors. They were well known by the jurists of the day. It thus seems implausible that a publication of arguments *already well-known to law-makers* would have any effect on the structure of the law.

Langbein offers a second objection: "The Roman-canon system . . . was simply unworkable without torture" (11). Thus, torture *could not* have been abolished prior to a change in the Roman-canon law. The 'fairy tale of humanism' (as Langbein calls it) claims that the eighteenth century destroyed torture, and that Roman-canon law fell in the next century. But if the Roman-canon system was untenable without torture this is an impossible sequence of events.

Langbein argues that the Roman system lost its force in the *17th century*, and that torture was eliminated as *unnecessary* once a new law of proof was established (the juridical view). Torture ceases to be part of our legal proceedings, on this view, not because we see it as problematic. We had *always* seen it as problematic. Torture falls away, rather, because of a change in *the epistemology of jurisprudence* in the legal systems of Europe. Langbein's defense of the juridical explanation involves two significant dimensions: changes in forms of punishment, on the one hand, and increased judicial discretion in examining available evidence and determining punishments appropriate in particular cases, on the other.

Changes in forms of punishment

With severe punishments, we ought to expect high levels of proof. To be convicted of a crime that will result in execution, for example, requires more than the say-so of a questionable source. This was a wisdom embodied in the courts of the late Medieval period. The 'blood sanctions' – crimes that resulted in death or dismemberment – required a high level of proof, given what was at stake. Consider the 1532 *Constitutio Criminalis Carolina*, a document that codifies the sanctions of the middle ages in the midst of their decline. It chronicles a variety of capital punishment.

> An ordinary murderer or burglar merits hanging in chains or beheading with a sword. A woman who murders her infant is buried alive and impaled, a traitor is drawn and quartered. Other grave offenders may be burned to death, or drowned, or set out to die in agony upon the wheel with their limbs smashed . . . For less grave offenses the Carolina prescribes afflictive punishments – flogging, pillorying, cutting off the ears, chopping off the fingers, cutting out the tongue – usually accompanied by a sentence of banishment. (Langbein, 27–28)

When the stakes are high, the standards of evidence must be too. Of course, it is easy for us to contend that the stakes did not *need* to be so high. Retrospect has its advantages, but on this point it seems unduly unfair. The concept of the 'prison,' as it is currently understood, was not available to the jurists of the middle ages. Prisons were originally *not* meant as places of punishment, but rather as places of detention, at least when it came to capital crime. For petty crimes, prisons functioned as places for those, for example, who were unable to pay fines for their crimes. There were thus, in essence, two *different* systems of punishment: one for capital crimes (where punishment involved the body of the convicted; it was enacted in death, maiming, public humiliation, and so on), the other for 'petty' crimes. The two forms of punishment in turn corresponded to two different systems of evidence (petty crimes did not require two eyewitnesses or a confession; torture was *never* used in such cases). For petty crimes, circumstantial evidence was sufficient. After all, convicting someone of a lesser offense (such as owing a small debt) would not result in the loss of life or limb. For capital crimes, on the other hand, a wrongful conviction would impose such a cost on the innocent that *any* conviction required something close to certainty.

Understanding the existence and future dominance of the prison is an important *additional* part of understanding the disappearance of torture given the link between evidential requirements and kinds of punishment. When the prison emerges as an alternative to loss of life and limb, the standards of evidence can *lessen*, as the consequences of wrongful conviction are not nearly so severe.

Economic pressures played a significant role in the emergence of the prison system. The road to the prison wove through two similar, prior institutions, prevalent in different parts of Europe: galley service in the Mediterranean, and the workhouse in the north. The increase in naval ambitions required a source of labor for ship propulsion. Rather than go without when regular supplies ran dry, "the practice began in the West of forcing condemned criminals to serve as oarsmen" (30). As Langbein argues, "the motivation for the galley sentence was strictly exploitative" (31). While the most notorious of criminals still faced execution, the Galley emerged as a surrogate prison: a place where criminals could be put to work, and which would act as a place of confinement. The death penalty was essentially traded for a life of enslaved labor. The emergence of the workhouse tells a similar story. It "arose to serve social purposes somewhat removed from the ordinary criminal law" (33). The workhouse evolved inland as well as on the coast. It was foremost a way of dealing with the destitute – but it served also to provide an alternative destination for those convicted. However, "it was not wholly exploitative," as the workhouse was thought to:

introduce the inmate to a regime of honest labor, it would train him in a working skill, and it would reform his character through discipline and moral instruction. Thus equipped, he could be released, no longer a burden to society. The workhouse would have reformed him. (35)

The idea that a criminal might be reformed is part of the rationale behind the workhouse. This was a fundamentally new idea about both the point of punishment (to reform rather than to enact justice on the body) as well as about the nature of human agency (it could be transformed through social institutions; one's nature is not written in stone). From here, it was a very short step to the notion of a rehabilitative prison, designed to alter *who* a prisoner was rather than to enact revenge on the flesh in the form of death or mutilation. As Foucault wryly remarks in exploring this shift in the penal system, "the soul [becomes] the prison of the body" (30): punitive law aimed, not to change the body as it saw fit, but to change the very *essence* of the prisoner.

The motives for a change in the penal system included "to reform offenders, to save the lives of skilled workers who could contribute to the mercantilist state, to render criminal sanctions more humane, and to exploit forced labor" (Langbein, 39). This provided an alternative to the blood sanctions for capital crimes: one no longer needed to be maimed or put to death when convicted of such crimes. The stakes were no longer as high when one was convicted of a crime, and this entailed that the need for *absolute proof* was no longer present: one's very life need not rely on the verdict.

Increased judicial discretion

In addition to changes in forms of punishment, an increased trust and reliance on judicial discretion involving punishment and the assessment of evidence contributed to the gradual obsolescence of torture. This was not a sea-change in the criminal system, however. The notion of judicial discretion in both of these areas *already existed* in dealing with lesser crimes. The novelty was to apply the criteria of evidence already in use for assessing petty crimes to the blood sanctions. Once this change in evidential requirements took place, torture was no longer required as a means for securing a 'full proof.' Indeed, the very idea of 'full proof' was no longer necessary for a conviction.

Judicial discretion in regard to punishment is captured in the legal concept of *poena extraordinaria* (discretionary punishment). While there was an obsession with eliminating the discretion of a judge in the law of *proof* in capital cases, there was no such obsession with sanctions. Judges could spare a convict from capital sanctions, and the proof available against a suspect could be used to measure the severity of an appropriate punishment under *poena extraordinaria*. Interestingly, even under Roman-canon law as it existed in the Medieval period, a person could be given a *lesser* sentence in the absence of full proof (i.e. even without the presence of two eye-witnesses or a confession). The legal concept of *Verdachtstraffe*, or punishment from suspicion, captures this peculiarity – though not quite literally.

> In truth, the *Verdachtstraffe* was *not* a punishment for mere *Verdacht* . . . It was a punishment imposed by the court when the court was persuaded that the accused was guilty, but when his guilt could not be established under the Roman-canon law of proof. (Langbein, 48)

Once again, we see here a recognition of the troubles with torture: even after torture, some of the guilty will not confess. At this point, a judge may, using his discretion, impose a lesser sanction based on the available evidence (perhaps all circumstantial). In essence, then, *Verdachtstraffe* acts as a safeguard against the 'robust ruffian' capable of withstanding being put to 'the question.'

In addition to this discretionary leeway regarding the imposition of sanctions, judges also had significant discretion in the evaluation of evidence. This discretion also had its roots in Roman law. It differed only in domain: in regard to petty crimes, a judge was permitted to independently evaluate the evidence against the accused. The concept of *Freie Beweiswurdigung* (independent judiciary evaluation of the evidence) only needed to be applied to capital cases to eliminate the need for the extraction of confessions. As Langbein puts it, "the courts did not have to invent this lower standard of proof, they had only to extend it." The standard in question was of "subjective persuasion rather than objective proof" (48). And by the 17th century, this *jus commune* was well-entrenched in criminal proceedings, and could easily supersede the strict proof requirements of the blood sanctions.

Ultimately, then, torture disappeared from the judicial proceedings because it becomes *unnecessary*.

> Punishment for serious crime no longer required full proof, hence in cases where the evidence was short of full proof it was no longer necessary to use torture to complete the proof . . . The new law of proof enabled the judge to do what the *jus commune* supposedly forbade him to do: he could now sentence a culprit to punishment on the basis of circumstantial evidence. (Langbein, 59)

And here, in a nutshell, is Langbein's thesis regarding the end of torture in the courts: changes in the law of proof caused the abolition of torture; the critiques of abolitionists *did not* lead to the end of torture, as there was no known workable alternative to the entrenched criminal proceedings. When an alternative was worked out *in the courts them-selves*, torture ultimately disappeared. Legislation reflected this change. It did not *produce* it.

The humanist view and the political view of the cause of the abolition of torture cannot account for the actual legislative timeline. Roman-canon law required torture to be workable. It was only when the courts found an alternative to traditional Roman-canon law that torture could be eliminated. This happened, not as a result of the deliberate efforts of a few exceptionally moral men, but as a result of the unintentional evolu-tion of criminal law.

There is an important lesson to be learned in Langbein's work on torture – one that will surface in several places in this book. It is all too easy for us to think of ourselves as knowing better than those in the *ancien regime* of law – to think that we have progressed, morally speaking, well beyond the naïve moral sensibilities of those who came before. This view of the evolution of torture in the courts (and generally) embodies significant problems: the view reads history 'Whiggishly,' to use an expression Richard Rorty once used in another context.[19] That is, it presumes our own intellectual and moral superiority. This is a danger-ous assumption, and one that can (and perhaps did) blind us to our own violent propensities. One of the greatest dangers in regard to torture – and a danger that has caused immense moral blindness – is that we are somehow beyond torture. This is a self-serving view of our place in the history of civilization; it is also likely a false one.[20]

Torture and treason: remarks on torturous punishment and the Inquisitions

In Ancient Greece and Rome, and during the middle ages, persons of status, although protected in most cases, could be tortured in cases of treason. The connection between torture and treason, however, runs much deeper than this. In fact, it is the permissibility of torture in the case of treason that largely explains the use of torture in two other theaters: in punishments, on the one hand, and in the inquisitions around heresy, on the other. No survey of the history of torture, however brief, can ignore these two arenas – arenas in which torture played a central part.

The connection between heresy and treason is seen in the way both of these notions are understood in the middle ages. Heresy, of course, involves the maintenance of beliefs that are against the prescribed beliefs set forth by the Catholic church – beliefs which are thought to be the uni-versal, correct words of God. To be guilty of heresy, then, is to be guilty of a crime against God, the punishment for which is no less than the damnation of one's eternal soul. Treason, on the other hand, involves the commission of a crime against the sovereign. One's actions are directed at a king, for example, and aim to thwart the absolute sovereignty of that king. Then, as now, treason was a crime against government. Given that a monarch embodied the state, however, there is an important difference between treason in the middle ages and treason as we find it today. Today, treason is a crime against the state, where 'the state' is understood as being an abstract entity. In earlier centuries in Europe, the state was anything *but* abstract: it was the flesh and blood of the sovereign. To act against the state was, essentially, to assault the very body of the sovereign; to assault, or attempt to assault, the monarch was an act which symbolically aimed to destroy the rule of law itself. Theoretically, this connection between the sovereign and the law meant that, in certain respects, *any* violation of the law constituted an attack on the monarch, and hence counted as treason (though this was obviously not carried out in actual judicial practices).

The connection between heresy and treason can be seen from either direction. The rule of the monarch was said to be held by divine right. God's law rules the world, but the monarch was God's law applied at the level of the state. An act of treason against a rightful king was thus *in itself* an act of heresy. It called into question God's law as it existed in concrete form in the state. From the other direction, *any* act of heresy amounted to a failure to recognize the legitimate authority of God, king of kings. Heresy was thus treason in the most profound respect: it was treason against *God*.

Under the power of the sovereign as embodied law, the abstract interests of something called 'the state' are not in question. What is in question by the commission of a crime is the legitimacy of the sovereign himself. It is for this reason that the 'festival of cruelty' must be public, and that it must exceed the crime in every respect. In this way, the divine right of the sovereign is made public, and thereby re-asserted against the criminal – and, indeed, on the body of the criminal. A well-known case of this exercise of brute power on the body of the condemned is offered by Foucault in the opening pages of *Discipline and Punish*.

On 2 March 1757 Maniens the regicide was condemned 'to make the *amende honorable* before the main door of the Church of Paris,' where he was to be 'taken and conveyed in a cart, wearing nothing but a shirt, holding a torch of burning wax weighing two pounds' . . . then 'in the said cart . . . the flesh will be torn from his breasts, arms, thighs, and calves with red-hot pincers, his right hand, holding the knife with which he committed the said parricide, burnt with sulphur, and, on those places where the flesh will be torn away, poured molten lead, boiling oil, burning resin, wax and sulphur melted together and then his body drawn and quartered by four horses and his limbs and body consumed by fire, reduced to ashes, and his ashes thrown to the wind'. (*Pieces originales*, 372–4)

'Finally, he was quartered,' recounts *Gazette d'Amsterdam* of 1 April 1757. 'This last operation was very long, because the horses used were not accustomed to drawing; consequently, instead of four, six were needed; and when that did not suffice, they were forced, in order to cut off the wretch's thighs, to sever the sinews and hack at the joints . . . (3)

Punitive torture, such as that described above, was used relatively continuously from antiquity to the 18th century and on. It is still used today.[21] What we see in this instance of torture are mechanisms of power exercised by a sovereign on that body which acted against it. "The mechanisms of power are strong enough to absorb, display, and nullify the enormity of crimes in rituals of sovereignty" (85).[22] And, indeed, the punishment *must* do this given the nature of the crime. "Besides its immediate victim, the crime attacks the sovereign: it attacks him personally, since the law represents the will of the sovereign; it attacks him physically, since the force of law is the force of the prince" (47).[23] There is an element of the sacred in this ritual that should not be overlooked. The spectacle is not really of the condemned suffering; the real spectacle is in the symbolic power of the absolute sovereign inscribed in all its force on the body of one who is not imbued with sacred power.

In the world of the sacral monarch, the scaffold was the site of a kind of passion play whose end was the confession of faith. This is an ancient script: the tortured body reproduces the power of the sovereign through the confession of faith. The violence done to the body is not mere negation. Rather, it is that creation through negation characteristic of sacrifice. Torture is, first of all, a form of sacrifice that inscribes on the body a sacred presence. Faith, politics, and torture were conjoined in a spectacle of sacrifice designed to produce in the audience a kind of terror – a combination of dread and awe before the sacred mystery of power. . . . Political power was stabilized by the transformation from mere fear of violent injury to awe before the sacred character of the sovereign. (25)[24]

It is hardly surprising, then, that "heresy was aligned with treason and both offences required the same proof" (4),[25] despite the fact that the prosecution of these respective 'crimes' occurred in different venues – one sacred, the other (at least nominally) secular. The inquisitorial process, as used in both the Roman and the Spanish Inquisitions, was not licensed by the state to administer punishment to those found 'guilty' of heresy.[26] Criminal punishment was a right of the sovereign, as ordained by God, and not a right of the church. Conveniently, this allowed the state to punish even those who would not confess to heresy (and hence who could not be proven to be guilty by the Inquisitors). Those who refused to confess adequately (from the point of view of the Inquisitor) could be dealt with by the law. These persons were often burned at the stake.[27]

> During the Inquisition, torture was not used for punishment, but as a means of eliciting truth. Inquisitors would not accept confessions as valid if they were made during torture sessions, since they had been obtained under terrible pressure. Instead, the victim of torture had to ratify his or her confession the day after the ordeal. (48)[28]

The connections between torture in criminal proceedings and in heretical inquisitions are unmistakable here. The *very same* restrictions on torture are used in the case of heretical inquisitions as in criminal proceedings. The church has borrowed its techniques from the law. Perhaps surprisingly, it *also* borrows its techniques from its own mystical traditions.

> . . . the fasts, vigils, scourging, and every other form of voluntary self-torture that the mystics inflicted on their own persons were turned against the heretics as an instrument of law. The Church . . . imagined the Holy Office as an arm of penance, spiritual reconciliation, and the restoration of the wayward back to the community of the faithful. Its tortures were modeled after ascetic practices, and even the burning of the heretic at the stake was based on readings of the scripture, and on the penitential model of purifying fires as a purgatorial blessing. (163)[29]

There are deep connections between the use of torture in the religious practices (particularly in the inquisition) and in the law courts of medieval Europe. These connections, however, should not obscure the fact that the powers exerted by sovereignty and church were conceptualized differently. The state was an organ of law, embodied in the king, while the church was an organ of spiritual teaching, in place putatively to save those poor souls who would otherwise be damned. While both juridical torture and the inquisition aim at eliciting *truth*, they do so for very different reasons.

> Much as chosen suffering sought to crush the rebellious will and thereby to make spiritual space for the indwelling truth of God, so too did judicial torture, by inflicting pain on the accused, seek to destroy the willfulness that diminished the truth of testimony. Truth was a spontaneous production, not a composed one . . . Torture inflicted pain as a means of achieving the spontaneous truth of the body rather than the composed truth of the mind. Torture sought the evidence of an animate body that could not dissimulate. (9)[30]

The case of punitive torture is different in many respects. Torture as punitive was an exercise of power against the body of its victim, designed to re-enforce the claim to legitimacy of the power in whose name the torture was conducted – namely, the sovereign.[31] This is markedly different from the use of torture in court proceedings as discussed above.

In the jurisprudence of Roman-canon law, the aim of torture was the production of truth. This is not to say that torture in the *ancien regime* did not *also* display the power of the state. It most certainly did. But it did so primarily through its role in criminal proceedings. As opposed to the older (Germanic) accusatorial system of law, where all criminal offenses were only between litigants (and the state played no real role), in Roman-canon law, torture demonstrates the power of the state to investigate and establish the crimes committed by its citizens. The existence of the state as a force that takes an active interest in the lives of its flock is inscribed in the very process of criminal justice: "we care about what you do," the state says, "and we care enough to secure the truth of what you do through subjecting your body to the *quaestio*."

We should not, however, mistake the introduction of torture into the criminal justice system for the introduction of corporal methods. As our discussion of the ordeals shows, corporal trials were already well-entrenched – and the existence of punitive torture pre-dates the use of torture in the legal mechanisms of the 13th century. "What Roman law brought into play was not so much the use of corporal punishment, but a renowned ideology of authority, the concept of heresy as treason against the central authority, and the notion of infamy (*mala fama*)" (Glucklich, 161). It was this ideology which led the Catholic Church from a policy in which torture was condemned to one where it was outright sanctioned.[32]

I have tried to sketch some similarities and differences between the various theaters of torture. Judicial torture is like inquisitorial torture in that both have something like 'truth' as their aim, albeit truth about very different things, and with significantly different (conscious) motivations. Punitive torture, by contrast, is uninterested in *discovering* truth through torture. Its aim is instead to *demonstrate* the already-known truth of the power of the sovereign by inscribing this power, in horrific and awe-inspiring splendor, on the limp and frail body of the accused. While judicial and inquisitorial torture also display the power of the courts and the church, this is not their explicit aim. Both judicial and punitive torture, however, are caught up in the operations of the state to a much greater extent than is inquisitorial torture. They both reveal the way that a state takes control of a body for its own purposes, whether that purpose is to demonstrate the power of the sovereign or to prove the validity of an accusation through 'rational' means. The inquisitorial use of torture, on the other hand, while not divorced from the revelation of power entirely, aims to justify itself in terms of the spiritual well-being of the tortured. Here, as in Greece and Rome, the use of pain is meant to guarantee the truth of what the tortured said, and the power of the articulation of this truth is designed (at least in principle) as an act of *mercy*. Souls are saved. In this respect, the Inquisition thinks of heresy as a form of the ticking bomb argument: the stakes are enormous, and any cost is to be paid.

Torturing a person to prevent them from eternal damnation is worth whatever cost it brings to the material body that houses an endangered immortal soul.

The re-emergence of torture in the state

Torture, as I said at the outset, has always been with us. It is thus somewhat misleading to talk about its 'abolition' and its 're-emergence.' What we *can* say is that torture played a large role in the court proceedings of antiquity until the seventeenth century – though admittedly changing its form for a while in trials by ordeal – and that it seemed to disappear from the explicit operations of the state, only to re-emerge as an engine of state in the twentieth century. Why did it re-appear?

In the influential *La Torture*, published in 1949, Alec Mellor suggests three reasons for this re-emergence:

1. A new conception of state as the site of power emerged in the form of totalitarian regimes.
2. New modes of warfare emerged that required immediate intelligence.
3. 'Asianism': a new exotic appeal regarding the spy, coupled with the view that no restraints should be imposed on the treatment of prisoners. (Peters, 106)

The new conception of the state, captured in totalitarian regimes like that of Hitler, Stalin, Mao, and Polpot, viewed the state as a means through which human civilization as such might be improved, and 'higher' forms of human beings might be created. This is captured in typical form in one of the many works dedicated to articulating a vision of the state as a means for the improvement of humankind.

> The fundamental idea is that the state is not a goal, but a means. It is certainly the preliminary condition for the formation of a human civilization of superior worth, but it is not the direct cause of it. (Hitler, *Mein Kampf*, II.2)

This view of the state as having a higher purpose, coupled with new levels of rationalization and bureaucratization and the silencing of dissent, set the stage for the full employment of modes of torture in a new vein. This was coupled with the modernization of warfare, which increased the need for quick intelligence. Espionage and counter-espionage grew in importance, as did special tactics for acquiring information from prisoners of war. As Peters remarks, at the turn of the twentieth century "the profession of spy began to lose its discreditable status and acquire some of the glamour that it has possessed until very recently" (108).

While Mellor's account provides some insight into 'new' torture, it is surely incomplete. Changes in medicine and religious practice led to a new way of thinking about pain, and this surely played a role in how the West conceptualized torture, as well as the way torture was put to use – though the role this played is difficult to specify.[33] In addition, while Mellor is surely correct to highlight changes in the modes of warfare in the twentieth century, more remains to be said on this front. To this end, Christopher Einolf has argued that three things explain the rise of torture in the twentieth century:

1. Changes in the quantity, intensity, and nature of military conflict . . .
2. The prevalence of civil conflicts in states divided along racial, ethnic, and religious lines . . . [and]
3. Changes in the nature of the sovereign brought about by an expanded definition of treason, and states that have become more effective at monitoring and prosecuting treason. (113)[34]

Items (2) and (3) offer supplements to Mellor's analysis, while item (1) clarifies Mellor's notion of 'new modes of warfare.' The supplements are certainly important. The role of race and what I will call 'Othering' (Chapter 9) is central to the policies of torture in the twentieth and twenty-first centuries.[35] Likewise, the changing nature of the state is crucial to understanding the expanded operations of the state, both in times of war and times of peace.[36]

As is obvious, the form in which torture re-emerges in the twentieth century at the hands of the state is quite different from the evidentiary use of it. It is also different from the punitive and religious uses to which torture was put in early periods. Einolf's assertion that all accounts of torture fail to explain the re-emergence and increase of torture in the twentieth century misses the mark. The explanations offered (by Langbein and Foucault, for example) explain why torture disappeared from a *particular institution*. These authors *do not* claim that torture no longer exists; they claim only that it no longer exists *in the same form*. As I will argue below, the accounts provided of the disappearance of older forms of torture by Foucault go a great distance in helping us understand the form modern torture takes.

As Edward Peters notes, Mellor's work begins to show us the form of modern torture, albeit in a preliminary way. Peters notes that Mellor shows us

how practices which began in the nineteenth-century as extra-legal began to become less repugnant to some branches of state authority, and when the law, which began the century as antecedent to and protected by the state, came to be, in a sense more thorough than Blackstone could ever have imagined, itself an 'engine of the state' and torture therefore an engine of the law. (*Torture*, 108)

A common practice up until the sventeenth century had become distasteful, but not distasteful enough to be driven out of society for good. Torture re-emerged in the apparatus of the state in the twentieth century, albeit in a different theater. Moreover, torture *increased*. A new system of surveillance and control came to dominate social space in the 19th century, and this was accompanied (as mentioned above) by a new conception of the nature of human kind: something that can be controlled by police, prisons, and additional institutions. These institutions, designed to control and re-shape human subjects, become the new sites of torture.

Here we can see the importance (once again) of Foucault's socio-anthropological approach to the explanation of changes in our punitive practices. The abolition of torture in criminal and punitive proceedings is coupled with the emergence of institutions that will themselves ultimately become the site of a more covert torture. As Peters claims, "the growth of state security police, political police proper, is perhaps the ultimate cause of the reappearance of torture in the twentieth century" (*Torture*, 114).

The change in our conception of the human being as malleable – as capable of reform – helped to eliminate torture from the courts, but it also made it possible for new forms of torture to emerge, and for torture to take on a novel character. It was in the twentieth century that we saw 'touch-free' torture coming to dominate the torturous actions of the state: the body is no longer the central site of torture. "The purpose of [torture specialists is] to treat their captives, not as objects of punishment, but as subjects whose perceptions had to be altered" (162).[37] Torture is directed primarily at the *person* rather than at the body. In *Preventing Torture*, Evans and Morgan note that this change is occasioned, in part, by the need to keep torture hidden.

> The technology of contemporary torture has largely been removed from the medieval museum of horrors. It generally lies more in the psychological manipulation of feelings and powerlessness and despair than the physical tearing of bodies. It leaves few visible marks. Because torture must be and is denied, it must be deniable. (43, cited in *Phenomenon of Torture*)

This is not to say, of course, that the body is irrelevant to torture. In fact, the body is essential, but it is not the place upon which justice is inscribed. The body now becomes *another instrument of torture* – something else which the state can use against the person being tortured:

> the most intimate and private parts of a victim's life and body become publicly available tools for the torturer to exploit as he will. The victim is completely exposed, while the torturer is free to conceal anything he likes, even those things to which a victim clearly has a right and a profound interest . . . the

asymmetry of power, knowledge, and prerogative is absolute: the victim is in a position of complete vulnerability and exposure, the torturer in one of perfect control and inscrutability. (Sussman, 7)

This is accomplished, not merely through the creation of intense pain *within* one's body, but by having one's body (rather than the torturer) be regarded as the very *cause* of one's pain. This is precisely the recommendation given in the CIA's *Human Resource Exploitation Training Manual*:

> The torture situation is an external conflict, a contest between the subject and his tormentor. The pain which is being inflicted upon him [the interrogatee] from outside himself may actually intensify his will to resist. On the other hand, pain which he is inflicting on himself is more likely to sap his resistance. For example, if he is required to maintain rigid positions such as standing at attention or sitting on a stool for long periods of time, the immediate source of discomfort is not the 'questioner' but the subject himself. His conflict is then an internal struggle. (L-12)

Modern torture thus aims to turn the body against the subject – to make it the very thing that will betray one – to make it one's fundamental adversary. Torture's change is *not* simply a product of the increased desire to hide torture. It is the product of a fundamentally different way of understanding the *victim* of torture: as a subject to be dismantled by the techniques of a science of discipline and control. Hannah Arendt makes a similar point when discussing the mechanisms of the concentration camps: "The aim of all of these methods, in any case, is to manipulate the human body – with its infinite possibilities of suffering – in such a way as to make it destroy the human person as inexorably as do certain mental diseases of organic origin" (199).[38]

As Arendt makes clear, torture still involves *pain* – but the use of pain does not merely concern the display of the sovereign's power, or the restoration of law. While these things may still function in the use of torture, they should not be regarded as the sole critical function of torture. The display in the power of the sovereign, as it existed in punitive torture until the end of the 18th century, demanded a *public* spectacle. This can be seen, for example, in the use of torturous techniques on *corpses*. Foucault makes this point with usual insightfulness:

> It is precisely after death that the public torture begins, because in the end it was less a question of punishing the guilty or of expiating the crime than of producing a ritual display of the infinite power to punish: the ceremony of punitive power, unfolding on the basis of itself and when its object has disappeared, thus works away on the corpse. (85)[39]

It would be foolish to claim that modern torture never involves spectacle. It is precisely *spectacle*, even in the modern world, that can reinforce, or even establish, the power of a regime.[40] Thus Kanan Makiya, discussing Iraq under Saddam Hussein's long rule, writes (in 1989) that

> The range of cruel institutional practices in contemporary Iraq – confession rituals, public hangings, corpse displays, executions, and finally torture – are designed to breed and sustain widespread fear. But those practices are also visible and invisible manifestations of power, extensions of, for example, the state's right to wage war on the nation's enemies . . . the 1969 hangings were a unique ritual, celebrating a new beginning [under Saddam Hussein] and not the continuity or stability of power. Because of the visibility of the occasion, the display of cruelty was intentionally excessive. (201)[41]

The theater of cruelty existed also in the show trials of Stalinist Russia, as well as more recently in the staging of photographs in Abu Ghraib.[42] These are not occasional anachronisms. The display of power – and particularly the power to dehumanize with impunity – is perhaps crucial to the very existence of a sovereign power that approaches absolute. I thus have no wish to deny that modern torture, much like torture in earlier centuries, might involve spectacle and the display of power. Even *secret* torture serves this function in certain respects. Knowing that one might be 'disappeared' at any moment can have a devastating effect on one's ability to navigate the world – and it certainly serves to remind one, at every turn, who is in control. Nevertheless, these similarities should not distract us from the very real differences between modern torture, on the one hand, and torture in its punitive and juridical contexts, on the other. Whereas punitive torture wrote the power of the sovereign on the body – even the *dead* body – of the accused, modern torture aims to eviscerate the *agency* of the tortured while leaving him his entrails. Whereas juridical torture used bodily pain as a means of gathering proof, ignoring entirely the *personhood* of the tortured, modern torture instead aims fundamentally at using bodily pain to break down personhood entirely.

Elaine Scarry's point that torture attempts to reduce a person to his body – to the singularity of pain experienced as one's body – is correct, and entirely compatible with my line of argument. The reduction of a person to her body is possible only because the subject has come to be constituted as fundamentally *more* than mere body. Evans and Morgan are thus wrong to criticize Foucault for purportedly claiming that "contemporary technologies of power rely on the control of the mind rather than the body; that there is no longer any need for the state to use torture when resort can be had to labor discipline, police surveillance, panoptic prisons, and judges using probabilistic reasoning" (23).[43] The 'need' for torture is a red herring here, as the power/knowledge structures Foucault aims to excavate are not the product of rational planning; they are instead the consequence of a change in the way we conceive of humanity. It is thus *irrelevant* that torture is not 'needed' in the disciplinary society. What Foucault's analysis enables us to understand is the new manner in which torture is carried out: the body becomes a means of controlling the mind.[44]

I am not suggesting that the change in our understanding of the human subject (along Foucauldian lines) *caused* the change in the way torture was practiced. A claim of such simplicity would be laughable. My claim, rather, is that the change in the way we collectively conceive of the subject made possible new techniques of torture.[45] Rather than controlling the body of the tortured *alone*, one now aims to undermine the very *agency* of the person being tortured.[46] This is accomplished in modern torture, as we will see, by making the body of the subject not merely a receptacle for painful experiences, but an additional *tool* of the torturer utilized for the express purpose of destroying the subjectivity that inhabits that body.[47]

The change in the way we conceive the human was necessary for the change in the way we conceptualize punishment, as Foucault contends. But the elimination of torturous punishment is not simply a step forward along the route of moral progress. The new anthropology recognizes a new source of weakness – a new thing against which the apparatus of state power can be thrown. Our new anthropology thus creates conditions for a new kind of torture – one which is, arguably at least, often more sinister than the wheel and the rack.[48]

Peters is thus correct when he says that "the coercive revolutionary state of the twentieth century could reintroduce torture into any or all of its procedures, for it had developed not only new powers, but a new anthropology" (Peters, *Torture*, 131). This new anthropology is precisely the one that Foucault so skillfully articulated in a number of his histories, most notably in *The Order of Things*.

> Before the end of the eighteenth century, man did not exist – any more than the potency of life, the fecundity of labor, or the historical density of language. He is a quite recent creature, which the demiurge of knowledge fabricated with its own hands less than two hundred years ago. (308)

The 'man' that emerges in the 18th century is one that is viewed as malleable, trainable, and who can be subjected to normalization through participation in institutions (such as the military, the university, the prison and the hospital). This new anthropology, in turn, creates the conditions under which a new kind of power can be exerted on human subjectivity. A condition for the possibility of a power which is all-pervasive – which operates essentially through observation and normalization through participation – is the emergence of the human being as an object of knowledge. Only when we come to view the human agent as a malleable object to be known and trained can power operate as an explanatory presumption. Towards the beginning of *Discipline and Punish*, Foucault remarks:

> Perhaps we should abandon the belief that power makes mad and that, by the same token, the renunciation of power is one of the conditions of knowledge. We should admit rather that power produces knowledge (and not simply by encouraging it because it serves power or by applying it because it is useful); that power and knowledge directly imply one another; that there is no power relation without the correlative constitution of a field of knowledge, nor any knowledge that does not presuppose and constitute at the same time power relations. (27)

This methodological suggestion provides a way of understanding why torture *changes*, as well as a way of understanding one of the conditions under which its re-emergence is enabled. Torture becomes less concerned with the body of the subject precisely because its aim changes in line with a new anthropology: torture aims to control the *agency* of the subject, not merely to utilize his body to write the power of the state. Controlling the body is no longer enough once a new anthropology emerges. One must now control *subjectivity itself*.

I suggest that a piece of the explanation of the re-emergence of torture lies in one of the conditions for its original elimination: a new conception of the human as something that can be manipulated and formed through the exertion of institutional power. It is this very fact that partially explains the proliferation of new kinds of torture *manuals* in the twentieth century: unlike the descriptions of torture offered in earlier epochs, the manuals of the twentieth century are guides for the manipulation of persons, not bodies. They emphasize the goal of destroying autonomy and personhood by turning a person against herself. The fluctuating person, capable of being reformed through moral instruction in the prisons of the 19th century, is the same subject that can be turned into a tool of the state through the manipulation of surroundings – through sleep deprivation, simulated execution, waterboarding, noise pollution, and the general maintenance of an environment where nothing makes sense.

> The 'questioner' should be careful to manipulate the subject's environment to disrupt patterns, not to create them. Meals and sleep should be granted irregularly, in more than abundance or less than adequacy, on no discernible pattern. This is done to disorient the subject and destroy his capacity to resist. (L-3)[49]

The hope and convictions of those who had lived through the atrocities of WWII led to stricter international legislation. After WWII and its attendant abuses, the nations of the world came together in an attempt to end the serious human rights abuses the world had seen (the Geneva Convention explicitly forbids any sort of torture, and attempts to fill in gaps in the earlier Geneva and Hague Accords). The 1948 Universal Declaration of Human Rights, Article 5, states that "No one shall be subjected to torture or to cruel, inhuman, or degrading treatment or punishment." Later, in 1984, the UN passed the UN Convention against Torture, which called for the compete elimination of torture: "No exceptional circumstances whatsoever, whether a state of war or the threat of war, internal political instability or any other public emergency, may be invoked as a justification of torture." These were hardly the only such international resolutions, treaties, and laws that were passed.[50]

But the story doesn't end in the totalitarian states of the twentieth century, or in the passing of international laws that explicitly forbid torture under any circumstances. For those of us who lived through the Bush administration, this has become even more apparent than it already was – but, I hasten to add, it wasn't nearly apparent enough. Many citizens of the developed West had been convinced that they were against torture, at least until it was convenient to be for it. Many citizens of nations like the US, Canada, and the UK had what I will call 'paper convictions,'[51] as well as the hubris to think that torture was not something nations as advanced as ours might be capable of. We have been proven sorely wrong.

Amnesty International reported in 2000 that over 150 countries had engaged in torture during the period between 1997 and mid-2000.[52] The numbers are not going down. The problem is recurrent, pervasive, and no one seems immune. To get a sense of the scope of the problem, I offer the following (incomplete) list of countries known to have engaged in torture in recent years.

1. Afghanistan
2. Algeria
3. Angola
4. Argentina
5. Brazil
6. Cambodia
7. Canada
8. Chile
9. China
10. Cuba
11. DR Congo
12. Egypt
13. El Salvador
14. UK
15. France
16. Georgia
17. Germany
18. Greece
19. Guatemala
20. Haiti
21. Honduras
22. Indonesia
23. Iran
24. Iraq
25. Israel
26. Italy
27. Kenya
28. Mauritania

29. Mexico
30. Morocco
31. Nicaragua
32. Nigeria
33. North Vietnam
34. North Korea
35. Paraguay
36. Russia
37. Saudi Arabia
38. Serbia
39. South Africa
40. South Korea
41. South Vietnam
42. Soviet Union
43. Spain
44. Sri Lanka
45. Sudan
46. Syria
47. Thailand
48. Turkey
49. Uganda
50. United States
51. Uruguay
52. Uzbekistan
53. Zimbabwe

The meaning of 'torture'

As I noted in Chapter 1, the term 'torture' is as difficult to define as a term can be. The varied history of torture is certainly part of the explanation of this difficulty. In the final section of this chapter, I want to explore how this situation has been made substantially worse by the movement of torture from a public practice to one that occurs in dark rooms, in secret sites, and under the cover of such disguises as 'national security.'

In Edward Peters' account of the history of torture, he recognizes the significant semantic confusion that has accompanied the departure of torture from the courtroom. As he notes, "torture slipped from a specifically legal vocabulary – in which it possessed specific meanings – into a general vocabulary of moral invective" (150). The nineteenth-century

> language of morality and sentiment, expanded and applied to increasing kinds and numbers of human relationships, widened the applicability of the term to all areas of human brutality, from the workplace to the home. Owners now tortured workers, husbands wives, parents children, criminals victims. All oppressors tortured all the oppressed. And torture thus entered a general vocabulary with sentimental and moral meaning. (151)

On Peters' (I think correct) view, this semantic slippage actually enables institutional powers to operate with ease in the use of torturous practices. "The term torture now exists in almost a wholly general vocabulary. And because it does, it is easy for torturers to deny what they're doing is torture" (Peters, 153). This has been nowhere more painfully realized in the recent past than in the rhetoric of the George W. Bush administration – an administration that claimed it did not torture while simultaneously engaging in sleep deprivation, waterboarding, prolonged solitary confinement, and the use of particular phobias against prisoners in an effort to terrorize said prisoners. In the memoranda of the Bush administration, the pliability of the term 'torture' is put to nefarious use. In a memo of August, 2002, for example, the Office of Legal Counsel claimed that:

> As we understand it, when the waterboard is used, the subject's body responds as if the subject were drowning, even though the subject may be well aware that he is in fact not drowning. You have informed us that this procedure does not inflict actual physical harm. Thus, although the subject may experience the fear or panic associated with the feeling of drowning, the waterboard does not inflict physical pain. As we explained in the Section 2340A Memorandum, "pain and suffering" as used in Section 2340 is best understood as a single concept, not distinct concepts of "pain" as distinguished from "suffering." *See* Section 2340A Memorandum at 6 n.3. The waterboard, which inflicts no pain or actual harm whatsoever, does not, in our view inflict "severe pain or suffering." Even if one were to parse the statute more finely to attempt to treat "suffering" as a distinct concept, the waterboard could not be said to inflict severe suffering. The waterboard is simply a controlled acute episode, lacking the connotation of a protracted period of time generally given to suffering. (11)

Of course, waterboarding was rarely used on a detainee only once. In fact, it was often used repeatedly over a period of days, weeks, or even months. Khalid Sheikh Mohammed, for example, was water boarded 183 times in March of 2003 while being held by the US in Guantanamo Bay. Abu Zubaydah was water-boarded 83 times in August of 2002 at the same facility.[53] The fact that this practice was known to be used, and could be used at any time, was in fact part of the cause of the psychological trauma experienced by detainees who were its victims. It is the anticipation of additional torture, survivors have sometimes remarked, that constituted the worst of the time they spent in detention. As John Perry notes in his analysis of torture,

> Many torture survivors report they experienced some of their worst anguish in the intervals between torture sessions. For the torturer, each session may last only a few minutes. For the victim, there is often no break; his or her mental anguish fills up the void between torture sessions. (107)

Even leaving aside this particular issue, Jay Bybee's[54] assumption that there is no suffering in waterboarding *in individual instances* is absurd. To make sense of this assertion, we need to pay special attention to Bybee's claim that a 'protracted period of time' is required for suffering. Because waterboarding typically does not last very long, Bybee claims, it cannot produce suffering.

Bybee's account of what suffering entails is absurd on several different levels. The claim that the psychological pain inflicted by waterboarding only lasts as long as the event of waterboarding strains credulity. People often report something akin to Post-Traumatic Stress after being assaulted. They tend to relive the assault in their minds, and this active remembering is the source of a great deal of suffering – often for years to come. This is particularly evident in cases of rape (often regarded as a type of torture). The duration of the actual rape is irrelevant to the suffering the rape causes, as the suffering continues well past the point when the rape occurs. Indeed, in certain respects, the *worst* of the suffering can come only after the act is complete.

There is no need to belabor the abuses of the Bush administration here. We will return to a thorough analysis of the legal legerdemain of the recent past in Chapter 8. The point I want to make here is that it is the *plasticity* of our current understanding of torture that partially explains the impunity with which it is done. A typical image of torture is nicely articulated by R. D. Emerick:

> Our core image of torture, I think, is captured quite fittingly by a Gary Larson cartoon. It depicts a skinny man, with unkempt beard, alone, in a dungeon, lying on the rack. Above him reads a sign, "Congratulations Bob, Torturer of the Month" . . . This image or exemplar is what I seem to invoke as a kind of place holder of contrast to my metaphorical employments of 'torture' [like 'this meeting is torture,' or 'going to the dentist is like torture']. It captures the understanding which is relied upon when I and others use 'torture' metaphorically. (5–6)[55]

As Emerick goes on to note, we have gone beyond the torture dungeon, even if our understanding lags behind. Our metaphors surrounding torture, however, run rampant: watching a film can be torture, as can a visit from the in-laws. "In the moral and sentimental universe, nothing may be torture, and, with a slight shift of perspective, everything may be torture" (153).[56] This slippage in meaning has significant consequences for debating torture. Indeed, as I have argued elsewhere, it is a failure to actually understand the empirical reality of torture that leads to its defense.[57] Ignorance of torture's empirical reality is something we shall return to again and again.

Notes

1. Demosthenes, 30.37, quoted in "A History of Torture," by James Ross, in *Torture: Does It Make Us Safer? Is It Ever OK?*
2. James Ross, "A History of Torture," in *Torture: Does It Make Us Safer? Is It Ever OK?*

3. Page DuBois, *Torture and Truth*, excerpted in *The Phenomenon of Torture*.
4. Ross, ibid.
5. Evans and Morgan, *Preventing Torture*.
6. We will return to this in the section on Torture and Treason.
7. See, for example, Malise Ruthven, *Torture: The Grand Conspiracy*.
8. England is an interesting exception to the claims here made about European torture. England's legal system involved the use of a jury, and hence did not face the same pressures as those on the continent. Torture in England was thus not part of judicial proceedings, which is not to say it wasn't used in other contexts. The Privy Council issued something close to 'torture warrants' for nearly a century during and around the reign of Queen Elizabeth I.
9. Bartlett, *Trial by Fire and Water: The Medieval Judicial Ordeal*.
10. From Ernest F. Henderson, *Select Historical Documents of the Middle Ages* (London: George Bell and Sons, 1910), pp. 314–317.
11. The social status of the witness, as well as his history, was relevant to both the weight of testimony and to its admissibility.
12. Ross, ibid.
13. Ross, ibid.
14. Even Angela Y. Davis, a leader of the so-called prison abolition movement, does not actually advocate an end to all incarceration. Davis is concerned, rather, with the way in which the current penal system duplicates the injustices of racism and slavery in a new institution. In calling for the abolition of prisons, she is calling for a recognition and rectification of the prison as slavery surrogate. See, for example, *Are Prisons Obsolete?* and *Abolition Democracy*.
15. See his *Torture: The Grand Conspiracy*.
16. Foucault, *Discipline and Punish*.
17. Langbein, ibid.
18. Beccaria was convinced to write a book on torture by one of its critics, apparently, and was coached along the way. See James Ross, "A History of Torture," in *Torture: Does It Make Us Safer? Is It Ever OK?*
19. See *Contingency, irony, and solidarity*.
20. Robert Mills has argued that our relationship to torture (and pain more generally) is closely connected to the Medieval relationship, although we manifest this in different venues. See his *Suspended Animation: Pain, Pleasure, and Punishment in Medieval Culture*.
21. This is true in many regimes in the world. Many contend that the long time period persons live on death row in the United States itself constitutes a kind of torture.
22. Foucault, *Abnormal*.
23. Foucault, *Discipline and Punish*.
24. Paul W. Kahn, *Sacred Violence*.
25. Evans and Morgan, *Preventing Torture*.
26. In the case of the Spanish Inquisition, the right to *carry out* the Inquisition

was granted by the monarchy. Ferdinand and Isabella of Spain, on March 31 of 1492, signed that 'Edict of Expulsion,' an order designed to rid Spain of Jews. This edict helped to create the Spanish Inquisition. Rather than leaving Granada, many Jews opted to convert to Christianity. This conversion made this class of person ('*conversos*') intrinsically suspicious, and automatically candidates for heresy. This is evidence for a partial separation of the investigation of heresy from the rule of law. If there were no such distinction, the edict would have been superfluous.

27. See Glucklich, *Sacred Pain*, Chapter 7.
28. John Perry, *Torture: Religious Ethics and National Security*.
29. Glucklich, *Sacred Pain*.
30. Lisa Silverman, *Tortured Subjects: Pain, Truth, and the Body in Early Modern France*.
31. My claim here is not that this was the *only* function of punitive torture. This would be absurd. Nor is my claim that there is a clean break in the primary function that punitive torture fulfilled. History is a messy business, and social institutions rarely (if ever) have a singular purpose. For a fascinating account of some of the different functions of punishment, see Mitchell B. Merback, *The Thief, the Cross and the Wheel: Pain and the Spectacle of Punishment in Medieval and Renaissance Europe*.
32. Early Christians (in Rome, for example) condemned torture, calling instead for mercy. The Catholic church's official policy was given by Pope Innocent IV on May 15th, 1253. It was subsequently confirmed by Alexander IV (1259) and Clement IV (1265). In 2004, Pope John Paul II condemned all torture as debasing humanity. See Perry, *Torture: Religious Ethics and National Security*.
33. For an account that attempts to spell out some of these changes, see Silverman, *Tortured Subjects: Pain, Truth, and the Body in Early Modern France*.
34. Christopher J. Einolf, "The Fall and Rise of Torture: A Comparative and Historical Analysis," *Sociological Theory*, 25:2, June 2007.
35. This point was made many years ago by Herbert C. Kelman, "The Social Context of Torture: Policy Process and Authority Structure," in *The Politics of Pain*.
36. Edward Peters cites the new power of the state, as well as its increased vulnerability, in accounting for modern torture. See *Torture*.
37. Rejali, *Torture and Modernity*, ibid.
38. Arendt, *The Origins of Totalitarianism*, cited in *The Phenomenon of Torture*.
39. Foucault, *Abnormal: Lectures at the College de France, 1974–1975*.
40. For an interesting discussion of this, see Judith Butler's *Precarious Life*, as well as Gordon Hull's compelling response, "One View of the Dungeon: The Ticking Time Bomb between Governmentality and Sovereignty," *International Philosophical Quarterly*, forthcoming.
41. From *Republic of Fear: The Politics of Modern Iraq*, excerpted in *The Phenomenon of Torture*.

42. For a fascinating account of the theatricality of torture at Abu Ghraib, see Stephen F. Eisenman's *The Abu Ghraib Effect.*

43. *Preventing Torture.*

44. As I noted above, modern torture frequently involves *both* psychological and physical torture. My remarks should thus not be understood to imply that we no longer use any kind of physical torture. My point, rather, is that the new torture of the modern era is made possible by a new understanding of the subject. This new understanding has not eliminated old forms of torture – a fact which some authors regard as a reason for rejecting Foucault's view. As indicated above, I do not think this is so. One can manipulate the subject through disciplinary practices that are remarkably violent. There is nothing in principle in Foucault's analysis that would prevent this, even if Foucault himself was not particularly clear on this point.

45. I thus agree with Rejali's contention, in *Torture and Modernity*, that Foucault does not explain the re-emergence of torture. I would insist, however, that Foucault's analysis is a part of the explanation of the changing *form* that torture takes.

46. This will be explored in detail in Chapter 4.

47. I of course do not intend to imply any sort of mind/body split in putting the point this way.

48. I will return to this point in Chapters 4 and 7.

49. CIA, *Human Resource Exploitation Training Manual.*

50. There was also the 1966 International Covenant on Civil and Political Rights, for example.

51. See Chapter 9.

52. See *Torture Worldwide: An Affront to Human Dignity.*

53. This was reported in the *IG Report* by the CIA Inspector General, John Helgerson. It has been widely reported in the media since this report became public.

54. Bybee was one of the lawyers, under the Bush administration, who had a hand in the crafting of 'the torture memos' – documents that gave legal cover to the United States for the use of torture. The US policy, and the conditions leading to it, will be discussed in Chapter 8.

55. "Politicizing 'Torture': Torturing a Metaphor," unpublished manuscript.

56. Peters, ibid.

57. See "It's About Time: Defusing the Ticking Bomb Argument." This point will re-emerge in several places in this book.

Chapter 3

The Wrongness of Torture: Identifying Torture's Unique Despicability

The torture debate

Torture persists – and so do the arguments in its favor. Torture is nevertheless nearly universally regarded as abhorrent, unlike so many other moral issues. The arguments offered in its favor are nearly all arguments from *exception* – arguments that defend torture as the lesser of two evils, but an evil all the same. In this chapter, I aim, at least in a preliminary way, to establish what it is that makes torture a wrong of this sort. Failing to identify this, in my view, has led to its defense. This, in turn, will mark the way to understanding what happens to the person tortured (Chapter 4), and then to assessing arguments for and against torture (Chapters 5 and 6).

The *prima facie* case against torture: models of torture's wrongness

Torture is one of a few actions that seems to be *obviously* wrong to virtually anyone.[1] Virtually no one defends the view that there is nothing wrong with torture, and I know of no such arguments in any serious academic journal or book. Indeed, the closest one comes to an argument that torture is *not* morally reprehensible in the majority of cases is from those who insist that there is no objective validity to any particular moral claim. The presupposition in all of the literature surrounding torture is that torture is *prima facie* wrong, and that any argument for its permissibility will of necessity be an argument for exceptions to an otherwise iron-clad moral rule: one simply should not torture, unless, of course (the defenders of torture maintain), this is the *lesser* of two evils. Only in such exceptional circumstances is engaging in such actions permissible.

Thinking clearly about the arguments for and against torture requires thinking clearly about its status as a near-universal wrong. There has been a tendency, in my view, to seriously underestimate the wrongness of torture, and part of this has been a failure to see precisely *what* is wrong with torture. Misidentifying torture's wrong-making features has the deleterious effect of weighing its potential merits in untenable ways. Thus, the place to begin our analysis is with what might make torture wrong. There seem to be two classes of candidates for torture's wrongness. The candidates are captured in a distinction between subject-referring wrongs, on the one hand, and other-referring wrongs, on the other. An action is wrong in the subject-referring sense if that action does damage to the person to whom the action is done. An action is other-referring if its wrongness consists primarily of the effects that this action will have on those *other than* the person to whom the action is done.

Obviously, these categories need not be mutually exclusive. *Any* instance of torture, it seems plausible to admit, will involve subject-referring harms. The point in distinguishing these two kinds of accounts of torture is to acknowledge that it is sometimes thought that the *effects* of torture (on the state, the citizens of a nation, the family of the victim, and so on) will be torture's primary wrong-making feature. The following four candidates represent some common accounts of torture's wrongness. The first three are subject-centered, while the fourth is other-centered.

> **Infliction of Pain:** torture is wrong insofar as it causes pain to the person being tortured.
>
> **Violation of Autonomy:** torture is wrong insofar as it violates the autonomy of the tortured, forcing her to undergo actions that no one would consent to.
>
> **Violation of Agency:** torture is wrong because it destroys the agency of the person to whom it is done.
>
> **Violation of Trust:** torture is wrong because it destroys the ability of citizens to live under a state with a sense of security.

Each of these accounts of the wrongness of torture has particular problems: there will be cases of torture that do not easily fall under any *single* account. This is perhaps to be expected, given that the term 'torture' is not precisely defined. In assessing these accounts of the wrongness of torture, then, our aim is not to isolate the *single* thing that makes torture wrong. In some sense, *all* of these things make torture a serious moral breach. Our aim, rather, is to attempt to discern what makes torture *uniquely* wrong – that is, it is to determine what makes torture unlike other things that are regarded as wrong, but not as *obviously* as wrong as torture is. None of this is (yet) to say, of course, that there might not be exceptions to the torture ban – instances in which torture turns out to be the *best* thing one can do, even though it is indeed an awful thing by anyone's lights. Before we can assess this latter issue, we've got to get clear about what makes torture the kind of wrong that it is.

Pain

The initial response offered to what makes torture wrong is typically the pain it inflicts. The wrongness of inflicting pain, however, is by no means as straightforward as it appears. Part of the issue in assessing the wrongness of pain involves the immense complexity of the phenomenon. Consider, for example, assessing the *level* of pain of someone who has gone to the emergency room due to a severe injury. In a study done by Ron Melzack and Patrick Wall, the findings on the correlation between injury and pain reported are quite telling:

> We examined the first 138 patients to enter, who were alert, rational, and coherent, 37 percent of whom said they did not feel pain at the time of injury. Of those patients with injuries limited to their skin, such as abrasions, cuts, and burns, 53 percent had a pain-free period. However, of those patients with deep tissue injuries, such as fractures, sprains, and stabs, only 28 percent had a pain-free period. The majority of these people reported the onset of pain within an hour, although some did not feel pain for many hours. (11)

The difficulty of predicting pain responses is illustrated here, and will be explored in much more detail below (Chapter 6: *Cannot predict pain response*). Wall argues, based on this research and much more, that one's *attitude* towards pain, as well as the state one is in, can affect the way that pain is experienced by the person on the receiving end of some painful occurrence. Put simply, responses to pain are multiple, and cannot be attributed to one particular brain activity. "The pattern of response varies from person to person, and within an individual it varies from one painful episode to another" (Wall, 76). Pain, in short, is not a uniform phenomenon.

In discussion of pain, moreover, it is often noted that pain *is a good thing* from the point of view of the species. While an oversimplification, the point that pain acts as a 'warning system' to an organism is at least partially true: the experience of pain stimulates a certain kind of behavior on the part of the organism. The oversimplified view typically appeals to the reaction the body undergoes when it comes into contact with a painful stimulus (a hot surface, for example). As it turns out, of course, a body will react to 'painful' stimuli even in the absence of pain receptors. Someone with congenital analgesia (someone unable to process pain signals) can still detect, by various means, when they come into contact with something that might be dangerous to them (such as a hot surface).[2] There *is*, however, a related function that pain certainly serves: it is crucial in allowing a body to heal, as it prevents an organism from utilizing whatever part of its body has sustained injury.[3] In this respect, it is a mistake to regard pain as something that is *entirely* negative, and equally a mistake to regard any instance of feeling pain as something to be avoided.

Even given that pain is not *intrinsically* an evil, one might still contend that it is the thing that makes torture the wrong that it is. After all, someone might argue, none of the benefits of pain are present in the torture case – or, at any rate, making an argument that these benefits *were* present would seem *ad hoc*, if not plain silly. So, the benefits of pain are not to be generalized: it is still the case that pain is something to be avoided, and that the infliction of needless pain constitutes a serious wrongdoing.

But there are complications to be considered with this view as well. Consider a series of cases:

Dentist
You go to the dentist for a routine cleaning. While there, the dentist notes several cavities. He has some free time that afternoon, so you have the cavities filled. Despite the use of pain medication, the procedure is quite painful.

Childbirth
You unintentionally get pregnant, and decide to have the child. Although you really do not want to experience the pain of labor, you opt to do so.

Tattoos, Piercing, and Scarification
You become fascinated with accessorizing your body. You begin with the standard forms of piercing: your ears, your nose, and your eyebrow. The pain in getting these piercings is not devastating, but, at least for some of these cases, neither is it negligible. From there, you decide to get tattoos in various places on your body. You eventually get a tattoo on your neck and head, despite having been told that this is one of the most painful places to receive a tattoo. Finally, you decide to experiment with scarification: the intentional burning of the skin in a way that leaves scar designs. This is certainly the most painful of the accessorizing you've done, but you feel it is worth it.

In each of these cases, we have pain that is a foreseeable consequence of particular events: the dentist's procedure will hurt, but it is worth doing given the overall benefit to one's health; childbirth is one of the most painful experiences one can undergo, and yet is often approached with excitement, and also often with the refusal to take any sort of medication to offset the significant pain involved; accessorizing one's body is done willingly and often with great enthusiasm, despite what can be considerable pain. No one, I think, would judge the dentist, the semen donor, or the piercer as guilty of wrong-doing in the standard types of cases, despite the fact that all of these persons are responsible for causing (in some cases more directly than others) a great deal of needless pain. In this respect, even inflicting needless pain need not constitute any moral wrongdoing. Regardless of whatever evolutionary benefit pain fulfills, it can also fulfill social functions, as well as highly personal ones. Even *intentional* and unnecessary pain need not constitute a harm.

There are two objections that one might raise on behalf of the pain thesis. First, one might argue that pain, in the above cases, is *incidental* to the actions in question. The dentist does not actually *intend* to cause the pain that he does. Invoking the doctrine of double effect, the pain in this case is a foreseeable but unintended consequence of the procedure. Provided we accept the doctrine of double effect, then, it is wrong to call the above actions cases of *intentionally* inflicting pain. The wrongness of torture, one might thus still maintain, is that the needless pain is *intentionally and willfully* inflicted.[4]

The second objection to the use of the above three cases runs as follows: pain is something that is willfully undergone in the above cases, but which is not thereby relieved of its character as a harm. This can be seen through a simple thought experiment: if these actions could be engaged in *without the pain*, they certainly would be. The pain in these cases is thus best seen as a *necessary evil* – but one it would be better to be able to forego if given the opportunity. As the expression makes clear, though, pain is still to be seen as an *evil* (loosely speaking, of course) – a harm that one submits to for the sake of some broader goal, but a harm all the same. The pain of torture is thus to be distinguished from the pain in the above examples, so the pain thesis is still a plausible candidate for the central wrong-making feature of torture. If it were not intrinsically harmful (and to be avoided), there would be no reason for persons engaging in the above actions to prefer that the actions in question be painless.

Once again, the situation is more complicated than these objections suggest. As it turns out, pain need not be something that is merely endured. While it is correct to point out that pain is *tolerated* in the above cases, this is not always so. Sometimes pain is *sought out* by persons. Likewise, pain is not always incidental to those actions we choose to engage in. There are cases in which we intentionally engage in actions that are *essentially* constituted by pain. These practices simply would not be what they are if they were not painful. Two examples should sufficiently demonstrate that pain can actually be regarded as a constitutive good, and hence that the pain thesis does not survive even in light of the above objections. The two examples are sado-masochistic bondage and certain forms of ascetic religious practice.

S/M

Sado-masochistic bondage involves the use of pain in an erotic, or at least semi-erotic, capacity. Typical kinds of S/M involve the use of clamps, weights, whipping, or even what is referred to, literally enough, as 'fist-fucking.'

In his fascinating account of Foucault's life, James Miller articulates what the S/M scene involves. I quote at length to give a more robust sense of some of the practices in question, as well as how painful such practices can be.

> [S/M] can be used to produce shattering states of intense 'suffering-pleasure' . . . [this involves being] bound, tied down, handcuffed, blindfolded . . . [it can also involve] "leather cockrings with pinpricks inside" – as the penis becomes erect, the prongs cut into its flesh, [or] a toy made of leather with metal rings which can be used . . . by hanging weights from the rings, thus pulling on the testicles.
>
> In 'tit torture,' the players use clamps, stretchers, and harnesses . . . sometimes with the nipple clamps attached to genital clamps. Fitted with adjustable screws, the clamps could be tightened gradually, delivering just the right dose of pain. "There comes a point in tit play when anything goes," explains Geoff Mains in *Urban Aboriginals*. "Pain of any form becomes sheer ecstasy. Hot candle wax dribbled over alligator clip. The most extraordinary pressure on muscles or connective tissue. The frontier between pain and pleasure has been crossed."
>
> Similarly with fist-fucking – the gentle insertion of one's hand and forearm up another person's ass . . . [There are also] a variety of far more unusual and voluptuously 'painful' scenes. [For example, one scene involves one person using] a lancet to pierce "the nipple, the skin of the penis," or the scrotum. (266–267)

The pain present in this case is anything but incidental; it is *essential* to the erotic satisfaction of the participants involved. Indeed, Foucault, an advocate and participant in such practices, thought that the intensity of 'suffering-pleasure' enabled one to access a truth that scientific discourse could not.[5] While this conception of S/M is likely a minority view, it nevertheless reveals what is *not* a minority conception of the importance of pain to such practices: the pain *is the thing sought*.

In this respect, certain forms of religious practice are surprisingly close to S/M. Rather than being incidental to the practice, pain becomes its central, defining feature. The use of pain in the context of religious ceremony is surprisingly common. Pain figures "prominently . . . [in] mourning rituals, pilgrimages, rites of atonement, vows and intercessionary rites, and celebratory performances of annual holidays . . . ritualized pain – self-flagellation, crucifixion, barefoot pilgrimages, walking on hot coals, rolling naked on a hard terrain, and so forth" (Glucklich, 35). The prominence of pain has been verified by empirical research.

> Self-mutilation is extremely pervasive in rites of mourning around the world. A recent survey of seventy-eight societies has documented thirty-one in which

self-injury prevails and thirty-two in which it is attempted in varying degrees
of success. Acts of self-hurting vary from mild hair-pulling and chest-beating
to extremely violent forms of self-abuse. (Glucklich, 35)

Rather than quibble about the extent to which any particular example
fits our standard notion of 'pain,' it is sufficient to demonstrate that
there are *at least some* cases of religious practice that involve excruciat-
ing pain. I will thus focus on one particular case, despite the fact that the
case can be made that pain exists throughout a variety of practices in
divergent religions, and strikes me as extremely compelling.[6] Providing
one such case is enough to show that pain, even when intentionally
inflicted and completely unnecessary, can actually constitute a perceived
good for an agent.

The Ascetic

A man devoted to practicing a particular religion has determined that the true
way to union with God is through engaging in particular kinds of painful
forms of worship. These forms involve whipping, self-mutilation, and other
kinds of what might be called 'self-torture.' Through engaging in these forms
of worship, the man believes, he can pay for his sin and come closer to divinity.

What the examples of *The Ascetic* and *S/M* demonstrate is that the harm
of pain can be transformed by the *meaning* that pain has for us. It would
be a misunderstanding, however, to think that the meaning of pain makes
it *cease to be pain*. As Glucklich remarks,

> In its relation to pain, the goal of religious life is *not* to bring anesthesia, but
> to transform the pain that causes suffering into a pain that leads to insight,
> meaning, and even salvation. This is the essential paradox of sacred pain: that
> the hurting body does not suffer silently. It offers a potential voice, if one has
> the tools to make the soul listen. (40)

In this example, as well as the *S/M* example, the pain presented is part of
the *intention* of the agent engaging in the actions in question. In the case
of sado-masochism, the presence of pain is central to the activities that
one intentionally engages in. Indeed, if the pain *were not present*, one
would not be engaging in the activity correctly. Likewise, in ascetic religious practices, the presence of pain demonstrates one's penance before
god. In asceticism and sado-masochism, pain functions as an *intended*
part of what an agent takes part in. In these cases, pain is *directly*
intended by the very person who will experience that pain, as pain is a
constitutive element of the practices themselves.[7]

Torture *also* involves pain intrinsically. If one were to remove pain
from the torture process, one would no longer be dealing with something

recognizable *as* torture. This point marks something in the deep structure of torture – that it is administered, to be sure, but also that it is something that is *experienced*. Torture is not merely some set of procedures or practices; it is also intrinsically something that is undergone. But as demonstrated by the above examples, undergoing unnecessary pain, even intentionally inflicted, need not constitute a harm.

These examples, as well as the others we have presented along the way, point to an important fact about pain: whether or not pain is judged a harm – indeed, the very way pain *is experienced* by those who are subject to it – depends on the *meaning* one attributes to the source of one's pain.[8] Given this, pain cannot be a wrong *simpliciter*. In some instances, on the contrary, it is the key to a meaningful life, sexual fulfillment, or some other valuable project.

There are two objections to the overall account of pain I have thus far given, as well as the argumentative strategy I have been employing. Dealing with these objections will, I hope, be a relatively easy task that has substantial payoff: we will be able to articulate an additional, independent argument for the inability of the pain thesis to account for the wrongness of torture. The two objections in question both center on the way we have been conceptualizing 'pain.'

1) *'Pain' is not a uniform phenomenon*
The analysis thus far has advanced utilizing an understanding of pain that is simply unrealistic both conceptually and biologically. Even in ordinary language, people distinguish different kinds of pain (the psychological and the physical for example). Likewise, investigations of pain at the biological level reveal that the way pain is processed is not a uniform phenomenon. In fact, 'pain' seems to designate very different processes, utilizing different neural pathways and different parts of the nervous system (A beta fibers, A delta fibers, and C fibers). To speak of the wrong of torture as consisting in 'pain,' construed monolithically, fails to acknowledge that we are not here dealing with *one* phenomenon, but with many. Helping oneself to different examples of pain that may be neurologically, biologically, and conceptually distinct, cannot demonstrate that pain *isn't central* to torture's wrongness. To infer this, in fact, could be like arguing that chess cannot be a game that uses pieces, and then highlighting a number of other games that involve no pieces (word games, mind games, and so on). Obviously, this form of argument cannot show what it intends to show. This is the case primarily because the notion of 'game' picks out a number of very different things related only through family resemblance. The same can be said of 'pain.'

This point is an important one, and one that has been routinely ignored. Indeed, a failure to recognize this diversity has often been regarded as the central failing among those who study pain. Glucklich, for example, expresses this exact concern with regard to analyses of religious forms of pain. These analyses "share this fault: They reduce all forms of pain to a single principle, and yet none of them gives any indication of the wealth of pain types being reduced" (32). Similarly, Patrick Wall, discussing neuroscientific attempts to explain pain, implores us to recognize its multiplicity:

> We should not be depressed that the most advanced modern techniques fail to show a single simple focus of brain activity associated with pain. Pain may be described as a single simple word, but it implies a class of responses involving many areas of our brains and bodies. The pattern of response varies from person to person, and within an individual it varies from one painful episode to another. (76)

This multiplicity of pain, however, actually speaks against the view I am currently criticizing, not for it. The problem with attempting to reduce the wrongness of torture to something called 'pain' is that this attempt *presumes* a uniform phenomenon, present universally in human life, which can adequately account for torture's wrongness. As we have seen, the variety of pain presents a substantial obstacle to this view. If, however, we *acknowledge* the multiplicity of pain, we need to appeal to something *other than* 'raw pain' as distinguishing the pain in torture from other, banal kinds of pain. Doing this, of course, is equivalent to discrediting the view that pain *alone* can explain torture's unique evil.

2) Pain vs. suffering

'Pain' is often regarded as something that is universally unwanted, even by definition. This view, however, is simply a failure to adequately distinguish *what* one experiences from *how* it is experienced. The conception of pain utilized so far is thus phenomenologically inadequate. It would be much more plausible to begin by distinguishing pain, on the one hand, from suffering, on the other. Glucklich makes this distinction as follows: "pain is a sensation that is tangled with mental and even cultural experiences . . . Suffering, in contrast, is not a sensation but an emotional and evaluative reaction to any number of causes, some entirely painless" (11). Given this distinction, suffering is a much more plausible candidate for the wrongness of torture.

I think we should accept the distinction between pain and suffering. But this does not yet help the case of explaining the wrong of torture – or at any rate, it does not help much. There is still a need to explain what transforms the one into the other, and for this pain alone, as we have seen, is inadequate. Thus, far from showing that an analysis of pain as the wrong-making feature of torture is still viable, the pain/suffering distinction further demonstrates why pain alone cannot fulfill this function.

At this point we can begin to see where the horror of torture lies: it is not in the pain itself, but rather in the *significance* of the pain for the agent being tortured. This is not to deny that the pain of torture is itself a harm. It obviously is. But the uniquely deplorable nature of torture, as we have seen, cannot be adequately explained in this way. On the contrary, it is the meaning attributed to the torture context that acts to make it as morally vile as it is. In the following two sections, we will have occasion to see this in more detail, first by investigating the loss of autonomy inherent in torture, and then by examining the deconstruction of the tortured's very humanity that naturally occurs as a result of torture. While the social cost of loss of trust will also be explored (Chapter 6: *Damages reputation of state and trust of citizens*), and is a significant harm incurred by torture, this does not capture the wrong done to the *tortured*.

Violation of autonomy

Return to the set of examples explored in the previous section: in *Dentist, Childbirth, Tattoos, the Ascetic,* and *S/M,* we are presented with cases where the normal harm of pain is morally transformed by the consent of those who undergo it. As I hope is obvious, this similarity highlights another candidate for the wrongness of torture: the violation of autonomy. While we have demonstrated that the presence of pain is inadequate as a measure of the moral permissibility of an action, we have not yet articulated one of the central reasons this can be so. The *meaning* we attribute to our pain, I have argued, has a significant bearing on the way that pain is experienced. The role of autonomy in the cases above allows us to see one way in which the perception of pain can be altered: pain becomes more bearable when we *choose* to engage in those activities that will be painful. This suggests a certain synergy between the two explanations we have thus far considered: certainly the pain of torture is not irrelevant to it, but neither is the fact that it is done against one's will. If torture did not involve the pain that it does, it would not be as wrong as it is (its wrongness, in many cases, would be that of coercion). If it involved the consent of the tortured, it would likely not be wrong at all (it would be a case of S/M, or something near enough).

In what follows, I would like to consider two arguments that suggest (wrongly, I will argue) that torture is wrong because it violates the autonomy of the tortured. The first argument concerns the morally transformative power of consent: if consent can change an immoral action into a moral one, one might argue, then it is the absence of one's consent that constitutes the wrongness of torture. The second argument involves the view that autonomy is intrinsically valuable, and hence that any violation of autonomy is to be considered a serious moral wrong.

Consent as morally transformative

The morally transformative power of consent suggests that it is the *absence* of consent which marks the wrong-making feature of torture. I have argued elsewhere for this view of consent in considering the wrongness of killing.

> Consent marks the difference between sex and rape, surgery and battery, torture and masochistic pleasure, and, I am suggesting, murder and assisted suicide. The condition of no prior consent specifies that a murder occurs (and not an assisted suicide) only when the person killed would not consent to the killing. If a violation of autonomy is a constitutive part of the wrongfulness of murder, then (to use Alan Wertheimer's expression) consent can be morally transformative (Wertheimer 2003; see also Wertheimer 2000). Because the absence of consent is necessary for murder, my giving consent can transform an impermissible act into a permissible one. There is nothing magical about this. There is a class of morally wrong actions that are morally wrong just insofar as they violate an agent's autonomy. If said agent gives legitimate consent, a violation no longer occurs. Thus, the very thing that made the action impermissible is no longer present. (13)[9]

The view of consent as morally transformative, I think, works well for a wide range of cases. This recognition marks an important one in moral philosophy, but it should not be exaggerated. There are, I would argue, plenty of actions that are morally wrong *regardless* of whether or not consent is given.[10] Likewise, even if an action's wrongness can be transformed through an act of consent, it does not follow that the wrongness of an action is constituted by an *absence* of consent. This requires some elaboration.

Consent transforms an impermissible action because an agent essentially *wills* (through the act of consent) those things to which the agent would (wrongly) be subjected. Put this way, it is apparent that what constitutes the wrong done to the agent is the very thing that must be consented to. But, as is equally apparent, one is not consenting to one's own consenting (i.e. one is not morally transforming one's own consent); the thing consented to is some *independent* thing, the nature of which is changed through the act of consent. This allows us to distinguish between the morally transformative *act* (consent) and the wrong that it thereby transforms (some wrong that might be done to an agent). Put another way, consent (act 2) changes the moral status of a separate action (act 1).

What makes an act wrong, we can thus see, need not be the absence of consent, despite the fact that consent can change the status of the action that would otherwise be wrong.

One line of argument showing this might run as follows: the fact that there is something *to be forgiven* after an event shows that the event was wrong. If it were automatically cancelled by the forgiveness, the forgiveness itself would be a self-undermining speech act: the very object of forgiveness would be *nothing to forgive* as soon as the decision to forgive had been made.

But perhaps, it might be objected, this is nothing to be surprised about. After all, after forgiveness has been given, it stands to reason that *there is nothing left to forgive*. This objection, it seems to me, is mere semantic play. It is true that forgiveness need not be perpetual (an action need only be forgiven once, not repeatedly), but this hardly entails that the event that *was forgiven* is no longer an event at all. The reason that forgiveness (in the usual cases) only needs to occur once is that the *nature* of the event being forgiven is changed by its forgiveness; it is *not* that the event itself changes. Put otherwise: forgiveness changes one's relation to an event, not the event itself.

In any case, we should concede that the *kind* of consent in question when considering *retrospective* consent must be rather different from consent that occurs prior to an event taking place. After all, 'retrospective consent' involves the alteration of an attitude that *already* exists to an event that has *already* taken place. Prior consent, by contrast, prevents certain kinds of attitudes towards an event from even forming.

There is a simpler argument for the view that retrospective consent does *not* eliminate the prior wrongness of an action. The very process of retrospective consent presumes that a wrong has occurred, and that to forgive this wrong is *not* simply to forgive the wrong-doer for not acquiring prior consent. Forgiveness for a wrong-doing involves forgiving *the wrong-doer* for the actions she undertook. What is to be forgiven is the wrong done, not the fact that consent was required. While it is true that, had consent been given, no wrong would have occurred, this does not mean that the *failure to seek consent* was what was morally wrong with the action.

This latter point is rather intuitive when one considers the alternative: if the wrong-making feature of an action is the absence of consent, it follows that widely divergent actions are wrong for *the same reason*. Certainly the wrong of theft, for example, has to do with the wrongful taking of property. Equally certainly, this wrongness is *not* equivalent to the wrongness of rape. Arguing that the absence of consent *constitutes* the wrongs present in these actions would produce absurd results: it would entail that rape and theft were wrong for exactly the same reason. This result is unacceptable, and we thereby have a powerful reason for thinking that, despite the ability of consent to transform immoral actions into morally permissible ones, it is not the absence of consent that *makes* these actions wrong.

This line of argument is sufficient, I hope, for showing that the wrongness of torture *does not consist in* the absence of the consent of those who are tortured. While torture certainly involves a violation of autonomy (insofar as it requires an absence of consent), this violation does not constitute the unique wrongness of torture.

Autonomy as intrinsically valuable

A simpler argument for the wrongness of torture postulates that one's autonomy is intrinsically valuable, and violations of our autonomy thus constitute a serious moral wrong-doing. As we have seen above, torture indisputably violates one's autonomy. The issue to be considered is whether or not this violation is the central problem with torture.

There are many instances where a violation of someone's autonomy is regarded as warranted, or even as necessary. Imprisonment, for example, marks one instance in which someone's autonomy is violated (one is imprisoned, presumably against one's will). Few people, however, regard absolutely no instance of imprisonment as justified. It thus appears that a violation of autonomy is not *in itself* an overriding reason for rejecting a particular practice. To claim that torture is a violation of autonomy, then, does not seem to sufficiently explain the wrongness we attribute to torture.

But perhaps this inference is too quick. Torture might also be warranted or 'necessary' (in some sense of this word) in much the same way that prison might be warranted. It would not follow from this, per se, that torture is not morally wrong, all things being equal. One might likewise contend that *imprisonment* is morally impermissible, all else being equal. The difference in cases of *justified* imprisonment is that other factors have overridden the presumptive moral value of preserving the autonomy of an agent. Imprisonment, the argument might go, is *morally wrong*, but it is nevertheless justified under the appropriate conditions. The wrongness of imprisonment consists precisely in its being a *violation of autonomy*. If there were no such wrongness to be overridden, there would be nothing problematic about imprisonment of the innocent.

This point strikes me as correct, but it does not show that a violation of autonomy is intrinsically wrong. All that is required to reject this view is a case in which one is morally required to violate another's autonomy. Given that one cannot be morally required to do something immoral (which would amount to a contradiction), one could not be required to violate autonomy (under any circumstances) if it were intrinsically wrong to do so. Moreover, there *are* cases when one is morally required to violate the autonomy of another – and these cases are hardly extraordinary. Here is one such case.

> Bill is pointing a gun at Sally. He will shoot her and kill her unless you intervene. All that is required for your intervention is that you take the gun from Bill's hand, thus inhibiting him from carrying out his wish to kill Sally. Absolutely no harm will come from you taking the gun from Bill. Moreover, minimal energy is required for you to take the weapon.

I take it as obvious that one is morally required to intervene in this case, despite the fact that this intervention would violate Bill's autonomy. This serves to show that a violation of autonomy is not *intrinsically* wrong. If it were, violating Bill's autonomy would be wrong, hence one could not be required to do it (on pain of contradiction).

To reiterate, I do not wish to deny that violating someone's autonomy is very often wrong – perhaps usually. My point here is that the violation of autonomy view of the wrongness of torture does not adequately explain the deep repugnance with which we regard instances of torture. I trust that *part* of what makes torture wrong is indeed that it violates one's autonomy (it is this, after all, which allows us to distinguish consensual sado-masochistic sexual relationships from torture) – but *only* part. The real wrongdoing of torture, I want to suggest – and this is the very thing that distinguishes it from other heinous acts of cruelty – is the way that it undermines the very humanity and agency of the person tortured.

One additional point needs to be made concerning the relationship between torture, on the one hand, and the violation of autonomy, on the other. When people focus on torture as wrong due to its violation of autonomy, they very frequently focus on torture as a fundamentally coercive practice. There is some merit to this point, but not enough to warrant such a universal account of torture's wrongness. As David Sussman argues,

> Torture should be distinguished from both coercion and brainwashing, even though all three may often overlap in particular cases. What is distinctive about torture is that it aims to manipulate its victims through their own responses, as agents, to the felt experience of their affects and emotions in a context of dependence, vulnerability, and disorientation. Coercion, in contrast, need only exploit the agent's rational responses to the cognitive content of these feelings. The coercer tries to influence his victims through their own appreciation of their reasons for action . . . Coercion, as a kind of hard bargaining by means of threats, involves too direct an appeal to its victim's rationality to count as torture. (Sussman, 9)

Coercion, in a very minimal respect, *requires* the autonomy of the agent being coerced. By the use of 'hard bargaining,' the victim of coercion is being asked to *choose* to engage in some kind of action, decision, etc. This, it would appear, misses an essential feature of torture (even though torture does, as Sussman admits, often involve coercion): torture *destroys* the person, and with this, it destroys the very capacity for rational deliberation.[11]

Violation of agency

Some of the most compelling literature on the wrongness of torture focuses not on the pain that torture produces, nor on the mere *fact* that autonomy has been violated. The focus, rather, is on the way that torture dismantles the agency of the person tortured. As is hopefully clear, this account of the wrongness of torture is *compatible* with the view that pain and the violation of autonomy are also partly constitutive of the wrongness of torture. As David Sussman argues,

> Unlike other kinds of unwanted imposition, pain characteristically compromises or undermines the very capacities constitutive of autonomous agency itself. It is almost impossible to reflect, deliberate, or even think straight when one is in agony. When sufficiently intense, pain becomes a person's entire universe and his entire self, crowding out every other aspect of his mental life. Unlike other harms, pain takes its victim's agency apart 'from the inside,' such that the agent may never be able to reconstitute himself fully. (Sussman, 14)

Elaine Scarry's magisterial *The Body in Pain* makes the same point:

> It is the intense pain that destroys a person's self and world, a destruction experienced spatially as either the contraction of the universe down to the immediate vicinity of the body or as the body swelling to fill the entire universe. Intense pain is also language-destroying: as the content of one's world disintegrates, so the content of one's language disintegrates; as the self disintegrates, so that which would express and project the self is robbed of its source and subject. (Scarry, 35)

In both of these cases, we see the close connection that exists, in the torture situation, between the pain inflicted and the way that this pain acts to undermine one's agency. In this respect, pain in torture is fundamentally *unlike* pain in religious practice or even injury. The pain one experiences is born of another agent whose very intent is to *destroy your agency* – to make you incapable of directing your own actions, and even incapable of determining the significance of the things that populate the world around you.

> Through the torturer's language, his actions, and the physical setting, the world is brought to the prisoner in three rings: the random technological and cultural embodiments of civilization overarch the two primary social institutions of medicine and law, which in turn overarch the basic unit of shelter, the room. Just as the prisoner's confession makes visible the contraction and closing in of his universe, so the torturer reenacts this world collapse. Civilization is brought to the prisoner and in his presence annihilated in the very process by which it is being made to annihilate him. (Scarry, 44)

The very things that make one human – that allow one to inhabit a civilization where one can live out one's subjectivity in concert with others in a context of common significance – become the tools through which one's agency is undermined. It is not simply that one's will is thwarted. This is a common enough occurrence. Rather, the conditions under which agency can be intelligibly exercised, and a life meaningfully lived, are turned against the agent that would inhabit such a meaningful world. Language becomes a tool for trickery; the artifacts of culture become the very objects through which culture is destroyed. The meanings that make us intelligible to one another are subverted by the torturer by redeploying these meanings in a way that makes any kind of autonomous action impossible. The effects are devastating.

When pain is inflicted, one can hope for eventual reprieve. When one is coerced, one can hope to regain the ability to carry out one's will once the coercing agent is removed. Not so with torture. The pain persists; autonomy is not simply thwarted while the torturer is present. Rather, one's agency – the thing that makes autonomy worth anything at all, and which provides direction and meaning for the deployment of autonomy – is crushed under the heel of the very things that had made it possible: language, interactions with others in meaning-laden contexts, and the artifacts of one's phenomenological world. Once agency is destroyed, unlike when autonomy is thwarted, agency *remains* destroyed indefinitely. As Jean Amery painfully and powerfully makes the point: "It is still not over. Twenty-two years later I am still dangling over the ground by dislocated arms, panting, and accusing myself" (Amery, 36).

There is much more to say about the way in which agency is destroyed by torture. The point of this chapter, however, is not to explore in detail the nature of the wrongness of torture (something I will take up in Chapter 4). Rather, my aim is to determine *what* that wrongness is. In the case of pain as well as the case of the violation of autonomy, we have seen that these things are wrong only insofar as they involve *more* than merely the sensation of pain, on the one hand, or something being done against one's will, on the other. Pain is wrong only when it is made into suffering – and the suffering present in torture is not explained simply by one's desires being thwarted. The wrongness of torture is unique in *how* one suffers and for what reason; the violation of autonomy in torture is unique in its nature – it is not merely that one's will is thwarted. Rather, one's very *capacity* to will is undermined.

Of course, one might point out that murder also undermines one's capacity to will – namely, by *eliminating* this capacity altogether. This is a valid point. For the time being, I will leave it as an open question whether or not the wrongness of torture is equal to or exceeds the wrongness of murder (for a discussion of this, see Chapter 5: *Argument from killing being worse than torture*). The point to be made here, though, is that while murder eliminates one's capacity to carry out one's will, torture does this in a very different way: unlike death, torture leaves its victim to suffer through his or her own inability to act autonomously. Death is certainly a great harm, but it is not a harm that continues to be suffered by the person who dies.[12]

There are two arguments that are worth making explicitly in defense of the destruction of agency as the central wrong-making feature of torture. First, the destruction of agency allows us to explain in sufficient detail what is missing in the previous candidates for this wrongdoing. Pain alone is not sufficient for a harm. Suffering, however, is – but the nature and extent of the suffering matters. What explains how pain becomes suffering – and grotesque suffering at that – is the destruction of the agency of the person who is tortured, and who must *continue* to suffer from this destroyed agency if he continues to live beyond the torture. Likewise, the violation of autonomy cannot account for the difference between torture and lesser instances where the violation of autonomy is a harm (such as imprisonment, for example). A recognition of the destruction of agency, however, allows us to make this distinction. Because the destruction of agency thesis explains both what the alternative theses capture and fail to capture, it is preferable to them both.

The second argument for the destruction of agency thesis is essentially an argument from exclusion: if we can show that the other candidates for the wrongness of torture are inadequate, and that this thesis does not suffer from their defects, we will have effectively shown that the destruction of agency thesis must be the correct one.

Of course, an argument by exclusion only works if all of the alternative (excluded) candidates have been considered. There is one candidate, however, that has not yet been considered: namely, that it is the social consequences of engaging in torture that make it the wrong that it is. In the next section, I will argue that this candidate cannot adequately capture the wrongness of torture.

Violation of trust

In articulating the negative consequences of torture, people frequently remark on the social mistrust that arises after one has been tortured. As Amery puts it: "Whoever has succumbed to torture can no longer feel at home in the world. The shame of destruction cannot be erased. Trust in the world, which already collapsed in part at the first blow, but in the end, under torture, fully, will not be regained" (40).

The question of the negative consequences of torture will be dealt with extensively in Chapter 6: *Damages reputation of state and trust of citizens*. The negative consequences arising from torture are indeed a *part* of any complete assessment of torture's wrongness. It is not, however, a candidate for what constitutes torture's central wrong-making feature. Of course, this assertion requires an argument to be plausible.

The wrong-making feature of any act must, quite obviously, specify those things an action involves that make it constitute the wrong that it is. For this to be achieved adequately, the wrong of the action must be appropriately connected to the person *wronged*. Put otherwise, if an account of the wrong-making feature of an action does not make reference to *the person wronged*, it has failed to capture what is wrong about an action.

Imagine, for example, that a person steals a car. Suppose that one negative consequence of stealing this car is that the person who stole it is under a lot of stress because of the theft: he is consistently worried that he will be arrested for his theft. If one were to claim that the central wrong-making feature of this theft was due to the stress it caused the thief, one would be making a serious mistake. The mistake, it is clear, involves misidentifying the victim of the wrong-doing. While it is true that the thief suffers a negative consequence, and that this consequence *adds* to the badness of the action in question, it would be a mistake to claim that this particular negative consequence was the wrong-making feature of the action. The wrong-making feature of the action, as this example hopefully makes clear, must make sense of the central wrong suffered as a result of the action. In the above example, the wrong committed clearly involves a wrong done to the person from whom the car was stolen.

So, how does this particular point relate to the wrongness of torture? The violation of trust, if it is to be a candidate for the unique wrongness of torture, cannot simply appeal to the negative *social* consequences of this violation. That is, if this account (or other more explicitly utilitarian accounts) tries to explain the wrongness of torture by appeal to its negative consequences for those *other than the person tortured*, such an account will prove inadequate, as it will not capture the harm done to the primary victim of torture.

What this entails is *not* that the violation of trust is not a candidate in the current discussion; it *does* entail that this violation can only be a candidate insofar as it is explained in terms of a harm done *to the person tortured*. What, then, is the harm done to the person tortured in the violation of trust? In fact, this harm is precisely what we see: an inability to exist safely in the civilized world – in the context of significance that allows the world to be meaningful to normal persons. This is precisely what is captured in Jean Amery's quote above: one loses one's ability to trust in others, and as this dies, so too does the nexus of shared meaning in which any agency is constructed, and within which it can flourish. After torture, all that remains is a shell of a person.[13]

A final note on deontology and consequentialism

In the above account of the wrongness of torture, I have not appealed in a doctrinal way to any particular meta-ethics. Considerations have ranged from rudimentary consequentialism to standard deontology. In my own view, this is the only way to approach ethical issues. To simply assume a meta-ethical standpoint and argue from its application strikes me as (usually) dogmatic, and likely to miss much of the moral terrain.[14] Rather than approach moral issues in this way, it seems to me, one should use all of the theoretical resources at one's disposal, whatever their prospects or problems. It is never enough to say, for example, that the *consequences* of torture are all that make it the wrong that it is. Such an account fails to capture the specificity of torture, as well as the specificity of its devastating consequences. Likewise, an appeal to something like universalizable maxims seems to reduce morality to consistency, and fails to capture the gradations of moral wrong-doing. Inconsistency is certainly something to be avoided. It is not, however, the *sole* mark of the immoral.[15]

The account I have given here of the wrongness of torture, I hope, has successfully avoided meta-ethical dogmatism. Nevertheless, it is worth noting that both consequentialism and deontology point to the same thing in the case of torture's wrongness. The consequences of torture are indeed atrocious, as is the pain that accompanies it – but these consequences (and the suffering they embody) cannot be adequately understood except by an appeal to the intrinsic worth of agency. Likewise, the intrinsic worth of agency must be conceptualized in relation to the suffering that agents are capable of undergoing. Does this make my analysis a consequentialist one or a deontological one? This is a question I decline to answer. Whatever answer I gave would be, in certain respects, a distraction from the central issue: moral wrongs are nuanced, complex things – and the unique wrongness of any particular act is not likely to be exhaustively explained by an appeal to any particular thing, be it consistency, agency, virtue, pain, consequences, or whatever.

It is also worth noting, though, that the analysis of the wrongness of torture I have given here is not only compatible with both deontology and utilitarianism. Other moral traditions, I believe, would yield similar results, though I will not consider these traditions in any detail here. To take two quick examples: Feminist ethics of many varieties, as well as virtue ethics generally, would point to the devastation of the agent as torture's central wrong-making feature: torture prevents us from seeing one another appropriately, from forming the kinds of relationships we ought to have, and from recognizing the ways our lives are intimately bound both to what we do and to other agents.

Having explored the wrongness of torture – what it is about torture that leads to its virtually universal condemnation – we are almost in a position to consider arguments suggesting that this universal condemnation admits of exceptions. Given its serious immorality in standard cases, we need to ask if there are conditions under which torture should nevertheless be permitted, or even encouraged. But before doing this, it is necessary to be as explicit and precise as possible about the effects of torture on the person who undergoes it. Only by facing the reality of torture squarely, rather than simply assuming we understand its nature, will we be able to grapple adequately with it as a moral problem.

Notes

1. Rape is another such action. In my view, these two actions are best understood as *of a kind*.

2. Various situational factors allow those with congenital analgesia to detect the danger. The reactions of others, the increase of one's own heart rate, fever, and so on all enable those with this condition to detect those things that we might normally detect through pain. This ability allowed one such person, for example, to be diagnosed with appendicitis. See Wall, *Pain: The Science of Suffering*, 50–52.

3. It is the absence of *this* detection of pain that spells trouble for those with congenital analgesia. Because it is not uncomfortable to walk on injured joints, for example, a person with this condition never gives their body sufficient time to heal. This leads to a deterioration of the joints, which in turn can lead to infection, and ultimately to osteomyeltis. See Wall, ibid.

4. This is the style of argument, incidentally, that was defended by the Bush Administration in various memoranda. If pain is not the specific intent of an interrogator (even though it is certainly foreseeable in the use of 'harsh interrogation'), then the action in question cannot be torture (which requires, on the Bush view, the *specific intent* to cause harm). According to the memoranda, an interrogator doing his job correctly will always have the specific

intent of acquiring actionable intelligence, and hence, on this view, *cannot* be engaging in torture, regardless of the methods he employs to extract said intelligence. This argument, along with the many others presented in these memoranda, will be explored in Chapter 8.

5. See James Miller, *The Passions of Michel Foucault*, and in particular pp. 268–270.

6. Glucklich makes an extraordinary case for this view, see *Sacred Pain*.

7. This marks an important distinction between sado-masochism, for example, and torture. Pain, after all, is not the *intention*, even indirectly, of the person who is tortured (though it is the intention of the torturer).

8. The significance of this will be discussed in greater detail in Chapter 6: *Cannot predict pain response*, below.

9. "Murder, Cannibalism, and Indirect Suicide: A philosophical study of a recent case," J. Jeremy Wisnewski, *Philosophy in the Contemporary World*

10. I have no need to delineate actions that fit this description. I am sure that there is much dispute surrounding virtually any example I might give here. Nevertheless, one such example strikes me as plausible enough, and worth mentioning explicitly. Any case involving 'consenting' to giving up one's capability in self-determination in one's future life strikes me as morally illegitimate (imagine someone consenting to live a life of total slavery). I have formulated this example in the way that I have to make it compatible with ending one's own life, whether in an act of assisted suicide or in an act of suicide that is not the result of a terminal medical condition. These actions may well be morally impermissible, but I do not wish to beg that question (or raise that issue) in this context.

11. Admittedly, I have not yet argued for this point in any detail. I will turn my attention to this argument in the next chapter.

12. I do not want to beg any questions here. If death *does* continue to be a harm (and I think it does), the harm is not because of the suffering one undergoes after the harm is inflicted. Let us grant that death is a harm, and continues to be a harm, after one's death. The point here is that this is not the sort of harm that is experienced by the victim of the harm.

    For a defense of the view that harms need not be experienced see Thomas Nagel, "Death," in *The Metaphysics of Death*. For a defense of the view that the dead can be harmed, see Bob Brecher "Our Obligation to the Dead." For the relevance of this to particular moral issues, see Wisnewski, "What we owe the dead," "A Defense of Cannibalism," "Murder and Indirect Suicide: A Philosophical Exploration of a Recent Case," and "When the Dead Do Not Consent: The Ethics of Non-Consensual Organ Use." All bibliographic information can be found in the bibliography.

13. I will discuss this in two places below, addressing the loss of trust on the part of the agent (Chapter 4), and on the part of others (Chapter 6: *Damages reputation of state and trust of citizens*).

14. For a defense of this approach to ethics, see my *Wittgenstein and Ethical Inquiry*.
15. I should add here that I do not think this is an accurate reading of Kant's ethics either. For a detailed treatment of this issue, see Wisnewski, Chapter 2, *Wittgenstein and Ethical Inquiry*.

Chapter 4

How Torture Unmakes Worlds

Torture's effects on the body

In Chapter 3, I argued that the wrongness of torture is captured in the way that it destroys the agency of the torture victim. The pain inflicted by torture, the destruction of dignity, and the effects it leaves on a society that allows it are all deeply troubling aspects of this dark practice. But none of this captures the uniqueness of its wrongdoing. The only thing that does, I have suggested, is the *way* it effectively dehumanizes and deconstructs the agents who are its victims: torture systematically removes the layers of meaning that make human life what it is; it destroys the trust we have in each other – a trust that makes possible our loving relationships and our care for both those close to us and those we've never met. In this respect, torture makes the human *inhuman* – it makes all that matters matter no more, all that enshrined the world in significance insignificant. Torture takes all of those things that are essential to the human condition – all of those things that make civilization possible – and destroys them. In this section, we'll look at what happens to those victims of torture who survive. We'll look at the (almost always underestimated) effects of torture on its survivors – on the way it not only disrupts life, but fundamentally destroys human character.

It is relatively easy to imagine the effects that some kinds of physical torture might have on a body: removed fingernails sometimes grow back in ways that appear abnormal, scarring is significant on those parts of the body subjected to physical brutality, the ability to stand and walk can be significantly compromised by *falanga* (a form of torture that involves repeatedly beating the soles of the feet), nerve damage is easily detectable in the wrists of those who have undergone *strappado* (a form of torture that involves binding the wrists behind the back, and then lifting the victim by his bound wrists).[1]

Other forms of torture are not as easily detected; effects on the body cannot necessarily be causally linked uniquely to torture. Being forced to undergo stress positions *does* have physical consequences – there is swelling, nerve damage, chronic pain, and so on – but, in many cases, courts have not judged these symptoms as sufficient for proof of torture.[2] The same can be said of sleep deprivation, solitary confinement, the use of phobias, sexual humiliation, forced nudity, exposure to extremes of heat and cold, light deprivation, and the use of environmental manipulations designed to destroy an agent's sense of stability and safety. And in some cases, even physical torture leaves no obvious physical effect at all. In waterboarding (*submarino*), for example, marks on the body are absent – despite the fact that this is often described as a most horrific experience.

All forms of torture (be it punitive, interrogational, terroristic, or judicial) – has one aim: the breaking of the agent. This conception of torture as destructive of agency, and as aiming at the 'breaking' of the subject of torture, has achieved near-universal recognition in the literature surrounding treatment of torture victims, and a growing recognition in other disciplines that aim to understand torture. Consider: "The objective of torture is to break down a person's integrity and personality" (131).[3] Torture has a singular goal: "to destroy the integrity of the human being in front of them, to isolate him from society, by using different methods of torture that deprive him of his fundamental trust in humanity and make him look crazy in the eyes of society. These people come to us with issues like mistrust, betrayal, rape, humiliation, ostracism, anxiety, and self-rejection" (143).[4] "Torture is intended to destroy and wipe out the victim's personality" (15).[5] Likewise, torture has a particular trajectory, where the end result is a destruction of the self. "It is as if the downward slope from power to powerlessness experienced in relation to the perpetrator has ripped apart the victim's ego into two or more pieces" (1)[6] Again: "The aim of torture is to destroy the individual's will, to break the individual down and obliterate a sense of autonomy and agency, thus turning that individual into a shell of a person who lacks the will to resist, or even to be human in the sense that being human requires personal agency" (127).[7]

The growing consensus around what torture aims to accomplish has been forged through intense work with those who have suffered it: "The victims describe the mental reactions after torture as the most disabling by giving them a feeling of having changed their personality . . . *the feeling of having a changed identity* is one of the most characteristic effects of torture" (134).[8] Another expert who has worked with survivors of torture notes that the trauma to agency effected by torture can last a lifetime (the term used in treatment is 'survivor' rather than 'victim').

Many survivors describe the psychological effects of torture as a shattering of one's personality, distorting perceptions, altering one's memories and experiences. Torture has profound and persistent consequences, which sometimes inexplicably, violently recur for years after the actual ordeal is over, causing extreme trauma, even years later. (135)[9]

Even ignoring the testimony of victims of torture, there is ample evidence that torture aims to destroy the human being tortured. Indeed, this is precisely what some 'interrogation' manuals state explicitly. The KUBARK manual, for example, states the following:

> It is a fundamental hypothesis of this handbook that these techniques, which can succeed even with highly resistant sources, are in essence methods of inducing regression of the personality to whatever earlier and weaker level is required for the dissolution of resistance and the inculcation of dependence. All of the techniques employed to break through an interrogation roadblock, the entire spectrum from simple isolation to hypnosis and narcosis, are essentially ways of speeding up the process of regression. As the interrogatee slips back from maturity toward a more infantile state, his learned or structured personality traits fall away in a reversed chronological order, so that the characteristics most recently acquired – which are also the characteristics drawn upon by the interrogatee in his own defence – are the first to go.[10]

The idea that the destruction of a person's agency is merely incidental to torture is thus seriously mistaken. This has led some to insist on a recognition of the destruction of the person as central to the very meaning of torture. One such definition runs as follows:

> any act intentionally performed whereby physical or mental pain or suffering is inflicted on a person for purposes of criminal investigation, as a means of intimidation, as personal punishment, as a preventive measure, as a penalty, or for any other purpose. Torture shall also be understood to be the use of methods upon a person intended to obliterate the personality of the victim or diminish his physical or mental capacities, even if they do not cause physical pain or anguish.[11]

Any definition of torture can be problematized, and this one is no exception. This definition does, however, allow us to recognize the irrelevance of the distinction between the two kinds of torture often characteristic of discussions of torture. In this definition, we understand torture in terms of its *aim* – the destruction of agency – and are not distracted by questions of particular technique.[12]

As we have seen (in Chapter 1: *Physical and psychological torture*), the distinction between 'psychological' and 'physical' torture has so plagued arguments surrounding torture that features of the constitution of torture have been utterly ignored. Given the brute physical effects of so-called 'psychological' torture, it is misleading to suggest that it is in any way fundamentally distinct from physical torture, as all torture is ultimately physical. While focus on the methods of torture has led to an insistence on the distinction between 'torture' and 'torture lite' – a distinction I have already discussed as being groundless – the real *effect* of torture has been largely ignored. Indeed, the insistence on the idea that only physical torture is 'real' torture explains why policy-makers in the United States have tried to 'justify' interrogation techniques that constitute torture by defining what is required to make pain and suffering an act of 'torture' in an utterly ridiculous manner.[13]

The distinction between physical and psychological torture cannot stand in any absolute sense. There are significant physical damages inflicted on victims of torture by the use of so-called 'psychological' torture; physical torture, in turn, involves substantial psychological trauma. In both cases, torture inscribes itself on both the body and the brain, and disrupts life for the survivor. This does not mean, however, that it is possible to easily draw isolated causal connections between torture and its traumatic effects with any certainty, and courts have been notoriously reluctant to accept claims of torture without such connections. The problem with this is, of course, that the absence of obvious evidence says nothing about whether or not torture actually occurs. As one researcher notes, "torture victims often experience physical symptoms for which there is no obvious basis" (145).[14]

Torture does, however, leave its mark on the brain. As neuroscience improves, it becomes easier to measure and map these consequences. This does not mean, however, that strict causal laws can be drawn from specific kinds of torture to specific brain trauma types, although this is hardly surprising given that identical painful stimuli can be experienced in radically different ways depending on factors such as age, culture, gender, religious beliefs, prior experience, and length of time torture lasts. The probability of ever being able to isolate neuroscientific laws that perfectly map out exact brain damage caused by specific acts of torture on specific persons is not particularly high (though there are some cases where this can be done with astonishing regularity). More plausible is an increased ability to recognize the way that trauma to the brain affects the rest of the body:

> three processes that result in permanent brain damage [are]: pain, environ-mental stressors, and sleep deprivation. Torture, whether inflicted by physical means such as beatings, or psychological through, for example, environmental manipulation, inflicts pain experienced in the brain and extending from there to all of the organs and physiological processes. (139)[15]

In several cases, particular techniques predictably produce changes in the brain in line with particular, well-documented conditions. "Even a few days of solitary confinement will predictably shift the electroencepha-logram (EEG) pattern toward an abnormal pattern characteristic of stupor and delirium" (115).[16] In other instances, the victim will undergo changes characteristic of Post-Traumatic Stress Disorder (PTSD). In fact, PTSD is a very common diagnosis for torture victims. As Wenk-Ansohn concludes, the intensity of PTSD can be predicted by the way a victim experiences torture: "the subjective appraisal of the torture event as being uncontrollable and unpredictable was repeatedly shown to be associated with higher perceived distress during torture and a greater likelihood of developing PTSD" (175).[17] Of course, one technique repeatedly advocated in engaging in torturous interrogation is to promote an environment that is both unpredictable and uncontrollable. A CIA interrogation manual, for instance, makes this point in reference to specific tactics:

> The 'questioner' should be careful to manipulate the subject's environment to disrupt patterns, not to create them. Meals and sleep should be granted irregularly, in more than abundance or less than adequacy, on no discernible pattern. This is done to disorient the subject and destroy his capacity to resist (L-3)

The loss of control undermines an agent's sense of autonomy and self-determination, as well as inflicting numerous symptoms on the victim that will sometimes endure for the rest of her life. As with other torture tactics, the brain reflects PTSD. Citing several studies, Fields concludes that "the symptom provocation in torture-related PTSD may alter neural activity in brain territories involving memories, emotion, and attention as well as motor control" (180).[18]

The claim that certain types of torture are not easily detectable should not be mistaken for the claim that these techniques have no physiological consequences. Any kind of trauma – and even stress – has physiological consequences. "Every organ in the body can be affected by torture" (158).[19] Thus, in the case of the tortured, certain disorders occur regularly: "gastroenteritis, respiratory infections, skin eruptions, and peptic ulcers are common" (180). John Conroy, in *Unspeakable Acts, Ordinary People* sums up some of the most common disorders resulting from torture.

> When Doctors Finn Somnier and Inge Genefke examined twenty-four torture survivors an average of 9.5 years after their torture (see "Psychotherapy for Victims of Torture," *British Journal of Psychiatry*, 1986, Volume 149), they found 71 percent had nightmares, 79 percent complained of headaches, 79 percent had impaired memory, 75 percent had impaired concentration, 75 percent experienced fatigue, 50 percent suffered from persistent fear and anxiety, 38 percent experienced vertigo, 21 percent reported sexual problems, and 13 percent tremors or shaking. (Conroy, 179–180)
>
> One study of Americans held as POWs during World War II and the Korean War ("Follow-up Studies of World War II and Korean War Prisoners," *American Journal of Epidemiology*, volume 92, no. 2, 1970) noted that in the first three years after their repatriation, POWs who had been held in Japan

showed a 50 percent increase in deaths over what would be typical of a similar group of white American males. Accidents, tuberculosis, and cirrhosis of the liver were the primary causes of those excess deaths. Suicides, though few in number, were about 30 percent more frequent than in control groups. (182)

Severe consequences are widely reported in the literature on treating the victims of torture. As Jacobson and Montgomery report, Juhler and Smid-Nielsen

found that up to 85 percent of the torture victims had symptoms from the central and peripheral nervous systems and that about half of these had corresponding physical findings. The victims complained of headache, poor concentration, inadequate memory, dizziness and fatigue . . . some survivors suffer chronic pain in the face and head, and also on their bodies because of nerve injury from beatings. (136–137)[20]

Moreover,

Approximately 75 per cent of the torture victims have short-term shooting pains around the heart, palpitations and difficulty with breathing. Abnormal physical findings are rare. Furthermore, about 75 per cent of survivors have gastro-intestinal symptoms; only 30 per cent have abnormal findings. Ulcer symptoms are common – for example, epigastric pain (hunger pain relieved by food). (137)[21]

But torture does not end with particular somatic symptoms and damage to organs. The very way in which a victim's body exists in the world changes fundamentally. "Torture, which attacks and wounds the self, often leads to a permanent condition of very intense excitement and hypervigilance" (Gurris, 33). This tension reproduces pain in an endless cycle:

Pain leads reflexively to countertension and this, in turn, to renewed pain, so that these events continue in a kind of vicious cycle. Psychogenic pains can, however, also arise without muscular tension; it is as though they are stored in a central location in the brain. They can be triggered by associated stimuli, experiences, or actions. (65, Gurris)

This state of constant tension reflects a new way of being in the world for the victim of torture, one characterized by a complete absence of at-homeness that frequently escalates into a state of near paranoia.

The use of various forms of humiliation, degrading treatment, threats, hunger and cold, isolation and other psychological methods during interrogations was found to cause 'persisting and paranoid anxieties, re-arousable by specific situations; persecution dreams, mood disturbances, suicidal tendencies, and shattering of confidence'. (599)[22]

The hypertension produced through torture also has detectable consequences in the way that the body of the tortured processes *any* pain signals. Citing several studies, Rona Fields notes that

> these studies and the most recent brain imaging studies that measure blood flow and metabolism in parts of the brain validate earlier hypotheses about measurable brain damage in survivors of psychological torture and coercion. After injuries (physical as well as psychosomatic), the brain and spinal cord rewire themselves, forming pain pathways that can become overactive immediately or years later. (153)[23]

The body internalizes its trauma, and this internalization multiplies the pain the body experiences. As we have seen, this internalization also manifests itself in conversion disorders of various kinds. The consequences of this internalization for the living agent, however, are crucial to understanding the mechanics of the distinct wrongness of torture. The loss of agency is not merely the product of the extensive damage done to the body of the tortured, whether that damage is direct or the product of displacement. The loss of agency has everything to do with the way this change in a victim's body, as well their relationship to themselves and others, is *experienced* by the agent. While there are subjective elements to this experience, there are also predictable results.

Tortured embodiment

For those who defend torture, there is often a clean distinction between the effects of torture on the body, on the one hand, and the effects of torture on the person, on the other. Initially, this view strikes many as an intuitive one: my body is not identical to who I am. My body can undergo significant changes without this changing my personhood. Losing a toe, for example, does not make me a different person. Thus, it is sometimes concluded, the body cannot be the defining feature of human identity.

This argument is correct so far as it goes – but it also seems to underestimate the significance of the body. While it is true that we are not identical to our body at any particular time, it does not follow from this that our body is not a crucial part of who we are – and of how we experience ourselves and the world around us. To understand the wrongness of torture, merely spelling out the effects that torture has on the body is inadequate. We must also tackle the question of how these changes in the body affect the very way we experience the world.

The positions our bodies occupy, as well as what our bodies are capable of, shapes the way we experience things – indeed, these things provide experience with a structure. Our experience is structured in terms of the possibilities of our living bodies: things are up or down, right or left, impassable or passable, and so on. This basic bodily orientation is fundamentally disrupted by torture.

The body, then, provides a sort of pre-reflective understanding – one that allows us to navigate and make sense of the world without the intrusion of theory or experiment. A corollary of this – one which Merleau-Ponty devotes much time to in his *Phenomenology of Perception* – is that changes to our bodies can alter the way we experience the world. Changes in what we are capable of, when these changes occur rapidly, can also lead to a sharp dissonance between our bodily consciousness and our reflective consciousness. One's body schema (the sense the body has of itself, of the way it occupies space) can conflict with one's reflective knowledge of one's body. This happens, for example, with phantom limb pains: one itches where there is no leg.

The abuse of the body, as it occurs in torture, can shape the way a victim of torture perceives the world. Nicolas McGinnis points out the relevance of these reflections in thinking through particular torture techniques.

> While sensory deprivation works by depriving the subject of the stimuli and motility required to sustain consciousness, stress positions direct the 'body schema' of the subject to work against itself, in a task whose continued successful performance will result in pain. The 'body schema' for Merleau-Ponty means that one's body is perceived as "an attitude directed towards a certain existing or possible task . . . a *spatiality of situation*." Since the spatiality of one's own body is task-oriented, is *directional*, the stress position is effective in sapping resistance and immediately distinguished from straight 'other-inflicted' pain. The other-directness is mitigated by one's own body schema incorporating the task as its identification, and as more time passes this identification becomes further anchored. As the position becomes difficult to hold, the subject's focus and concentration on maintaining it only serves to confirm the situation's hold on the body schema. (McGinnis, 13)

This phenomenological conclusion articulates the very aim of torture: victims are reduced to the particular situation, and understand themselves in terms of it. The world a victim inhabited ceases to be available: he *is* a tortured body. Again, McGinnis:

> From the thesis that consciousness is irreducibly *perceptual* we begin to understand why sensory deprivation can have such damaging effects on the individual subjected to it. With no patterned stimuli or perception to 'latch on' to, as it were, consciousness loses its orientation to the world. Without this

world-directionality, without a "world to live through" consciousness does not become merely *unanchored* – for this identifies it as somehow existing separately – but senseless (here making use of the multiple meanings in French of *sens* as Merleau-Ponty often does: direction, sense and meaning). (7)[24]

As we have seen, the effects of torture on the body do not end here. The body, as our "perspective on the world," bears the continued brunt of torture. Pain is persistent even long after torture is over. Thus, one's very body becomes the consistent reminder of what one has endured. "The body . . . seems to want to reflect the agony it is living through, its every wound and devastation" (Gurris, 31). In certain respects, such somatic memory is the *function* of chronic pain – the lived body experiences its history in the present, through recurring experiences resulting from conversion of the trauma into somatic reality. The victim of torture quite literally embodies her trauma. It is this that leads one researcher to contend that *"Pain is embodied memory"* (Wenk-Ansohn, 58).

Torture, in this respect, is inescapable. The torturer has inscribed his work onto the body, and the body refuses to forget what the torturer has done. The tortured's living, organic existence in the world thus becomes the heart of her alienation from the world. Intense pain, as we have seen, rips one out of the sharable world through which that world is intelligible. It is fundamentally isolating. Scarry's claims about pain, cited earlier, are worth remembering:

> It is the intense pain that destroys a person's self and world, a destruction experienced spatially as either the contraction of the universe down to the immediate vicinity of the body or as the body swelling to fill the entire universe. Intense pain is also language-destroying: as the content of one's world disintegrates, so the content of one's language disintegrates; as the self disintegrates, so that which would express and project the self is robbed of its source and subject. (Scarry, 35)

It is in the initial isolation of pain that agency begins to break down.

> The most intense feeling we know of, intense to the blotting out of all other experiences, namely, the experience of great bodily pain, is at the same time the most private and the least communicable of all . . . Pain, in other words, truly a borderline experience between life as 'being among men' (*inter homines esse*) and death, is so subjective and removed from the world of things and men that it cannot assume an appearance at all. (50–51)[25]

But agency is not destroyed by pain alone. If this were so, no one would be an agent. In the trauma of torture, as we have repeatedly seen, pain stays with the agent, pervading his bodily existence. This is characteristic of chronic pain. Byron J. Good offers the following description of his interaction with 'Brian', a victim of chronic pain:

> In Brian's world, the body has special primacy . . . It absorbs the world into itself, floods out into the world and shapes not only his experience but the experienced world . . . His body comes to dominate his consciousness, threatening to unmake the everyday world . . . We act in a world *through* our bodies; our bodies are the subject of our actions, that through which we experience, comprehend, and act upon the world. In contrast, Brian describes his body as having become an object, distinct from the experiencing and acting self . . . the body takes on agency over and against the self . . . pain is the central reality; it dominates experience and expression . . . Verbal objectification, the extension of the self into the world, and thus the self authored in the process, is dominated by pain. But since others doubt the word, they doubt the world and its author . . . As a consequence, the self and the world of the pain sufferer are threatened with dissolution. (38–40)[26]

The case of torture, however, exacerbates the experience of pain with a recognition of the *significance of this pain* as a reminder of one's utter humiliation and dehumanization at the hands of another. Torture leads us to understand our pain as a mark of the inhumanity that our fellow human beings are capable of. Afterwards, "the victim has suffered physical pains and other symptoms that have taken away any joy with respect to his body" (141).[27] The very methods of torture aim to make the living body something that is no longer the tortured's being-in-the-world. As Arendt remarks, discussing the use of such tactics by the Nazis:

> The aim of all these methods, in any case, is to manipulate the human body – with its infinite possibilities of suffering – in such a way as to make it destroy the human person as inexorably as do certain mental diseases of the organic type. (199)[28]

We come to dissociate who we *were* from who we are now. The victim is no longer at home in the world, or even in his own body. "Through torture, the unity of body and soul (psychosomatic unity) within the person is significantly and profoundly disturbed" (30).[29] Even the capacity we have to allow our bodies to recuperate from the work it undergoes – work which is itself often meaning-given,[30] the capacity for which torture also diminishes[31] – is undermined by the experience of torture.

> Torture victims usually only sleep for a few hours a night . . . Torture victims do not share their painful memories with others. They are alone with them and

afraid of becoming insane. Nightmares and flashbacks, however, are normal reactions to what they have gone through. (135)[32]

> Individuals experiencing such environmental restriction find it difficult to maintain a normal pattern of daytime alertness and nighttime sleep. (116)[33]

The inability to share the painful experiences she has gone through mark the second dimension of the destruction of agency. As we have so far seen, the body, as a 'nexus of leaving meanings,' turns a person's very being into a constant reminder of the horrors of a previous torture. As Amery remarks, "Whoever was tortured, stays tortured. Torture is ineradicably burned into him, even when no clinically objective traces can be detected" (Amery, 34). This continuing living torture also eradicates the social *habitas* that makes human agency what it is.

Torture's destruction of the social world

Discussing the effects of seeing one's family tortured, Jacobo Timerman writes:

> The entire world of affection, built up over the years with utmost difficulty, collapses with a kick in the father's genitals, a smack on the mother's face, an obscene insult to the sister, or the sexual violation of a daughter. Suddenly an entire culture based on familial love, devotion, and the capacity for mutual sacrifice collapses. Nothing is possible in such a universe, and that is precisely what the torturers know. (69)[34]

Victims of torture often are incapable of rejoining family life. Divorces are common, as are instances of blind rage. As is obvious, the shattered world of the torturer makes it incredibly difficult for the victim to relate to others in normal ways. This has the further effect of increasing that agent's isolation, and thereby his misery. As Jean Amery claims, reflecting on his experience at the hands of the Gestapo, "torture is the total inversion of the social world" (135)[35] – a world that is essential to our living a human life.

> No human life, not even the life of a hermit in nature's wilderness, is possible without a world which directly or indirectly testifies to the presence of other human beings. All human activities are conditioned by the fact that men live together. (Arendt, 22)

The public world in which we live is destroyed both in the moment of torture, as well as in its aftermath. The pain inflicted on the tortured during interrogation serves to sever her connection to a world of significance, and this severance continues in the body as it carries its pain forward into future experience.

Normally, the absence of pain is no more than the bodily condition for expe-
riencing the world; only if the body is not irritated and, through irritation,
thrown back upon itself, can our bodily senses function normally, receive what
is given to them. (Arendt, 113)

Getting help from psychologists, it turns out, is also incredibly difficult
for the victim of torture. As one group of clinicians characterizes the
problem,

serious symptoms include *anxiety, sleep disturbances, and nightmares*, often
combined. The anxiety is often chronic, and may be present even during sleep.
Torture victims try to suppress their anxiety, but they are seldom successful;
it is easily aroused and increased by associations with torture. People who
have been isolated in small rooms during torture become very anxious and
afraid when they are enclosed in small places, such as hospital examination
rooms, lifts, and so on. The same anxiety is provoked when they have to meet
authorities, especially uniformed ones, to the extent that they fail to come to
appointments because of fear. Their very low self-respect and their suspicion,
coupled with fear, make it impossible for them to explain themselves vis-à-vis
authorities. In particularly stressful situations, their fear may lead to panic so
that they suddenly have to leave the room. (134–135)[36]

This state of fear, as noted above, makes it incredibly difficult for victims
of torture to pursue any kind of therapy, and even more difficult for
therapy to be carried through to success. Even posing questions via a
standard questionnaire – a procedure often used to introduce patients
to the therapeutic process – can "lead to an intensification of treatment"
(160).[37] Moreover, "many seem to lack drive and vitality, appearing
numb and tense, but they can also be excessively irritable and lose all
control of themselves as they succumb to rage" (1).[38] Nor can therapists
simply turn to the use of pharmacology to solve the problems of the tortured.[39] The problems for clinicians are exacerbated by the very things
they hope to deal with.

Since it is not easy for refugees to size up our Treatment Center, a certain
mistrust prevails at the outset of our communication with patients . . . Many
patients cry when talk turns to forms of torture that have injured their dignity.
Some patients suddenly turn mute and slump into their pain; some patients
jump up, become restless, sweat and tremble as they describe what happened.
(159–160)[40]

The fear experienced by the victim of torture is, in certain respects, justified. Their lives are marked by persistent suffering, a past from which
they cannot escape, and a body that carries their experiences with them

in everything they do. The trauma characteristic of torture can also re-
emerge at any moment – when one is driving a car, playing with one's
children, having dinner.[41]

> Contrary to recollections of everyday events, flashbacks are experienced as if
> the event is occurring at the moment . . . once the recollection of the torture
> scene is triggered, it will result in a 'here and now' perception and the trauma-
> tized survivor may experience a flashback. (176)[42]

Flashbacks are a common occurrence. The experience of torture *does
not* stay in the past – it lives in both the present (through conversion
disorders) and the future (through the constant possibility of flashbacks).
Traumatic experiences "tend to be memorized more deeply under the
influence of adrenaline and other stress hormones. Traumatic experiences can therefore enter consciousness spontaneously or turn into dream
images. Even in old age they can surface again after a long latent period,
as if they were leading an autonomous existence" (190).[43] This happens
despite the fact that there is memory *loss* in other areas: short-term
memory is damaged, for example, and many patients find it difficult to
remember specific details accompanying their torture (e.g. dates, names,
times of day).[44] Resurfacing trauma – trauma re-lived in the course of
everyday life – hampers the ability to find successful treatment, and it
further erodes a person's trust in the ability to even *be* helped.

> A positive course of treatment is fundamentally handicapped by the way in
> which the omnipotence of the perpetrators and the powerlessness of their
> victims lives on in the inner psychic reality of the latter. (Haenel, 8)

The inability to seek help from those in the medical profession, however,
is not limited to those in mental health. The presence of medical personnel within torture situations creates problems with getting treatment for
the physical ailments associated with torture.

> Doctors use too many techniques that are similar to the kinds of tortures
> experienced by survivors. This applies not only to actual physical techniques
> but also to the ways in which doctors examine and interrogate their patients.
> Doctors have to exercise tremendous care in the way they speak and treat
> their patients for the patients themselves can no longer effectively distinguish
> between what is torture and what is medicine. (174)[45]

The loss of trust in others is exacerbated by the typical reactions of
those the torture victim confides in. This includes those they encounter
when seeking asylum in other countries.[46] "When episodes of torture
are portrayed, typical human reactions include downplaying it, denying

it, avoiding it, and tuning it out" (155).[47] While this kind of coping mechanism on the part of those who hear stories of torture is perhaps understandable – they are attempting to avoid a recognition of the depths of human depravity – it reinforces the feelings of alienation that partially constitute the world of the victim. In fact, such tactics are not exhaustive: victims also encounter challenges to their stories from others, and in many cases, blame for the atrocities that have happened to them. The tortured person

> feels incompetent and unable to cope with the challenges of his life situation, a state of mind that has been termed 'demoralization'. Feelings of guilt and shame, alienation, isolation from and resentment towards the surroundings are part of this state of mind, restricting the way the individual perceives himself and his possibilities in life. (146)[48]

Feelings of guilt and shame, in fact, are extraordinarily common, though not universal. The use of certain techniques is designed precisely to produce just this effect. There are reported cases of torture by inserting objects into the rectum, and of forcing persons to drink their torturer's urine.[49] "The purpose behind these torture methods injurious to the sense of honor is not confession; rather, its aim is the dissolution of personal identity. The greater the horrors portrayed, the more fragile the remnants of identity, the greater the likelihood that the victim will lack credibility" (166).[50] The social world that allows us to live in a meaningful context becomes one where the tortured is abandoned, where there can be no help to be had, and in which the basic trust that allows us to exist in communal fashion has been utterly crushed.

Other aspects of the destruction of agency

The social world of the tortured is first eroded in the experience of a pain that reduces his world to the singular experience of extreme pain inflicted by an Other. This experience, however, continues long after the torture is complete: he feels isolated and alienated, unable to find himself in the ordinary activities of those who occupy his world. This isolation and alienation unmakes his world – it strips it of meaning as it strips the very notion of 'civilization' of any content.

> For the victims, torture is unpredictable in a way that is unlike anything they have ever known before, and at the same time it is unavoidable and usually uncontrollable. For these reasons, torture is something that cannot be mastered. The almost always unanticipated breakdown of the self, of the self's values, leads to the experience of one's own total failure, to self-blame, and therefore to overwhelming feelings of shame. (Gurris, 29)

The loss of autonomy and self-determination begins in the moment that torture begins, and manifests itself later in the inability to control one's emotions (shame is ever-present, rage frequently erupts), one's experiences (flashbacks are common), or one's body (pain is chronic, disorders emerge, sometimes without any obvious physical cause). The sorts of decisions one used to make are no longer easily made (to go to the doctor, to play with one's children). Even one's understanding of everyday objects becomes something *forced* upon the victim by the experiences he was subjected to: the objects of ordinary life that were used in the torture session – the chair, the hammer, even *language* – now has a deeply humiliating significance. The aim and consequence of torture are total destruction of the self via the destruction of all those things constitutive of humanity: being with others, using language, and exercising one's will.

> It no longer fits into our familiar maps of thought and evaluation for a grown human being to become completely helpless, to cry or beg for mercy, to void the bowels and pass urine in the panic of uncontrolled anxiety, to wish simply to be killed at last instead of having to vegetate, and to have even this last bit of autonomy refused. Under these circumstances, naked biological survival can lead the tortured person to betray anyone and everything. So after torture the victim finds that he is still somehow alive physically but has been psychologically destroyed. (Gurris, 31)

Pain itself works to undermine our sense of self, as well as our capacity to guide our own lives. David Sussman, as we saw in Chapter 3, makes this point with impressive clarity and force. His remarks are worth repeating:

> Unlike other kinds of unwanted imposition, pain characteristically compromises or undermines the very capacities constitutive of autonomous agency itself. It is almost impossible to reflect, deliberate, or even think straight when one is in agony. When sufficiently intense, pain becomes a person's entire universe and his entire self, crowding out every other aspect of his mental life. Unlike other harms, pain takes its victim's agency apart 'from the inside,' such that the agent may never be able to reconstitute himself fully. (Sussman, 14)

As we have seen, the pain present in the torture situation pervades the life of the torture victim, extending into one's everyday life, and dismantling one's capacity to function with that life. The same can be said of other tools of the torture chamber. Not only the implements of torture, but also its associative content – smells, sounds, words, and sights – all carry with them a new significance after the torture event. These things, directly and intentionally involved in the willful restructuring of one's experience, spell the death of one's agency, as well as the death of any meaningful notion of 'civilization' as opposed to 'barbarity.' The very things that are regarded as the *source* of civilization are re-tooled to unmake it. Technology, law, and language, normally hallmarks of civilized society, become the means through which civilization is destroyed. It is hardly surprising, then, that one can never return to the world as it was before torture occurred.

One of the central methods used in torture is to produce dependence on the torturer. Indeed, this is crucial to achieving the goal of torture: the destruction of the victim's sense that they have any power. Again, Sussman:

> The victim is completely exposed, while the torturer is free to conceal anything he likes, even those things to which a victim clearly has a right and a profound interest . . . the asymmetry of power, knowledge, and prerogative is absolute: the victim is in a position of complete vulnerability and exposure, the torturer in one of perfect control and inscrutability. (Sussman, 7)

Multiple interrogation manuals and studies make precisely this point: inducing in the victim a sense of total helplessness both isolates the individual and makes it more likely for the individual to lose any sense of himself as an agent. Even the agent's pain, something usually regarded as private, comes to be something that is not the agent's own. It becomes a tool to be used to dismantle its possessor. "What the torturer does is to take his victim's pain, and through it his victim's body, and make it begin to express the torturer's will" (Sussman, 21). And the body continues to do this even when the torture is complete.[51]

Does torture always result in the destruction of agency?

It is sometimes argued that the consequences attributed to torture are not *necessary* consequences, even if they are probable ones. So far as it goes, this argument is correct: there are instances where torture methods have been applied, and the victim of these methods has not been broken by them, or where victims seem to recover from the unmaking of the world.[52]

The argument that torture will not necessarily produce the unmaking of agency, however, does not have any straightforward consequences. If it is meant to show that torture can be acceptable in certain cases, it is surely a very misleading way of proceeding. The fact that a practice aimed at the destruction of agency might not achieve its goal is hardly evidence that the practice is sometimes acceptable. If the very aim of torture is the destruction of agency, whether to terrorize, to gain information, or some other such thing, the fact that cases of torture might not have these results only shows that torture is not always successful. The same is true with any and every practice that faces the constraints of the empirical world. This fact, it seems to me, is irrelevant to our assessment of the *nature* of torture as well as to its moral assessment.

In this respect, the argument that torture does not always destroy agency is a red herring (and it is actually generous to call this an argument – it is more realistically simply an empirical observation). Much as the fact that certain baseball games do not *necessarily* have at least nine innings (because of rain, natural disaster, or what have you) tells us nothing about the nature of baseball, neither does the existence of people surviving torture tell us anything about its practice. The aim of baseball is to have at least nine innings. It sometimes is unable to do so because of unforeseeable obstacles. The aim of torture is to destroy the agent – this is not merely a foreseeable but unintended consequence, as I hope this chapter has demonstrated. To point out that torture sometimes fails to achieve the goal postulated in torture manuals, however, is irrelevant to determining what torture *aims to do*. To say otherwise would be as crass as saying that torture does not always destroy the capacity for agency because sometimes a person is executed before the torture is complete. This is true, of course, but this is one truth that is at best unhelpful; at worst, it blinds us to the devastation that is the nature of torture.

Concluding remarks

At this point, both the kinds of torture and its significant effects have been addressed. Only now can we begin a meaningful discussion of the arguments that torture is, in exceptional cases, morally permissible. Too often, I have repeatedly urged, such arguments are presented without any concern for the physical and psychological realities of torture – and this willful ignorance about the nature of torture has significant consequences for the way the discussion goes. This, I think, is particularly applicable to the use of the so-called 'ticking bomb argument.' It is for this reason that I have not introduced the arguments for and against torture without first offering some significant background on what torture *is* and what it *does*. It is only after grounding ourselves in the reality of torture that we can even meaningfully *raise* questions about whether or not it is permissible, and under what conditions it might be so. This will be the focus in the following two chapters.

Notes

1. These effects are documented widely in the literature on torture.
2. This is less true now than it used to be. See Reyes, "The worst scars are in the mind: psychological torture," *International Review of the Red Cross*, September 2007, Volume 89 Number 867.

3. Lone Jacobson and Edith Montgomery, "Treatment of Victims of Torture" in *An End to Torture*.

4. Britta Jenkins, "There, Where Words Fail, Tears are the Bridge: Thoughts on Speechlessness in Working with Survivors of Torture" in *At the Side of Torture Survivors: Treating a Terrible Assault on Human Dignity*.

5. Pieter Kooijmans, "Torturers and their Masters" in *The Politics of Pain*.

6. Ferdinand Haenel, "Foreign Bodies in the Soul" in *At the Side of Torture Survivors: Treating a Terrible Assault on Human Dignity*.

7. Terry Kupers, "Prison and the Decimation of Pro-Social Life Skills" in *The Trauma of Psychological Torture*.

8. Lone Jacobson and Edith Montgomery, "Treatment of Victims of Torture" in *An End to Torture*.

9. Fabri, "Treating Torture Victims," in *Torture: Does it Make Us Safer?*

10. KUBARK, pagination missing (Sec. VII.A.7).

11. The Inter-American Convention to Prevent and Punish Torture, Article 2.

12. There is a tendency to forget that even 'minimal' procedures, when used repeatedly over a long period of time, or in conjunction with other 'minimal' procedures, can indeed constitute torture. I am indebted to Reyes' discussion of these points in "The worst scars are in the mind."

13. See Chapter 8: *The Constitution, US Law, and the Unitary Executive, Again*.

14. Lone Jacobson and Edith Montgomery, "Treatment of Victims of Torture" in *An End to Torture*.

15. Rona M. Fields, "The Neurobiological consequences of Psychological Torture," in *The Trauma of Psychological Torture*.

16. Stuart Grassian, "Neuropsychiatric Effects of Solitary Confinement" in *The Trauma of Psychological Torture*.

17. Claudia Catani, Frank Neuner, Christian Wienbruch, Thomas Elbert, "The Tortured Brain" in *The Trauma of Psychological Torture*.

18. Claudia Catani, Frank Neuner, Christian Wienbruch, Thomas Elbert, ibid.

19. Sepp Graessner, "Two Hundred Blows to the Head: Possibilities and Limits in Evaluating the Physical Aftereffects of Torture" in *At the Side of Torture Survivors: Treating a Terrible Assault on Human Dignity*.

20. Lone Jacobson and Edith Montgomery, "Treatment of Victims of Torture" in *An End to Torture*.

21. Lone Jacobson and Edith Montgomery, ibid.

22. Hernan Reyes, "The worst scars are in the mind: psychological torture" *International Review of the Red Cross*, September 2007, Volume 89 Number 867.

23. Rona M. Fields, "The Neurobiological consequences of Psychological Torture," in *The Trauma of Psychological Torture*.

24. Nicolas McGinnis, "Phenomenology, Interrogation and Biopower: Merleau-Ponty on 'Human Resource Exploitation'."

25. Hannah Arendt, *The Human Condition*.

26. "A Body in Pain – The Making of a World of Chronic Pain" in *Pain as Human Experience: An Anthropological Perspective.*

27. Lone Jacobson and Edith Montgomery, "Treatment of Victims of Torture" in *An End to Torture.*

28. Hannah Arendt, *The Origins of Totalitarianism.*

29. Gurris, "Psychic Trauma through Torture – Healing through Psychotherapy?" in *At the Side of Torture Survivors.*

30. See Hannah Arendt, *The Human Condition.* "The task and central greatness of mortals lie in their ability to produce things – works and deeds and words – which would deserve to be and, at least to a degree, are at home in everlastingness, so that through them mortals could find their place in a cosmos where everything is immortal except themselves." (19). Marx, as is well known, makes a similar point about the centrality of creative labor to human existence.

31. See Bent Sorensen, "Torture and Asylum" in *An End to Torture.* The after effects of torture can be "so severe that the person has difficulty in, or is not capable of, performing normal work" (172–173).

32. Lone Jacobson and Edith Montgomery, "Treatment of Victims of Torture" in *An End to Torture.*

33. Stuart Grassian, "Neuropsychiatric Effects of Solitary Confinement" in *The Trauma of Psychological Torture.*

34. Jacobo Timerman, *Prisoner Without a Name, Cell Without a Number,* quoted in Hector Timerman, "Torture: A Family Affair" in *Torture.*

35. Quoted in *The Phenomenon of Torture.*

36. Lone Jacobson and Edith Montgomery, "Treatment of Victims of Torture" in *An End to Torture.*

37. Sepp Graessner, "Two Hundred Blows to the Head: Possibilities and Limits in Evaluating the Physical Aftereffects of Torture" in *At the Side of Torture Survivors: Treating a Terrible Assault on Human Dignity.*

38. Ferdinand Haenel, "Foreign Bodies in the Soul" in *At the Side of Torture Survivors: Treating a Terrible Assault on Human Dignity.*

39. See, for example, Başoğlu et al., "Amitriptyline for PTSD in a Torture Survivor: A Case Study," for a useful account of the limited effectiveness of drug-therapy.

40. Sepp Graessner, "Two Hundred Blows to the Head: Possibilities and Limits in Evaluating the Physical Aftereffects of Torture" in *At the Side of Torture Survivors: Treating a Terrible Assault on Human Dignity.*

41. It is for this reason that treatment centers must avoid looking 'institution-like,' among others. As Marianne Kastrup notes, "an institution-like environment might easily bring memories of prison and torture back to the victim and should be avoided as much as possible" (282), "Coping with Exposure to Torture."

42. Claudia Catani, Frank Neuner, Christian Wienbruch, Thomas Elbert, "The Tortured Brain" in *The Trauma of Psychological Torture.*

43. Sepp Graessner, Salah Ahmad, and Frank Merkord, "Everything Forgotten! Memory Disorders among Refugees Who Have Been Tortured" in *At the Side of Torture Survivors: Treating a Terrible Assault on Human Dignity.*

44. Ibid.

45. Darius Rejali, *Torture and Modernity: Self, Society, and State in Modern Iran*

46. See Sepp Graessner, Salah Ahmad, and Frank Merkord, "Everything Forgotten! Memory Disorders among Refugees Who Have Been Tortured!" and Christian Poss, "Legal Status, Living Conditions, and Health Care for Political Refugees in Germany", both in *At the Side of Torture Survivors.*

47. Sepp Graessner, "Two Hundred Blows to the Head: Possibilities and Limits in Evaluating the Physical Aftereffects of Torture" in *At the Side of Torture Survivors: Treating a Terrible Assault on Human Dignity.*

48. Lone Jacobson and Edith Montgomery, "Treatment of Victims of Torture" in *An End to Torture.*

49. See, for example, Sepp Graessner, "Two Hundred Blows to the Head: Possibilities and Limits in Evaluating the Physical Aftereffects of Torture" in *At the Side of Torture Survivors: Treating a Terrible Assault on Human Dignity*, where a detainee reports precisely these things. Detainees at Abu Ghraib also report being urinated on, as well as being anally raped by guards. See, for example, the detainee report in *The Phenomenon of Torture*, as well as the ICRC report on conditions at Abu Ghraib.

50. Sepp Graessner, "Two Hundred Blows to the Head: Possibilities and Limits in Evaluating the Physical Aftereffects of Torture" in *At the Side of Torture Survivors: Treating a Terrible Assault on Human Dignity.*

51. I would be remiss not to at least mention the sexual dimension of torture. The use of sexual humiliation, as well as rape, is a common torture practice. Like other forms of torture, the use of the sexual identity of a victim *against* that victim serves to cut off the victim from this dimension of his agency, and this can produce substantial problems for living a life that is regarded as fulfilling, as well as to specific problems in treatment. See, for example, Inger Agger, "Sexual Torture of Political Prisoners: An Overview."

52. Senator John McCain, for example, might constitute one such instance. Despite being tortured for seven years while serving in Vietnam, he has since had a successful career in politics.

Chapter 5

Thinking through Torture's Temptations

Part One: Arguments For Torture

Introduction

Having examined the many faces of torture, and having suggested that its unique wrongness is found in its degradation of agency, I will now turn my attention to the various arguments offered in its favor.

As I have noted, torture is almost universally regarded as a serious wrong. Many arguments for torture thus begin with a thought experiment – the 'ticking bomb' – designed to call into question the claim that torture is always impermissible. It is not used to argue (so far as I know) that torture is *always* permissible.

I will only touch on the ticking bomb thought experiment here (for a sustained critique, see Chapter 6: *Criticisms of the ticking bomb*) concentrating instead on more general cases for torture for the following reasons:

First, the ticking bomb argument is what is frequently called a 'wedge argument' – it is meant to make us think about whether or not we *actually* accept the idea that torture is in fact *always* impermissible. As such, it is the point of departure for thinking about the issue of torture; it is not where the argument comes to an end. In fact, this argument is not an argument at all. It is an intuition pump. One might accept that torture is permissible in such a case but deny that there ever *are* such cases, and hence defend an absolute moral and legal prohibition.[1] The ticking bomb case is thus insufficient to justify torture, as even its adherents will admit.[2]

Second, as I hope to show in Chapter 6, the ticking bomb case admits of some unique confusion.

The arguments for torture can be seen as falling into two broad, sometimes overlapping categories: arguments from mitigating circumstances, on the one hand, and arguments from warrant, on the other. Almost all arguments accept that torture is *prima facie* wrong, but that this wrongness is significantly mitigated by certain kinds of circumstances (threats to national security, the risk of many innocent lives, and so on). Another kind of pro-torture argument maintains that there are cases in which torture is *warranted* by the actions of others (these include arguments invoking what justice requires, or what is warranted based on non-reciprocity, and so on).

Arguments for torture

The ticking bomb

Recent years have seen increasing numbers of articles and books devoted to demonstrating the severe problems with ticking bomb reasoning.[3] This is hardly surprising, given the extent to which and frequency with which the ticking bomb case is invoked. It has many variations, but its central outline is as follows.

Ticking Bomb Scenario

Officials have recently captured a person with information regarding the whereabouts of an explosive device set to detonate in an urban area. It is also known that this device will detonate within the next six hours, making evacuation of the area impossible. It is known that torture will be effective on this person, and that it will be effective in time to defuse the bomb and save thousands of lives. No other means of interrogation can be assured of equal success.

There are two broad pro-torture positions that tend to result from ticking bomb scenarios. One position, championed by Alan Dershowitz,[4] is that the ticking bomb argument gives us a substantial reason for implementing an actual policy of torturing persons – a policy replete with judicial oversight reminiscent of the *ancien regime*.[5] Another position – and one that is by far the most common – is that the ticking bomb argument demonstrates that torture is *morally* permissible in particular cases.[6] As such, the ticking bomb argument *does not* have any particular bearing on questions of policy. Indeed, many argue that torture ought to be legally prohibited *in all cases*, but concede that the ticking bomb argument shows that the universal illegality of acts of torture can in some cases be overlooked.[7] This is precisely the view that was defended by the Israeli Supreme Court, which argued for an absolute ban on torture, but acknowledged that a necessity defense could be used when this law was broken.[8] Importantly, this *is not* the same as allowing a policy of torture. It is, rather, a way of acknowledging that certain violations of the law admit of *ex post* ratification. Others have argued that the ticking bomb case provides another case where civil disobedience would be justified.[9]

The minority position is the Dershowitz view – a view that has been criticized from a variety of angles. The majority view is that torture should be banned absolutely as a legal matter, *and* that it might nevertheless be morally permissible in certain cases. This view is articulated, for example, by John Parry and Richard Posner.[10] Parry claims that "we cannot completely reject the evil of torture as a method of combating terrorism, regardless of what international law provides. If torture provides the last remaining chance to save lives in imminent peril, the necessity defense should be available to justify the interrogators' conduct" (158). "Torture may be a legitimate option – the lesser of two evils – in rare circumstances" (160). Posner's view is no less clear: "what is required is a balance between the costs and the benefits of particular methods of interrogation . . . Certainly the costs include the horror that the term 'torture' evokes, but the costs can be outweighed by the benefits if torture is the only means by which to save the lives of thousands, perhaps tens or hundreds of thousands, of people. In so extreme a case, it seems to me, torture must be allowed" (293).

In a recent paper, "Torture, Terrorism, and the State: a Refutation of the Ticking bomb Argument," Vittorio Bufacchi and Jean Maria Arrigo claim to offer a refutation of the Ticking bomb Argument. Their aim is to argue for "the unconditional refutation of any attempt to justify torture, under any circumstances" (355).[11] The scope of the refutation, we can see, is meant to apply to *all* cases of the ticking bomb argument. To this end, Buffacchi and Arrigo argue that ticking bomb cases commit two fallacies: 1) a deductive fallacy, such that the inferences drawn from the ticking bomb scenario simply do not follow from its premises, and 2) a consequentialist fallacy. Concentrating for a moment on the 'deductive fallacy' alleged to occur in the ticking bomb case will help us to understand the underlying *point* of ticking bomb arguments. I here quote at length:

> The Deductive Fallacy occurs when a certain argument infers invalid conclusions from certain premises, either because the conclusions rest on a different set of premises, and/or because the premises don't support the conclusions. The ticking bomb argument follows a deductive line of reasoning concerning the efficacy of torture interrogation.
>
> (P1): Terrorist is captured
> (P2): If the terrorist is tortured, he/she will reveal information regarding the location of the primed bomb before the bomb detonates.
> Therefore (C1): Terrorist ought to be tortured.
> Therefore (C2): The information regarding the location of the primed bomb is retrieved.
> Therefore (C3): The bomb is found and disconnected before it explodes, saving the lives of many innocent people.

There are two sets of problems with this argument. The first problem is that the Conclusions C1, C2, and C3 do not follow from premises P1 and P2. In order to draw these conclusions, other 'invisible' premises must be in place. The second problem is that the premises (both visible and invisible) from which the ticking bomb argument deduces its conclusions are illegitimate, being questionable from an empirical point of view.

In order to deduce Conclusions C1, C2, and C3, all the above premises are required:

(P1*): It is almost certain that this is the terrorist holding information regarding a primed bomb.

(P2): If the terrorist is tortured, he/she will reveal information regarding the location of the primed bomb before the bomb detonates.

Therefore (C1): Terrorist ought to be tortured.

Therefore (C2): The information regarding the location of the primed bomb is retrieved.

(P3): It is almost certain that the terrorist will reveal the correct information.

Therefore (C3): The bomb is found and disconnected before it explodes, saving the lives of many innocent people.

All the premises in the argument are contentious from an empirical point of view. (360–361)

The remarks made by Bufacchi and Arrigo are quite compelling in one respect. As a deductive argument, the one presented above is indeed problematic. Bufacchi and Arrigo criticize this view for the right reasons: intelligence is always fallible, torture is not always effective, torture is less likely to work in short time spans, torture elicits false information, etc. On all these accounts, the criticisms offered are spot on.

But Bufacchi and Arrigo are guilty of presenting a straw-man conception of the logic of the ticking bomb case. If someone utilized the ticking bomb argument as a *deductive device* to justify torture, they would be committing a series of logical errors. Bufacchi and Arrigo have successfully and skillfully shown this. This, however, is not typically how the argument is used (in fact, I do not think I have *ever* seen it used this way). The ticking bomb argument is used, rather, as a way of demonstrating that the moral ban on torture has particular limitations. The argument works much like any intuition pump: it shows us that there are cases where our intuitions about the absolute moral impermissibility of some x are not nearly so strong as we initially thought. Once this is established, to borrow George Bernard Shaw's famous wit, we only need to haggle over the price – that is, we only need to determine exactly what conditions must obtain for torture to be allowed. Thus, the claim of a 'deductive fallacy' in this context strikes me as a red herring: *all* intuition pumps commit this kind of fallacy if we construe them as deductive arguments. The ticking bomb argument amounts, essentially, to the claim that there are cases under which a rational and moral person will be willing to condone torture. As such, I do not think

Bufacchi and Arrigo have adequately demonstrated that the 'Deductive Fallacy' refutes the argument – unless it refutes all devices used to test our intuitions.

Admittedly, Bufacchi and Arrigo have shown that the ticking bomb (TB) case is unrealistic – but there has never been any doubt about *that*.[12] The issue is what can be inferred from the thought experiment as a whole (as well as the intuitions it generates). The issue is *not* whether the concocted scenario justifies *by itself* a policy of torture. By itself, the scenario justifies nothing – except perhaps the view that we should re-examine our intuitions about the absolute impermissibility of torture.

The ticking bomb case is meant to demonstrate that our intuitions against torture are not nearly as absolute as we might perhaps think. The majority of people facing this case (according to its proponents) will endorse the use of torture. It is irrelevant (again, according to its proponents) that such cases are exceptionally rare – or even nonexistent. The point of the thought experiment is not to justify torture in only such cases. Rather, the point is to demonstrate that *there are* cases in which torture would be permissible. Only after establishing this conclusion can we then go on to draw more substantive conclusions about *when* torture is justified. Once we have determined that it *can* be justified, the argument runs, we can then explore the limits of its justifiability.

Arguments from mitigating circumstances

The moral responsibility to save lives

The force of the ticking bomb scenario comes primarily from what is at stake: lives will be lost if one does not torture. The number of lives, of course, depends on how the case is constructed – but the more lives, the greater the sense of obligation one might feel to engage in whatever is required to save those lives. Any refusal to torture in such a case is often regarded with disdain: to refuse to torture, the argument runs, is to place one's own moral purity over the lives of the people who would otherwise be saved. In this respect, the decision to *immorally* torture is a decision to sacrifice one's own moral standing for the greater good. To fail to do so strikes some as grotesquely selfish.

> To do otherwise [than torture] – to give up the chance to find your soldier lest you sully yourself by authorizing torture of the person who possesses potentially lifesaving information – is a deeply immoral betrayal of a soldier and countryman . . . pure pacifism, like no-torture absolutism [is] a form of moral foolishness, tinged with moral vanity. (315)[13]

There is an important point lurking behind the bile and rhetoric here: morality demands the sacrifice of self-interest – and this might well mean that, in certain cases, one must even sacrifice one's own moral purity if there is something much more important on the line. This presents a philosophical perplexity for anyone interested in moral philosophy: is it possible that a (normally) immoral action can be morally required?

We should tread carefully here. The claim that one should torture in the above instance is based on a certain conception of morality – one that relies on both deontic and consequentialist considerations. Obviously, the number of lives at stake ups the ante considerably. A failure to torture, *ex hypothesi*, will result in a great loss (the consequentialist consideration). The criticism of a refusal to torture, however, is not merely a consequentialist criticism. In fact, it is a criticism of motivation. The wrong done involves a failure in respecting those who will be sacrificed on the altar of one's moral purity. It also involves a claim that *not* engaging in the act of torture would be an instance of egoism: one is motivated by self-interest in moral purity rather than in the lives of those to be saved (a deontic consideration).

While rhetorically very powerful, this kind of criticism is philosophically confused. No one defending the claim that one should not torture is motivated (at least not explicitly) by selfish considerations[14] – a motivation that would indeed be deeply problematic. On the best reading, the motivation in question involves a respect for moral absolutes: human dignity has no price, the traditional deontologist claims, and hence the numbers game cannot be played when dignity is at issue.

But the view that numbers are irrelevant is problematic. Few would claim that the wrong done by killing one person was the same as the wrong done by killing one million. This suggests that numbers *must* matter in some way, even if it isn't precisely clear *how* they matter. It is likewise problematic to assume moral absolutes, for all the standard reasons. Strictly speaking, however, these points are irrelevant to the above response: the point is that one cannot criticize the advocate of absolute prohibition for having selfish motives. This is simply a caricature. If there is a criticism to be made, it must be that the deontologist, in the ticking bomb case, fails to see the importance of the loss of lives that will occur if one does not engage in torture.

This criticism, however, also strikes me as something of a caricature. Even the advocate of absolute prohibition would regard the decision not to torture as a tragic one – as a case where it is impossible to act without significant harm coming to someone. In this respect, the deontologist might argue, the choice here is akin to that of the character Sophie in William Styron's novel (and the subsequent Academy Award-winning film adaptation) *Sophie's Choice*, where Sophie must choose which of her two children is allowed to live. No choice, in this case, is an innocent one – each choice will have severe repercussions – that's what makes the decision a tragic one.

This is not to say that a deontologist will *necessarily* refuse to torture in the ticking bomb scenario. On a traditional Kantian model, having a maxim to save as many lives as possible could easily be universalized, and might well justify the use of torture in this case. Alternatively, one can appeal to the view that the dignity of the torturer *requires* that one carry out torture, provided that there is ample warning of what consequences will follow if one refuses to provide the needed information. If the tortured chooses to remain silent, despite knowing that she will be tortured, torture itself would constitute a way of respecting the will of the torturer. Kant offers a similar argument for the death penalty.[15] In some cases, respecting a person might well require executing them. Analogously, one might argue that torture could instantiate just this kind of respect.

Ultimately, I do not think the analogy works, but whether or not it does is not relevant here.[16] The issue under consideration is how to understand the refusal to torture in the ticking bomb case. Many deontologists argue that it *is* impermissible for the standard sorts of reasons (it violates the dignity of the tortured, it reduces the tortured to a means to an end, and so on). The issue is not whether this is the position dictated by deontology (a question, which, I will confess, does not strike me as very important). The issue, rather, is *on what grounds* this decision is to be criticized. As we have seen, criticizing someone for refusing to torture based on motivations of selfishness or a failure to appreciate the significance of the loss that will occur both misconstrue the decision itself. Likewise, an insistence on torturing despite one's squeamishness sounds a lot like 'don't be a sissy' – a claim that is based on the kind of normative masculinity and sexism that is inappropriate in moral deliberation.[17]

So, where does this leave us? Critiques of the absolute prohibition of torture – of the decision *not* to torture in the ticking bomb case – are left with an appeal to the greater good. What is interesting about this appeal, of course, is that it relies on empirical considerations. And it is at this point that the ticking bomb argument begins to break down. Many argue that *any* use of torture will have massive negative consequences – that it will destroy the credibility of the nation that tortures (or the person, for that matter), that it requires institutions for training torturers that would have serious negative impact on the quality of life for anyone in such a society, that is would ultimately produce more terrorists, and so on.[18]

The advocate of the ticking bomb case might well insist that torture would prevent more harm than it caused – but this insistence is simply dogmatic. There is a good deal of empirical evidence regarding the use of torture having an effect on particular societies – evidence that is not entirely consistent. The dogmatic assertion that torture will *necessarily* have a positive net outcome is to mistake faith in a process for an argument that justifies it. No one would deny that saving lives is of crucial moral consequence – but it isn't everything. If we are to honestly assess the harms prevented and produced, the significance of a ticking bomb case is anything but clear.

These kinds of considerations are behind what Buffachi and Arrigo call the 'consequentialist fallacy,' mentioned above. The consequentialist fallacy 'points to the empirical evidence suggesting that the negative consequences of implementing a policy of torture interrogation outweigh any possible positive consequences; therefore arguments for torture interrogation of terrorists can be refuted on consequentialist grounds' (355). Insofar as the aim of the argument is to demonstrate that torture *policies* have a net negative outcome, Buffacchi and Arrigo successfully make their case. The case against institutionalized torture is presented here in summary:[19]

> The accuracy and speed of virtuoso torture interrogation dictate long advance preparation and coordination, and ultimately corruption, of many key social institutions. The principal parties actually include the medical establishment, the scientific establishment, the police, the military establishment, the judicial establishment, and a great many innocents falsely tortured.
>
> It may appear that damages to democratic institutions are negligible compared to deaths of innocents because institutions can be repaired but the dead cannot be resurrected. Yet in country after country where alleged national security threats have resulted in the torture of domestic enemies – including Algeria, South Africa, Chile, Argentina, Uruguay, El Salvador, Guatemala, Ireland – human rights researchers have shown the failures of various programs of social repair. Criminal trials, truth commissions, reparations to victims, and community mourning rituals have all proved inadequate. Part of the difficulty of social repair is the high proportion of innocents who are tortured. Realistically, the moral calculus of the ticking bomb argument should weigh (a) the evil of the murders of innocent victims against (b) the corruption of key social institutions, the evil of torture of many innocents mistakenly tortured, and the ruination of many torturers. (367)

Buffachi and Arrigo take this result to be a refutation of "the consequentialist reasoning used to justify interrogations" (362). As they put it:

> We believe the ticking bomb argument ultimately fails as a consequentialist argument because it ignores the intensive preparation and larger social consequences of state-sponsored torture. The validity of any consequentialist argument rests on a costs and benefit analysis. We argue that empirical evidence clearly suggests that institutionalizing torture interrogation of terrorists has detrimental consequences on civil, military, and legal institutions, making the costs higher than the benefits. (362)

The problem here is as follows: not all consequentialist defenses of torture – and certainly not all uses of the ticking bomb argument – advocate torture *policy*. A refutation of the view that we should implement a torture policy, it must be admitted, does *not* constitute a refutation of the ticking bomb argument itself. The Consequentialist Fallacy shows that any *policy* of torture will have ill-effects such that said policies cannot be justified on consequentialist grounds. While this is not an unimportant result, it is not a refutation of those who utilize the ticking bomb argument for *exceptional* cases (and this is how most philosophers who are fans of this thought-experiment use it). To make this argument would require that we argue that all torturers must be trained – even to successfully perform a single act of torture (a point I will return to in Chapter 6: *Professional torturers: Where policy and exception overlap*).[20]

But suppose we changed the thought experiment to preclude the possibility of the negative consequences outweighing the positive ones. Could we expect those who refuse to torture to then change their position? Perhaps we could, perhaps not. Of course, whether or not we could convince someone to change his position is not the best measure of the force of an argument, as virtually everyone knows. Changing the thought experiment, however, has certain restrictions, the primary of which is that the thought experiment must be constrained by the nature of the thing discussed. Can we imagine torture that has had no negative consequences? For reasons I will provide in the next chapter, I do not think that we can. Once we ground ourselves solidly in the empirical reality of torture, we see that it *inevitably* has negative consequences – on the tortured, the torturer, those who become aware of the torture, and so on – though the nature and extent of these obviously cannot be decided in advance. Consider, by analogy, this version of the ticking bomb thought experiment:

> Imagine that you could torture a person without them knowing it, and with absolutely no negative consequences, in order to save a million lives. Would you do it?

Saying that one would not torture in such a case sounds absurd. All of the objections to torture seem to have been removed. If this does not seem the case, simply change 'person' to 'tin can'. Would you torture a tin can to save a million lives? The obvious answer is 'yes.' But notice that this thought experiment no longer seems to be *about* torture. I do not know what it is about, to speak frankly. To be *about* torture, the thought experiment must involve something that can reasonably be described as 'torture' given what we know about it. What we know, at least, is this: torture has negative consequences, and it is used against beings who *experience* the torture, and who are deeply affected by this experience.

The imperative to 'save lives' in the ticking bomb case is insufficient to warrant assenting to torture, and the criticisms against those who do refuse assent are inadequate. In the long run, it simply is not clear that lives *will* be saved, or that less harm will result from torture than will be prevented. To make this claim requires an additional premise – namely, that torture is the *only* way to save lives. Thus, to justify the use of torture requires something like an appeal to the *necessity* of torture – and precisely these kinds of arguments have in fact been made. In the following three sections, we will consider some popular appeals to necessity as justifying torture.

Argument from need for intelligence gathering in 'new wars'

In this section, we'll explore the idea that the use of torture might, on a regular basis, be justified by appeal to utilitarian considerations. It is just this sort of view that continues to be advocated by former Vice President Dick Cheney.

> When we get people who are more concerned about reading the rights to an Al Qaeda terrorist than they are with protecting the United States against people who are absolutely committed to do anything they can to kill Americans, then I worry . . . These are evil people. And we're not going to win this fight by turning the other cheek.
>
>   If it hadn't been for what we did – with respect to the . . . enhanced interrogation techniques for high-value detainees . . . then we would have been attacked again. Those policies we put in place, in my opinion, were absolutely crucial to getting us through the last seven-plus years without a major-casualty attack on the US. . . .[21]

As the former Vice President makes clear, torture is portrayed as the only way to deal with the 'evil doers' that aim to eradicate Western civilization. The argument here, as offered by US Officials, is not that we are under threat. This has been perpetually the case for virtually every nation in the world. As such, the existence of a threat is insufficient to warrant the use of torture. The argument, rather, must additionally stipulate that the current enemy is unlike any other, and hence that *only* torture will allow us to defeat this particular threat.[22]

This last point highlights that the argument we are considering is a version of the 'necessity' argument for torture. If torture is required to save one's life – or even the life of another – it is, according to one version of the necessity defense, excusable to engage in it. Importantly, this is *not* the same as saying that torture, in such cases, is *legal*. The standard necessity argument is a *defense* of engaging in illegal action, which claims that the illegal action in question was the only way to save someone's life.

Determining necessity is no easy task. One is dealing with the logic of counterfactuals, as well as with incomplete knowledge. Simply *believing* that an action is necessary does not make it so. Even when a *claim* of necessity is warranted, it doesn't follow that a necessity defense is legitimate. If, for some bizarre reason, one could only save oneself by killing an infant (perhaps to harvest its organs, unavailable by any other means), few would claim that this killing was justified, despite the fact that it was necessary.

What we see here, then, are two cautionary notes about the necessity argument: 1) determining necessity is an incredibly difficult business. This is not to say that there are not instances of such defenses being successful. It *is* to say that it will not be obvious, *a priori*, which situations will fit this category. 2) Even if necessity can be claimed with justification, a necessary immoral action is not *automatically* a justified action. Sometimes, an action simply *cannot* be justified, despite its status as necessary to preserve one's own well-being.

What this suggests, of course, is that morality will sometimes demand extreme acts of self-sacrifice – even the sacrifice of one's own life. While there are those who would object to such extreme cases of sacrifice, I find such objections groundless. In certain respects, *all* morality demands acts of self-sacrifice. Minimally, if one's desires conflict with the demands of morality, we are required to act against our desires. There is no difference in principle between this instance of self-sacrifice and one that requires sacrificing one's life.

As Larry May has pointed out, many distinguish between necessity *simpliciter* and military necessity. Even if the above conditions for claiming necessity *do* apply in a criminal case, it is not clear that one can extrapolate from this to establish conditions for the actions of nations. Nations and individuals, after all, are different beasts.

> The principle of military necessity is different from the defense of necessity . . . the defense of necessity is indeed a post-hoc or post-factum defense . . . many believe that there is a principle of military necessity that establishes pre-emptory authorization, that is, where a State is permitted to use otherwise impermissible tactics in certain cases of extreme emergency. The two ideas are related in that they both concern what it is necessary to do to achieve a certain very important objective. But, at least according to many Just War theorists, military necessity is not merely a post-factum defense for normal soldiers to employ but a full-blown justification for a State to initiate otherwise prohibited action against an enemy. (203)[23]

As May goes on to point out, the International Law Commission maintains that necessity can be legitimately invoked by nations to ensure the protection of certain vital interests – provided that the threat is imminent, that there are not available alternatives, and that the action carried out "does not seriously impair an essential interest of the State or the States towards which the obligation exists, or of the international community as a whole" (204).[24] As this makes clear, international law does not allow *carte blanche* when it comes to claims of necessity.

The issue at stake is whether these conditions are met when the need for so-called 'enhanced interrogation' is invoked by politicians like Cheney. The three crucial questions, in the current context, are as follows:

1. Is there an imminent threat that will cause harm sufficient enough to warrant violating the laws of war?
2. Is the use of torture the only reasonable means by which to prevent the harm to be inflicted?
3. Would the use of torture cause more harm than it would prevent?

I will examine each of these conditions in what follows.

A. Imminence

The vast use of 'enhanced interrogation' in the United States' military and CIA strains the notion of 'imminence' to its breaking point. This is one condition that was not met by the policy promoted by the Bush administration. In other instances where a policy of torture has been invoked to defend national security, we find similar results: those picked up by the British in 1971 and subjected to 'The Five Techniques' had virtually no intelligence value.[25] The widespread use of torture by the Nazi Gestapo and the USSR's later-named KGB typically operated on suspicions, and torture was used in fishing expeditions, as well as to get additional names of those suspected of acting against the state. The same thing happened under Mao in China and Polpot in Cambodia.[26] Likewise, in the Argentinean 'dirty war,'[27] the Brazilian military state,[28] the Greek junta,[29] and in Islamic Iran,[30] the policy of torture proceeded by working on (largely unreliable) tips, and aimed often to suppress dissidents rather than to stop attacks. Even in the case of Israel, which has been subject to attacks for decades, the courts have rejected the claim that the threat of such attacks is sufficient for the use of torture as an established interrogation technique. If the historical record is of value here, we have every reason to believe that the appeal to torture policies is not backed by recognition of actual imminent threat.

B. No alternative

Despite the historical record, there have been reported cases of 'ticking bomb' scenarios. Even if there *is* a legitimate case of a terrorist posing an imminent threat, the nagging question is whether or not torture is the only efficient means to extract the information necessary to eliminate the threat. In every purported 'ticking bomb' case cited in the literature, there is reason to believe that alternative means of intelligence gathering would have been equally, if not *more*, effective. As we will see in Chapter 6: *Torture doesn't work*, there is some reason to suspect that torture *does not work*, at least when we understand 'working' to mean producing results that could not be obtained in other, less harmful ways.

C. Harm prevented and harm caused

The effects of utilizing a policy of torture have been seriously underestimated. To have persons capable of using torture effectively requires significant amounts of training. This is not merely because a person has to learn a certain range of techniques; it is also because the normal moral reactions to torture have to be subdued. In many cases of training torturers, this process is achieved by gradually introducing persons to the torture situation, subjecting these persons to torture, and inducing in these persons a post-traumatic personality (for a detailed discussion, see Chapter 7: *Cannot predict pain response*). Moreover, the training of torturers who would be capable of torture has substantial costs to the society that *houses* such training institutions, both in the way that a nation perceives its government, and in the way this nation is perceived in the international community (see Chapter 6: *Damages reputation of state and trust of citizens*).

There is thus substantial reason to think that torture cannot be defended by appeal to necessity, even when this appeal is grounded in military necessity (as opposed to the necessity defense).

Do we have different intelligence needs?

As seen in Cheney's quip, and in much post-9/11 rhetoric in the United States, people often claim that we need to be able to utilize interrogation methods that have been traditionally illegal because we are facing an enemy unlike any enemy we have faced before. There are two points that need to be made in response: first, it is simply false. Second, it presumes that torture is effective as a means of intelligence gathering, and hence begs the question in favor of torture.

Because I devote substantial time arguing that torture is ineffective in the next chapter, I will concentrate for the moment on the claim that terrorism presents a unique kind of enemy. The uniqueness of this enemy, it is often said, consists in the enemy's operating in small 'cells,' not being able to be identified by uniform, and being willing to hide among civilians even at their (the civilians') peril. There are *many* conflicts that have fit precisely this model. I will mention only two here: the Vietnam conflict and the American Revolutionary War.

In Vietnam, it was common for the Viet Cong to hide among civilians, to recklessly endanger civilian lives, and to operate in small units in largely independent ways. The policy of the United States during that conflict was to abide by the strict law of Geneva. The argument of the

Viet Cong, on the other hand, was that the laws of war did not apply, as the United States had embarked on an illegal war. They thus refused to respect the demands of the Geneva Accords, despite the fact that the US insisted on these accords in its official policies (this is not to say, of course, that there weren't significant abuses – such as the massacre at Mai Lai). The point here, of course, is not to defend the actions of the United States in this conflict. The point, rather, is that the appeal to a new 'enemy' is simply rhetoric.

In the American Revolutionary War, likewise, the Continental Army often did not utilize uniforms. There were also bands of civilian soldiers that operated more or less autonomously beside the better organized Continental army. Such soldiers, moreover, often hid among civilians. As is well known, the British soldiers engaged in brutal tactics against revolutionary Americans. These tactics were criticized in no equivocal terms by General Washington as abhorrent. When citizens of the United States claim to face a new enemy, and hence to require the use of torture, there is a deep irony, if not simply an ignorance of their own history. As a citizen of the United States, I am forced to recognize that *we* were very much like the enemy we now face – albeit with a very different ideological justification for our actions.

Of course, it might be argued that the British use of torture justified this. Alternatively, it might be argued that the Continental Army was fundamentally *unlike* terrorist organizations in that it did not resort to massive civilian casualties to achieve its goal. I have no wish to consider such responses in the current context. It is easier to simply concede them, and then to note why they are irrelevant. If the central 'newness' of the enemy we face has to do with a willingness to kill thousands of innocent civilians, there is an even *more* powerful case to be made that the enemy is anything but new. In other contexts, the US has killed thousands of innocents (Native Americans, the Vietnamese, the Japanese), and we have faced enemies that have done the same (the Nazis, for example).

There thus seems to be ample reason to reject the two central features of the claim that we are in a 'new war' that requires 'new techniques.' The conflicts we face are not without historical precedent, and the justification for the 'new techniques' is entirely lacking.

Walzer's "dirty hands" argument
A variation on the above argument can be found in the idea that politicians have a responsibility to engage in ostensibly immoral actions based on their political position. This is referred to in the literature as 'the problem of dirty hands,' based on Sartre's play by the same name, and largely due to Michael Walzer's seminal discussion in "Political Action: The Problem of Dirty Hands."[31] Walzer still provides the best account of the central issue:

I do not think I could govern innocently; nor do most of us believe that those who govern are innocent . . . even the best of them. But this does not mean that it isn't possible to do the right thing while governing. It means that a particular act of government (in a political party or in the state) may be exactly the right thing to do in utilitarian terms and yet leave the man who does it guilty of a moral wrong. The innocent man, afterwards, is no longer innocent. If on the other hand he remains innocent, chooses, that is, the 'absolutist' side . . . he not only fails to do the right thing (in utilitarian terms), he may also fail to measure up to the duties of his office (which imposes on him a considerable responsibility for consequences and outcomes). (61–62)[32]

One oft-discussed case of dirty hands is Harry S Truman's decision to use the atomic bomb against Japan at the end of World War II. The central issue is whether or not the use of such non-proportional force – force that caused the death of thousands of civilians – was justified by Truman's obligation as president to the citizens of the United States to defend their lives above the lives of non-US citizens. The decision to kill thousands of civilians, from the perspective of just war theory, is deeply immoral. The basic principle of proportionality is violated in near-immeasurable terms. In this sense, Truman is guilty of gross immorality. But the issue does not end here. Was this immoral action one that was, in a certain respect, *required* by Truman's obligation to protect the citizens of the United States?

This is the same problem posed by torture in an age of terrorism. Despite torture's immorality, one might argue, our leaders have the political obligation to engage in it in order to protect the lives of citizens. The politician, in other words, has an obligation to dirty his hands in the muck of immoral action.

> Far greater moral guilt falls on a person in authority who permits the deaths of hundreds of innocents rather than choosing to 'torture' one guilty or complicit person . . . To condemn outright torture [in the form of] coercive interrogation, is to lapse into a legalistic version of pietistic rigorism in which one's own moral purity is ranked above other goods. This is also a form of moral laziness. (87–88)[33]

The argument here depends on showing that torture *must* be moral if there are conditions under which one can be morally obligated to carry it out. On this view, politicians have such on obligation based on the roles they occupy. Accepting office entails accepting a set of duties one would otherwise not have. By accepting a public office, one vows to protect the public that one represents. As Walzer notes,

> we can get our hands dirty in private life also, and sometimes, no doubt, we should. But the issue is posed most dramatically in politics for three reasons

that make political life the kind of life it is, because we claim to act for others but also to serve ourselves, rule over others, and use violence against them. It is easy to get one's hands dirty and it is often right to do so. (69)[34]

Despite wide opposition to the idea that torture ought to be a policy of particular nations, a surprising number of jurists, philosophers, and political scientists nevertheless defend the idea that torture should be permitted (morally speaking) even while it remains illegal. In this respect, many resolve the problem of dirty hands by concluding that, as lamentable as it is, we want leaders willing to get their hands dirty – to compromise their moral purity by ordering immoral courses of action.

There are several lines of response available to this position in general, as well as regarding the question of torture in particular. As is obvious, one could not possibly have an obligation to dirty one's hands with techniques that are ineffective, or when there are readily available alternatives. Thus, this argument can only work if the 'hand-dirtying' in question will in fact achieve the result it was meant to achieve. If this does not happen, then dirtying one's hands becomes not only unjustified, but despicable.

There are also more general problems with the argument that politicians should dirty their hands. As Paul Gilbert argues, "although the duty of a statesman is to his own citizens, he must be mindful of the consequences of his acts for others, since his fellow statesmen have analogous duties" (44). When getting one's hands dirty, the aim is to protect those people to whom one has a special obligation. It thus follows that one should *not* get one's hands dirty if such an action would produce a greater harm than it would prevent. In the case of terrorism and torture, there is reason to suspect that the use of torture has actually *made things worse*. As Gilbert notes, it is arguably the case that "the War on Terror, as an ostensible defense of Western interests, has destabilized many predominantly Muslim states with potentially disastrous consequences" (44).

We must also be wary of the effects allowing illegal techniques to be employed will have on the decisions of the enemy. Utilizing brutal techniques can provide one's enemy with a reason for thinking that they face a barbarous nation. It can also serve as an indication that complaints made *about* a nation are in fact justified. It would be surprising if such claims were not made by members of Al Qaeda in relation to the actions of the US and UK. Dirtying one's hands can thus *increase* the opposition one faces. It can provide further justification for the very attacks one aims to prevent. Dirty hands might also inspire rage, or even lead to an increase in the number of enemies one has.[35] In this respect, a strict adherence to the rule of law might well be, in a case where it is tempting to torture, the true 'lesser of two evils.'[36]

Of course, one might argue that a *failure* to torture would violate the trust of the citizens one is trying to protect. This might be the case even if torture did *not* work. On this view, a certain behavior is expected from the leadership. If a leader is perceived as failing to protect the lives of her citizens, the argument goes, this will undermine the authority of the leader in question, and upset the trust essential to democratic communities.[37]

There are two responses to be made here. First, it is simply assertion that citizens will be outraged by a failure to torture, or that their trust will be undermined. In fact, there is good reason to think that the *use* of torture might have this result to a much greater extent. If one comes to recognize that the leadership is willing to violate the rule of law, this could undermine one's sense of security in a nation that is *supposed to be* a nation governed by law. Of course, this is an empirical question, not merely a conceptual one. It also presumes that citizens will be made aware of cases in which torture *should have been used* and wasn't. Perhaps cynically, I have difficulty imagining that this would happen. Far more likely, if an instance of a leader refusing to torture became public, the question of whether or not torture was warranted would be precisely what was at issue – it would not simply be assumed.

But presume for a moment that trust would be destroyed by failing to order torture (something I find implausible, to say the least). What follows from this (and this is the second response to the above argument) is *not* that one should torture. All that follows is that one should *claim* that torture has been ordered, and this has been done to protect the lives of citizens. The only reason actual torture should be ordered and carried out, then, is if we knew it would work, and that the harms to citizens would be less than if said torture was *not* carried out. No such certainty is available, and hence there is good reason to refrain from dirty hands in the case of torture, even if there are other instances where it might be justified.

A final criticism of an appeal to the notion of dirty hands in the context of the torture debate is worth mentioning. It is *at least* questionable whether or not we should speak in terms of 'justification' when considering putative cases of dirty hands – cases that are meant to be exceptional. As Andrew Fiala has argued,

> To deal in exceptions is to continue to encourage this sort of slippage [into increasing frequency and extremity of violence]. If there are exceptions, they should not be a standard part of our moral vocabulary; nor should they be legalized and regularized as policy. Rather, they should be viewed with fear and trembling as abysses into which the real world pushes us. Indeed, rather than claiming that an exception could be 'justified,' perhaps it is better to admit that exceptions are not justified at all. As exceptions they fall outside the scheme of justifications.[38]

This is surely a criticism that *must* be considered by any argument in favor of torture. If the very language of justification precludes appeal to emergency situations, we may well have to set aside the very idea of torture being justifiable in the moral sphere. While I find this suggestion an interesting and (partly) compelling one, I cannot in good faith end our analysis of those arguments in favor of torture based on it. I cite it here to note that there is a meta-ethical difficulty surrounding the very idea of the justification of exceptional, emergency situations.

From self-defense

In "Can the War against Terror Justify the Use of Force in Interrogations?", Miriam Gur-Aye argues that self-defense

> justifies the use of force against an unlawful attack. Self-defense is not limited to defending one's own self; it applies also when third parties are being attacked. Like necessity, the use of force seeks to prevent an imminent danger to legitimate interests. Unlike necessity, preventing the danger in cases of self-defense does not involve the sacrifice of innocent people's interests. The self-defender repels the attack by using force – at times even deadly force – against the attacker who has unlawfully created the danger. The moral basis of self-defense is, therefore, stronger than that of necessity. (194)

From this analysis of self-defense, Gur-Aye proceeds to argue that torture is best understood under this particular model.[39] The "one person who is not defenseless in ticking bomb cases is the terrorist who has planted the bomb. He has full information . . ." (192). This information, in turn, is the key to securing our own defense against an unlawful attack, as well as in securing the defense of countless others sure to be harmed (or killed) by the detonation of the bomb.

Of course, as Gur-Aye recognizes, self-defense does not justify *every* response to one's attacker. It justifies only those actions that are absolutely necessary to thwart one's attacker. Thus, it is not the case (though it is often thought to be) that one is justified in killing an assailant if that person attacks one. Killing someone, even an attacker, is permissible only if killing the assailant is the *only* means one has to protect one's own life. If there are alternatives (for example, fleeing the scene of attack, or detaining one's attacker through force), then killing is unjustified. These two conditions might be called the 'necessity condition' and the 'absence of alternatives condition.' These conditions can be elaborated as follows:

Necessity Condition
One's actions to defend oneself against another person are justified only insofar as these actions can be reasonably thought to be the only *effective* means of self-defense. This condition explicitly regards what one is justified

in doing *directly* to a perpetrator. *If one is justified in inhibiting the actions of an agent, that person is justified only in doing what can reasonably be deemed necessary in saving oneself.*

Absence of Alternatives Condition

One is only justified in acting against another (threatening) agent if there are no alternatives to such actions that one could easily take. The 'absence of alternatives' specified here concern alternatives to acting directly against a perpetrator. In other words, self-defense does *not* always justify inhibiting another agent's actions. Sometimes, when alternatives to interfering with an agent are available, one is *only* justified in carrying out these alternatives.[40]

The second condition follows from the first one. If one is entitled to engage in violent actions in self-defense *only if* these violent actions are reasonably thought to be *necessary* to defending oneself, it would follow that no action directly against a perpetrator is justified if an alternative to such direct action is available (in the *Abusive Paraplegic* case, one can simply move out of the reach of the abuser).

These conditions, perhaps not surprisingly, mirror self-defense law. One might here object that what is justified under the law is not to be conflated with what is justified morally. After all, a common objection runs, there have been many laws which were morally suspect (slavery, for example), and many things which might be morally suspect are legally permissible (the death penalty, for example).

This is an important objection, but one which does not here find adequate footing. To say that the moral and the legal are not co-extensive is a valid point, but it does not follow from this that *no* legal principles are also moral ones. In the case of the legislation surrounding self-defense, this seems particularly evident. The principle of '*lex talionis*' has been defended in many contexts. While it is perhaps best known as a principle meant to govern punishment, this principle has also been a central principle in the just war tradition. In both cases, the principle is advocated as a moral *restraint* on what is legally permissible. 'The principle of proportionality' concerns what can *justly* be done to a person in response to actions they have carried out. It has been advocated as an extra-legal concept that ought to be embodied in law, as it articulates the appropriate moral limits of what one agent (or a state) can do to another.

So, self-defense is permissible only insofar as it follows the basic principle of proportionality. This is how self-defense is understood when it is used as a defense of torture: given the threats of a terrorist attack, the argument goes, we are justified in utilizing even extreme, extra-legal methods to prevent the attack in question. Torture, while normally impermissible, is justified in this context precisely because it is a proportionate response to the threat of a terrorist attack.

This argument initially appears quite compelling: a person to be tortured is directly responsible for a major threat against oneself (and others). Torture is presented as a means to preventing this threat. Given the standard thinking about self-defense, despite the normal moral impermissibility of torture, it is tempting to conclude that, in this case, we *should* permit torture. But the defense is not nearly as powerful as it initially appears. Several objections to the use of this defense are immediately available.

First, the argument from self-defense is question-begging. It simply presumes too much. Self-defense is viable, as noted above, only if there are no other *viable alternatives*. It is contentious, to say the least, to claim that there are such cases when it comes to torture. In fact, as I will argue (Chapter 6: *Torture doesn't work*), we have some reason to think that torture *working* is the exception rather than the rule, and that it never works in a way that would justify it.

Second, there is an important disanalogy in the self-defense case. The standards of just war do not seem to apply in the case of torture. One's right to kill the enemy, for example, is warranted only because the enemy has an identical opportunity. Once one is captured, however, no reciprocal threat exists. As Henry Shue has put this point in his seminal paper, "Torture":

> At least part of the peculiar disgust which torture evokes may be derived from its apparent failure to satisfy even this weak constraint of being a 'fair fight.' The supreme reason, of course, is that torture begins only after the fight is – for the victim – finished. Only losers are tortured. A 'fair fight' may even in fact already have occurred and led to the capture of the person who is to be tortured. But now that the torture victim has exhausted all means of defense and is powerless before the victors, a fresh assault begins . . . In this respect torture is indeed not analogous to the killing in battle of a healthy and well-armed foe; it is a cruel assault upon the defenseless. (130)[41]

This point applies, *mutatis mutandis*, to the case for self-defense. One cannot use a self-defense justification against a threat that has already been neutralized. The terrorist *himself* no longer poses any particular threat. Of course, *the bomb* still poses a massive threat. But, in the case we are imagining, the terrorist no longer has any control of the bomb. To invoke self-defense as a justification for torturing this terrorist, then, is deeply misleading.[42] Consider an analogous case:

Mad Dog 1
A man has raised and trained a dog to be totally vicious. The dog will attack anyone he is able to, and the dog's owner is responsible (at least in part) for

this. While walking down the street one day, you see this man with his dog. He also sees you. For some reason, the man turns his dog loose, and the dog charges at you, prepared to attack.

The question in this case is as follows: are you justified, from self-defense, to attack the man who unleashed the dog? Importantly, you may well be justified in attacking the man, but the attack would by no means be best understood as an instance of *self-defense*. An attack on the man would be justified, if it were justified at all, because he has needlessly and recklessly endangered your life. (I am doubtful that such retributive attacks are in fact justified, although certainly some type of punitive action *would* be justified). The threat upon your person is *the dog*, and the dog is no longer under the control of its owner. Even though the owner is responsible for the dog being the threat that it is, and for willingly and knowingly allowing the dog to attempt to harm others, the owner *himself* has ceased to be a threat altogether. To claim that an attack on the man would be justified by self-defense, then, seems absurd.

Perhaps the case would be different if attacking the man would *stop* the dog. This might make the case more closely parallel to the case of a terrorist with knowledge of the whereabouts of a bomb.

Mad Dog 2
A man has raised and trained a dog to be totally vicious. The dog will attack anyone he is able to, and the dog's owner is responsible (at least in part) for this. While walking down the street one day, you see this man with his dog. He also sees you. For some reason, the man turns his dog loose, and the dog charges at you, prepared to attack. You can stop the dog's attack by attacking the man.

Even with this modification of the case, an appeal to self-defense strikes me as highly problematic. There are two reasons for this.

1) A case like the one we have constructed presumes that torture will work, as torture is meant to be analogous to attacking the man in order to prevent the dog's attack. (I will return to this in Chapter 6: *Torture doesn't work*)
2) Attacking the man to prevent the dog's attack still does not appear to be a straightforward case of self-defense, at least as 'self-defense' is usually understood.

Self-defense involves engaging in some act of violence or coercion against that person who poses an immediate danger to you. In the modified case, the owner does not pose any danger to you. Thus, while you would be justified in preventing the dog from carrying out his attack on principles of self-defense (by killing it, if that were necessary), attacking the man would not *strictly speaking* count as an act of self-defense, as the man poses no immediate danger.

As is obvious, one might nevertheless be *justified* in attacking the man in order to save oneself. My point here is that the attack would not be an instance of self-defense. To bring out why, consider two additional cases:

Death Machine 1
Imagine a man has constructed a machine that is connected to his heart. The machine (something of the science fiction type) will kill you if it is allowed to operate. The only way to stop the machine is to kill the man (thereby stopping his heart).

In this case, killing the man seems to be a case of self-defense. Even though the man is not *directly* what is threatening to you (the machine poses the immediate danger), two additional conditions are given that meet the conditions of self-defense: 1) the only way to prevent your death is by killing the man (there are no available alternatives), and 2) the man is directly responsible for the threat to your life. The most that could be claimed would be necessity.

Condition (2) is crucial to the above case. This condition precludes the possibility of claiming self-defense in killing persons who pose no danger to you. (Imagine an analogous case in which the only way to stop the mad dog is by killing an innocent bystander. Even if this *were* justifiable (and I doubt that it is), it couldn't be argued that you were justified by virtue of self-defense. After all, the threat on your life was not *due to* the innocent person).

Condition (1) is no less important: if there were alternative ways of stopping the machine that *did not* involve killing the man, and which did not involve the substantial harm that killing does, self-defense would not justify the killing. Consider:

Death Machine 2
Imagine a man has constructed a machine that is connected to his heart. The machine (something of the science fiction type) will kill you if it is allowed to operate. There are two possible ways to stop the machine: (a) kill the man (thereby stopping his heart), or (b) unplug the machine.

In *Death Machine 2*, self-defense clearly would not justify killing the man. The alternative involves virtually no harm compared to killing: one need merely unplug the threatening machine.

These cases, I think, reveal why *Mad Dog 2* is not a case that could justify attacking the dog owner. The issue here is straightforward: you could *also* stop the dog attack in other ways that would not involve such a high degree of harm (you could attack the dog rather than the man).

These thought experiments, I hope, reveal what is problematic about an appeal to self-defense as an argument for torturing someone for the whereabouts of a bomb. First, the terrorist, having already planted the bomb, no longer poses an immediate threat to you. But, second, even if torturing the terrorist would *prevent* a harm to you, it does not follow that you are justified in torturing the terrorist out of self-defense. For this to be justified as self-defense, three conditions would have to be met: 1) the threat to you would have to be immediate, 2) torturing the terrorist would have to be reasonably expected to prevent the threat and 3) there could be no alternatives to the torture that involved significantly less harm than torture.

None of these conditions are met. As we have already pointed out, the threat is not *immediate*. Even though the terrorist is the cause of the threat, the terrorist *himself* is not the threat. As we will see below (see Chapter 6: *Torture doesn't work*), torture is *not* particularly likely to work. In fact, the *more* immediate the threat of the bomb, the *less* likely it is that torture will work (I will argue for this point in Chapter 6: *Cannot predict pain response*, when providing a refutation of the untoward use of the ticking bomb scenario). Finally, and related to the last point, traditional means of interrogation and intelligence gathering *are* available alternatives to torture, and these (obviously) involve significantly less harm to the perpetrator.[43]

These arguments have been explicitly directed at *one type* of defense of torture (namely, the defense of torture as an instance of self-defense). It does not follow from my criticisms of this defense that there are not *other* possible defenses. All we have so far established is that this particular avenue to torture's defense is not one that can be travelled. It is now my task to turn to other avenues, and to argue that these are just as impassable as this one.

Arguments from warrant

From deterrence

Another way to defend the use of torture by a nation is to invoke the appeal to deterrence. If we utilize torture, the argument goes, our enemies will be *less* likely to engage in violent acts of terrorism against us, for fear that they too will be tortured. As of this writing, I know of no actual published defenses of torture that utilize this line of reasoning. It is given voice, however, in classrooms and in the blogosphere, and so is worth considering.

This thesis strikes me as completely unjustified, and highly unlikely, for three reasons: first, the data we have collected on the deterrent effect of punishment suggests that these forms of punishment (i.e. more severe kinds of punishment, such as the death penalty) have no measurable positive benefits. In fact, some studies suggest just the opposite: crime rates actually *rise* after an execution.[44]

Why then do some believe that such a deterrent effect exists? Sadly, the answer seems to be that one extrapolates from one's own fear of certain punishments to everyone else in the world. 'I'm afraid of torture, the death penalty, prison, etc,' the reasoning seems to go, 'so everyone else must be as well.' This inference, I hope obviously, is completely unjustified. It presumes 1) that fear is a greater motivating factor than other things, and that 2) one's individual psychology is an adequate sample for the psychology of others (such as murderers and terrorists). Both of these claims are deeply problematic, if not demonstrably false.[45]

Secondly, there is reason to think that engaging in harsh forms of treatment of terrorists will actually lead to an *increase* in the number of sympathizers with terrorist organizations.[46] Far from deterring potential terrorists, it looks as though the use of torture might actually help to *create* terrorists by justifying some of the criticisms such organizations make about the state in question.

Finally, there is at least one documented case in which *not* using torture (on the part of the United States) acted as an incentive for a known terrorist to become a useful informant, providing intelligence on Al Qaeda's command structure.[47]

One final point remains to be made about arguments from deterrence. This kind of argument, it seems to me, even if it were successful, could be no more than a *supplemental* one. Even if torturing would deter future acts of violence, it does not follow from this that there are any mitigating circumstances that might warrant the use of torture. If no case could be made for instances of torture that would override its *prima facie* moral repugnance, its deterrent effect would not justify using torture. This is not a rejection of utilitarian forms of argument. My point here is rather about what the utilitarian value of deterrence would warrant in terms of practice. If a belief that a nation engages in torture deters terrorists, all that follows from this is that we should attempt to make people think that torture is a likely consequence of terrorist activity. One way to do this, of course, is to actually engage in torture. Another way to do this, however, is to simply *pretend* to have such a policy. Such subterfuge would prevent the wrong of torture while securing the benefits (here assumed only for the sake of argument) of deterrence.[48] Thus, as we can see, the argument from deterrence could only supplement another argument for torture's permissibility. On its own, all that it justifies is presenting oneself to the appropriate audience *as if torture were one's policy*.

As punishment[49]

One argument, often implicit in arguments for torture, is the idea that perpetrators *deserve* what they get, and hence normal constraints simply do not apply. Charles Krauthammer is explicit on this point, though claims this is not his reason for advocating torture: "Khalid Sheihk Mohammed, murderer of 2,973 innocents, is surely deserving of the most extreme suffering day and night for the rest of his life" (314). No one would deny that criminals should be brought to justice. What is at stake here is whether or not there are legitimate *limits* to what justice can demand. The strict retributivist view maintains that the punishment should be on par with the crime committed. On one reading of retributivism, certain crimes are so depraved that virtually *any* kind of punishment could be permitted – including torture.

This argument is more common in the philosophical literature than one would expect. There are two aspects of the argument that need to be separated and assessed. The first is that the *guilt* of a person is morally relevant to whether or not they can justifiably be subjected to torture. Tibor Machan makes this point as follows:

> (extreme) violence may indeed be morally justified at times but only if some measure of moral guilt is present or highly probable on the part of the party about to experience violence. Yet all this still restricts the moral justifiability of extreme violence (within the context of a just legal system) to the personal domain – accordingly, I should not torture someone I knew to be entirely innocent of the relevant evils even if his or her torture would secure some great good; I *may*, however, use torture if some probable or demonstrable guilt is present in the party to experience the torture and the end of the torture is itself worthy. (94)[50]

The view that the guilt of a person is relevant to whether or not it is acceptable to torture him has some empirical support. Fritz Allhoff conducted experiments indicating that a subject's willingness to engage in torture correlates in a statistically significant way with knowledge of the guilt of the person to be tortured.[51]

The second aspect of the above argument to be noted involves the application of the principle of *lex talionis*. The claim made is that the guilty party must be punished strictly according to the crime he has committed. Torture is warranted, it is argued, because it is *proportional* to the crime. To fail to torture, the argument goes, would be to fail to achieve justice in the case. This argument has been made by Stephen Kershnar. Summarizing the argument in question, Kershnar writes:

> A particular amount of punishment is justified if and only if that amount of punishment is deserved and the desert claim is not overridden. Deserved punishment is punishment that is equal to the amount of harm that typically results from acts of the type that the fully culpable wrongdoer performed. In the case of multiple murderers or people who perform serious violent acts

in addition to murder, the deserved punishment must involve torture. The legitimate desert claim is not overridden by objections based on the Kantian concern that persons be treated as ends, the intuitive distaste that many persons have for torture, the likely consequences of institutionalized torture, the likely biased implementation of torture, and the heightened care needed for the intentional infliction of harm. Hence, in some cases, all things considered, torture ought to be imposed as punishment. (55)

There are several responses to this line of argument that are worth making. As noted above, the view that torture can be used as punishment is based on a particular understanding of the principle of *lex talionis*. I do not wish to dispute that this is one reading of the principle – but it is not the *only* way of understanding the principle, or even the best way. As Kershnar uses the principle, *lex talionis* prescribes what must be done for justice to be carried out: the severity of the crime dictates the severity of the punishment. This is the lynch pin of Kershnar's entire argument. If *lex talionis* does not demand particular punishments, the argument falls apart. Thus, if it is possible to construct an alternative reading of the principle, we will have shown that Kershnar's argument does not yet justify the claim the torture ought to be used to punish people. To make that case, he would owe us a defense of his reading of the principle over its alternatives.

The alternative understanding of *lex talionis* reads it as a *limiting* principle rather than as a positive one that prescribes particular punishments. The alternative understanding of *lex talionis* regards the principle as a merely negative one: it tells us what the limits of punishment can be in any particular case. Historically, this seems to be the origin of the principle. It emerged in response to wildly disproportionate punishment being used in response to relatively minor offenses. The thief was put to death; one who insulted another was severely beaten, and so on. *Lex talionis* emerged as a means of precluding such disproportion in carrying out justice. A person should not suffer a much greater harm than the one they inflicted. This does not entail that the criminal *must experience* an equivalent harm. It entails that punishments are not to exceed a certain level; it does not entail that they *must* be at the very level they are not to exceed.

There are at least two considerations that speak in favor of understanding *lex talionis* as a limiting principle rather than as a positive, productive one. First, this understanding of the principle seems to be much more in line with our intuitions about what justice requires. It reflects the widespread belief that rapists should not be raped, and that murderers should not be murdered (this is a minority view in the United States; it is anything but a minority view in Europe).

Second, *lex talionis* as a limiting principle makes room for the category of mercy. If this principle dictates the level at which a punishment must be executed, any act of mercy would become an act of injustice. Even in cases where victims forgave their assailants, justice would require that they be punished in accordance with the harm they inflicted. Mercy itself would be a violation of the dictates of justice. While this view might be the correct one, it is not obviously so – and, in fact, it seems to me clearly false. Mercy is a crucial moral category, and one that even has a place in legal contexts (persons can 'throw themselves on the mercy of the court').

Another interesting criticism of the view that torture should be used as punishment has been offered by Andrew Sullivan. On this view, the crucial problem with using torture as a punishment involves the way we understand the perpetrators of crimes that would *warrant* torture. According to defenders of torture like Charles Krauthammer, crimes that warrant torture are so severe that these crimes prove their perpetrators do not deserve to be treated with the same respect that human beings normally do – they are, in effect, 'moral monsters.' As Sullivan points out, re-categorizing certain persons as moral monsters effectively robs them of responsibility for their actions – and hence of the justification for punishing them with torture. As Sullivan put the point,

> to reduce [persons] to a subhuman level is to exonerate them of their acts of terrorism and mass murder – just as animals are not deemed morally responsible for killing. Insisting on the humanity of terrorists is, in fact, critical to maintaining their profound responsibility for the evil they commit. (321)[52]

There is also a practical problem with the use of torture as a punishment, though it is perhaps a problem with any punishment. Inflicting pain on a person is anything but a science. Different persons respond to different techniques in no discernible pattern. The continuous use of pain, moreover, can damage the ability of a person to process pain signals when subjected to techniques that have formerly been proven effective. Moreover, the claim that persons ought to be tortured ignores the harm this does to *the torturer.* As we will see, torturers are often afflicted with Post-Traumatic Stress Disorder. In addition, making a person capable of torture requires significantly desensitiving him to human suffering, and this can have extraordinary effects on the ability of a person to live a fulfilling life. (We will return to this in Chapter 7: *Damaged agency: The effects of torture on the torturer*).

These objections are sufficient, I think, for rejecting the view that torture is warranted as a form of punishment. Torture does not obviously follow from the principle of *lex talionis*, and the view that it does proves inimical to the very idea of mercy. Torture as punishment also risks alleviating our worst criminals of responsibility for their actions, and hence of a major justification used to legitimize punishment. Utilizing torture as a punishment would risk causing a good deal of harm to those who were employed as professional torturers. Finally, there are significant practical difficulties in the actual administration of torture as punishment.

As response to non-reciprocity

Motivated by a social contract view of the problem of torture, as well as a reciprocity reading of the Geneva Conventions, some theorists claim that torture is permissible if one's enemies are not holding up their end of the bargain. Casey and Rivkin argue in just this way in their discussion of obligations under the Geneva Convention:

> First, the text of Common Article 1 does not directly address the question of reciprocity, but only requires the parties to "respect and to ensure respect for" the treaty "in all circumstances." Both respecting the treaty and ensuring respect by other parties are obligations equal in dignity, and how these requirements can be met is left to the parties. Second, Common Article 2, governing the Convention's application, itself clearly contemplates that reciprocity will be the rule in certain critical circumstances. In this respect, it provides that a nonparty state may obtain Geneva benefits, but only if "the latter accepts and applies the provisions thereof." If merely accepting Geneva's obligations is insufficient to guarantee its benefits to a nonparty, there is little reason to interpret the treaty to afford those guarantees, in the face of a widespread or systematic failure of compliance, to a party. (208)

There is much that is problematic in this view of treaty obligations under Geneva, in my view. In particular, the argument ignores the substantial language in the Convention that explicitly states that certain modes of behavior are *never* permitted (such as torture). The analysis also ignores the other significant treaty obligations that most (if not all) parties to the Geneva Convention have since ratified – treaty obligations that, in no uncertain terms, reject the use of torture in *all circumstances*, even if there is a threat to national security.

Rather than exploring these problems with the argument offered by Casey and Rivkin, I want to extract what I regard as one of the central points: namely, that the reciprocity of another nation or organization is relevant to the obligations we have to that nation or organization. On the strongest reading of this line of argument, a nation is under an obligation *not* to torture *only if* members of that nation are not themselves being subjected to such actions.

The idea that reciprocity (or its absence) dictates one's moral obligations is, in my view, a deeply problematic one (though I would not deny that reciprocity is sometimes relevant to determining *particular* moral obligations). One of the primary problems with this view is that it makes moral conduct entirely contingent on the actions of others: it is wrong to cut you because you *do not* cut me, for example. The problem with this line of argument should be familiar: the wrongness of any particular action is reduced to a singularity: an action is wrong *because it violates reciprocity*. This seems to ignore the different *kinds* of wrong actions, as well as the intuitive idea that some harms are in fact greater than others (if all wrongs stem from violations of reciprocity, it seems to follow that all wrongs are equivalent). An additional problem is in the downward moral spiral created by this conception of moral obligation. If my moral obligations are limited by what others do, and others are not reciprocating my actions, I can give up the moral boundaries I am currently respecting. This, in turn, might well create a further deterioration of treatment, which would in turn lead me to restrict my moral boundaries even less, and so on *ad infinitum*.

Of course, we should distinguish concepts of reciprocity in relation to military affairs from concepts of reciprocity within the context of determining the bounds of individual morality – but the distinction is not as sharp as it might initially appear. After all, individual actors carry out military operations, and military operations are ordered by individuals. Nevertheless, there is a distinction to be made here. Most, I think, will reject the view that reciprocity is the proper basis of moral obligation (for the reasons briefly sketched above). Some of these same persons, however, would argue that in military operations reciprocity plays a different role. Likewise, some will argue, in line with Casey and Rivkin, that reciprocity plays a *crucial* role in understanding the treaty obligations we are under when conducting warfare. Because the reciprocity view of individual moral obligation seems so obviously false, I want to concentrate here on what the principle of reciprocity can tell us about what's permissible in military affairs, given various treaty obligations. My main objection to this line of argument is that it fails to actually *justify* the use of torture. I will briefly elaborate.

Even if the above reading of the Geneva Accords is correct, it simply does not follow that the use of torture is warranted. The role of reciprocity in the Geneva treaty only shows that one does not have *treaty* obligations to refrain from torture. It doesn't follow from this that engaging in torture is permissible. The most this argument could show is that the use of torture would not be wrong *based on the violation of a treaty*. This is hardly the same thing as torture *not being wrong*. To make that case, one would need to appeal to arguments other than the one from non-reciprocity. One might argue that torture was necessary to win a conflict, to address threats to security, to save lives, or for some other reason (arguments that, as we have seen, are quite problematic). The absence of reciprocity may well remove one roadblock to the use of torture; it does not clear the way.

Argument from killing being worse than torture

A final argument to be considered runs as follows: killing is worse than torture. It is sometimes permissible to kill. Therefore, it is sometimes permissible to torture.[53]

There are several questions here. One of these concerns what the nature of the comparison is in fact supposed to be. Is killing 'worse' in the sense that it causes a greater harm to the victim? Or, is killing 'worse' in the sense that it is a greater moral wrongdoing than torture? In most of the cases where this argument is used, the two questions become tied together: torture, the argument runs, causes a great harm to its victim, but this harm is not so great as the harm inflicted by killing that agent. Killing is a worse thing to do *because* it is a greater harm to the person killed.

In Chapter 4, we explored the consequences of torture on its victim. We are now in a much better position to assess whether or not this argument is effective. Death, it hardly bears repeating, is a great harm to the person who dies – at least in most cases. What do we make, then, of people who, after torture, long for this harm? One conclusion to be drawn here is that death is to be preferred to the harm that results from torture. If this were not so, there would be no clear explanation for the recurrence among victims of torture: suicidal ideation, on the one hand, and actual suicide, on the other. Jean Amery, whom I have had occasion to quote several times in this study, ultimately ended his own life. He could not live in the world constructed by torture. The thought of following just this course is a common one: "Some patients depict themselves as endangered; their daily fantasies revolve around different ways to take their own lives" (167).[54] Many claim they would rather be dead.[55] In some ways, the beginning of torture is the beginning of one's slow descent into death.[56]

> At the moment of victimization, the individual begins to die a slow death, which very few others can comprehend. The perpetrators see her as less than human; they strip her of her dignity, her sense of control, and her link with humanity. She begins to question the horrible reality before her eyes. Shattered by the very face of evil, treasured values of community, trust, and hope are lost in an instant – in their place are alienation, betrayal, and despair. (15)[57]

To live in a shattered world like the one here described leads many victims of torture to suicidal thoughts, and sometimes to suicide. Exact data on the extent of this is difficult to acquire, as most testimony comes from those who seek professional help. Many others refuse to seek this help, often out of fear and humiliation. In some respects, a certain level of health is already presupposed by even *seeking* professional help. For those who cannot seek such help, things are likely even worse – though this is hardly imaginable. As one survivor remarks, "People around me were celebrating my miraculous return while I was mourning my death" (16).[58]

The fact that many torture victims do not commit suicide should not be regarded as evidence for the view that death is regarded as worse than a continued life. In many cases, the torture victim exists in a kind of limbo where the distinction between life and death seems unintelligible – a condition that begins in torture and can persist afterwards. As Helene Jaffe reports of one torture survivor, "he told us that while he was being tortured he had gone through a whole period when he did not know if he was dead or alive" (137).[59]

The act of suicide, moreover, is an act of *agency*. Many victims of torture feel entirely powerless, moving through life as through a fog, alienated and helpless. To act on suicidal ideation, in this respect, is not something we should expect – it would represent precisely the kind of exercise of agential control that torture destroys.

These considerations, coupled with the more complete analysis of the world of the torture victim offered in Chapter 4, warrant the claim – at an absolute minimum – that we should not think it is *obvious* that killing is worse than torture. Frankly, the opposite of this strikes me as very plausible, and this is because to undergo torture is to undergo a destruction of agency very akin to having one's self murdered, but with one crucial difference: after one's destruction, one must live through its effects.

One reply to this view that is sometimes offered is that torture does not *necessarily* produce the destruction of agency in question. Because of this, it is argued, killing *must* be worse than torture, as it necessarily causes a great loss to its victim. Torture is only *likely* to cause such a loss. Although we have had occasion to consider this argument already (Chapter 4: *Concluding remarks*), it is worth reiterating and expanding the point made there.

In the above objection, 'killing' is taken as a success term: that is, it is regarded as an action that has successfully been carried out. One attempted to accomplish a particular goal (to kill), and one success-fully completed this task (hence, one killed). Unfairly, I think, torture is *not* regarded as a success term. One carried out particular proce-dures designed to accomplish a particular task (the destruction of agency, as we saw in Chapters 3 and 4), but one *might not have been successful*.

In this comparison, the odds are stacked against torture. The reason for this, I want to suggest, is *not* that killing is in fact necessarily harmful to its victim while torture might not be. The reason, rather, is that we are comparing an action *attempted* and an action *completed*. As such, the comparison is not an appropriate one. A better comparison might take two distinct forms:

1) Is attempted killing worse than attempted torture?
2) Is successful killing worse than successful torture?

I do not know the answer to (1), above. In fact, there is probably not a general answer to this question, as it will depend on the circumstances surrounding each thing attempted. The answer to (2), however, *is* clear – at least if I've made a powerful enough cause for the harms inflicted on a person by torture: torture is a kind of death, but one that is stretched out over days, months, and years. One experiences one's world as utterly inverted, and devoid of the meaning-given features that make our lives *human*. In this respect, to live a life after torture, when torture has been successfully carried out, is to live a life of suffering and despair, where our normal relationships have been so completely compromised that we are no longer capable of functioning in the world. In this respect, question (2) is very much like asking if a life of total suffering that ends in death is better than simply dying.

Conclusion

In the preceding pages, we have considered a range of arguments offered in favor of torture, both as policies to be administered by nations and as actions permissible in certain kinds of exceptional cases. As I hope to have demonstrated, all of these arguments are deeply problematic, though some are more so than others. In the following chapter, we will look in detail at the arguments against torture. We will begin with a reconsideration of the ticking bomb case and the various problems this thought experiment faces.

Notes

1. This position has been dubbed 'practical absolutism' by Michael Davis. See his "The Moral Justifiability of Torture and other Cruel, Inhuman, or Degrading Treatment."
2. I will return to this point in the following section.
3. See, for example, Bob Brecher, *Torture and the Ticking Bomb*; Vittorio Bufacchi and Jean-Maria Arrigo, "Terrorism and the State: A Refutation of the ticking bomb Argument;" J. Jeremy Wisnewski, "It's About Time: Defusing the Ticking Bomb Argument;" J. Jeremy Wisnewski and R. D. Emerick, *The Ethics of Torture* (Continuum, 2009).
4. See Alan Dershowitz, "Tortured Reasoning," in *Torture: A Collection*, ed. Sanford Levinson, and Alan Dershowitz, *Why Terrorism Works*.

5. John H. Langbein, *Torture and the Law of Proof*; John H. Langbein, "The Legal History of Torture," in *Torture: A Collection*, ed. Sanford Levinson; Alan Dershowitz, "Tortured Reasoning," in *Torture: A Collection*, ed. Sanford Levinson.

6. Mike Bagaric and Julie Clarke, *Torture: When the Unthinkable is Morally Permissible*; Oren Gross, "The Prohibition on Torture and the Limits of the Law," in *Torture: A Collection*; Miriam Gur-Arye, "Can the War against Terror Justify the Use of Force in Interrogations? Reflections in Light of the Israeli Experience," in *Torture: A Collection*; Richard Posner, "Torture, Terrorism, and Interrogation," in *Torture: A Collection*, ed. Sanford Levinson.

7. Oren Gross, "The Prohibition on Torture and the Limits of the Law," and Miriam Gur-Arye, "Can the War against Terror Justify the Use of Force in Interrogations? Reflections in Light of the Israeli Experience." Both in *Torture: A Collection*, ed. Sanford Levinson.

8. *Supreme Court of Israel Judgment*, in *The Phenomenon of Torture*.

9. Oren Gross, "The Prohibition on Torture and the Limits of the Law," in *Torture: A Collection*, ed. Sanford Levinson.

10. John T. Parry, "Escalation and Necessity: Defining Torture at Home and Abroad," in *Torture: A Collection*, ed. Sanford Levinson; Richard Posner, "Torture, Terrorism, and Interrogation," in *Torture: A Collection*, ed. Sanford Levinson.

11. Bufacchi, Vittorio, Jean-Maria Arrigo. "Terrorism and the State: A Refutation of the Ticking Bomb Argument."

12. There is one respect in which the 'realism' of a thought experiment is crucial to its success – namely, the thought experiment must be coherent. I will return to this point in Chapter 6.

13. Krauthammer, "The Truth about Torture" in *Torture*, ed. Levinson.

14. I will not consider the pedestrian view that everyone is motivated by selfishness. If this were the case, the critique of selfishness in the above case would be meaningless, as one couldn't avoid this motivation. Moreover, psychological egoism seems to me to have been decisively refuted, and in many fields to boot (evolutionary psychology, for example, has successfully dismantled this view, as have various philosophers. See, for example, Robert Wright, *The Moral Animal*, and Joel Feinberg, *Harm to Others*).

15. See *The Metaphysics of Morals*, 6:331.

16. See Chapter 3, *The Ethics of Torture*, for the arguments demonstrating that the analogy is faulty.

17. See Rejali, "Torture makes the man" in *On Torture*, ed. Hilde. I return to this point in Chapter 6.

18. I will consider each of these claims in Chapter 6.

19. One of the primary articles used to defend the negative effects of torture policy here is L.E. Fletcher and H. Weinstein, "Violence and social repair: rethinking the contribution of justice to reconciliation," *Human Rights*

Quarterly 24, 3 (2002): 573–649. I cite it here to give credit where credit is due.

20. In an earlier article (from which some of this section is drawn), I criticized Buffachi and Arrigo for not actually refuting exceptional cases of torture. I now think my criticisms were too harsh. Everything one needs to offer a refutation of the TB case is contained in the idea that all torture requires training, and that training requires institutional support. My criticism of Buffachi and Arrigo at this point is much milder: they did not explicitly distinguish policy and exception, nor did they explicitly make the argument (one I think that was available to them) that even 'one-off' torture requires training institutions. Arrigo, however, has argued powerfully for this view in "A Utilitarian Argument against Torture Interrogation of Terrorists."

21. See John F. Harris, Mike Allen, and Jim VandeHei, "Cheney Warns of New Attacks," *Politico*, February 4, 2009, cited in Danner, *New York Review of Books*, April 2009, Volume 56, Numbers 6–7.

22. The idea that we face a new kind of enemy is deeply questionable, as I will argue below. For an excellent discussion of this issue, see Liam Harte, "Could New Terrorism Exist? A Philosophical Critique of the 'Expert Analysis'" (unpublished manuscript).

23. Larry May, "Torturing Detainees During Interrogation."

24. The International Law Commission, Article 25, State Responsibility principles, Report to the General Assembly (2001), quoted in May, op cit.

25. See John Conroy, *Unspeakable Acts, Ordinary People*.

26. This has been widely documented. Jonathan Glover provides a useful overview of these cases in *Humanity: A Moral History of the 20th century*.

27. See Mark Osiel, *Mass Atrocity, Ordinary Evil, and Hannah Arendt: Criminal Consciousness in Argentina's Dirty War.*

28. See Huggins et al., *Violence Workers: Police Torturers and Murderers Reconstruct Brazilian Atrocities.*

29. See Rejali, *Torture and Democracy.*

30. See Rejali, *Torture and Modernity.*

31. This article originally appeared in *Philosophy and Public Affairs*. It has subsequently been anthologized in numerous volumes.

32. In *Torture*, ed. Levinson.

33. Jean Bethke Elshtain, "Reflection on the Problem of 'Dirty Hands'" in *Torture*, ed. Levinson.

34. Walzer, ibid.

35. I will argue for this view at greater length in the following chapter (*TB as producing more terrorists*).

36. This is a point made by Castrasana in "Torture as a Greater Evil" in *On Torture*.

37. I will not consider cases in which non-democratic governments refuse to torture, and thereby might undermine the trust of the citizenry. My suspicion is that these cases will be similar enough in outcome.

38. Andrew Fiala, "A Critique of Exceptions: Torture, Terrorism, and the Lesser Evil Argument."
39. Jeff McMahan presents a similar view, though in my view it is far less sophisticated than the model provided by Gur-Aye (which is surprising, given the high-esteem in which I hold most of McMahan's work). See his "Torture, Morality, and Law."
40. There are several additional requirements to justify violence in self-defense. I will return to these below.
41. To say that the tortured has the defense of giving up whatever information he or she possesses, I think, is to misunderstand what kind of harm such a revelation might entail for the terrorist. As Tindale has effectively argued, giving up one's identity – the very things that make one who one is – cannot be expected as one side of a fair exchange (which seems to be what some imagine torture to be). See Tindale, "The Logic of Torture."
42. I thus disagree with Miriam Gur-Aye's assertion, cited above, that the "one person who is not defenseless in ticking bomb cases is the terrorist who has planted the bomb" (192).
43. One might argue that there is one case where these conditions are met: the ticking bomb case. I will deal with this case in detail below (Chapter 6: *Criticisms of the ticking bomb*).
44. See *Sociological Snapshots*.
45. I will return to this below. See Chapter 6: *Small (and unrepresentative) sample*.
46. I will discuss this at greater length in Chapter 6: *TB as producing more terrorists*.
47. See 'The Dark Art of Interrogation,' A&E Television Network, 2005.
48. Jeffrey Reiman has made this point in relation to the death penalty. See his "Against the Death Penalty."
49. In an earlier draft of this book, I considered 'revenge' as a category under which one might attempt to justify torture. I have since eliminated this category for two reasons: 1. Revenge picks out a motivation for an action, not a justification for an action. 2. Any justificatory power the concept of revenge might have would be sufficiently similar to the justificatory power of the notion of punishment (one motivation for punishment, after all, is revenge). For these reasons, I will not consider revenge as a category of justification unto itself.
50. Tibor Machan, "Exploring Extreme Violence (Torture)."
51. See Chapter 5 of his forthcoming *Terrorism, Ticking Time-Bombs, and Torture* (Chicago: University of Chicago Press).
52. Sullivan "The Abolition of Torture," in *Torture: A Collection*.
53. This view is defended, for example, by Seumas Miller. See his "Is Torture Ever Morally Justifiable?"
54. Sepp Graessner, "Two Hundred Blows to the Head" in *At the Side of Torture Survivors*.

55. See 166, op cit.
56. Interestingly, there appears to be some correlation between the techniques of torture one undergoes and the suicidal ideations one experiences. See Ferrada-Noli et al., "Suicidal Behavior After Severe Trauma, Part 2: The Association Between Methods of Torture and of Suicidal Ideation in Posttraumatic Stress Disorder."
57. Sister Dianna Ortiz, "The Survivor's Perspective," in *The Mental Health Consequences of Torture.*
58. Quoted in Ortiz.
59. Helene Jaffe, "How to deal with torture victims."

Chapter 6

Thinking through Torture's Temptations

Part Two: Arguments Against Torture

Introduction

We have now explored, in detail, arguments for the use of torture. We explored the arguments offered for the general use of torture, considering the most common argument for its exceptional use only briefly (the ticking bomb case). Because the ticking bomb case has played such a definitive role in the arguments used to advocate torture, I will begin with an analysis of the problems with it. I have chosen to separate my critique of the ticking bomb (TB) case from those where things are less certain: perhaps there is only a high probability that we have someone with the requisite information; there is only a *chance* that torture will be effective; we might have several weeks to carry out the interrogation, rather than only a few hours. I have done this despite some significant overlap in criticism of the ticking bomb case and the more general arguments offered in favor of torture. One reason for this is pedagogical: in articulating the many problems with the ticking bomb case, we will come to see much about the nature of interrogational torture that is directly relevant to larger questions surrounding the institutional use of torture.

Criticisms of the ticking bomb

Unrealistic

The first response to the ticking bomb argument almost inevitably concerns how decidedly unrealistic it is. This is a fact that no one disputes. And concessions about the irrealism of the scenario are extensive: it is unrealistic epistemologically, psychologically, and in terms of the efficacy of torture. According to the defenders of torture, however, this is irrelevant: the point of the ticking bomb scenario is not to justify torture in a case *just like* the ticking bomb case. There are no such cases – or, at least, the existence of such cases is hotly contested. The point of the ticking bomb scenario is to test our intuitions about the supposed absolute prohibition against torture; it is not about the realism of the case that is used to test our intuitions.

So far as it goes, this is an accurate way of describing the point of the ticking bomb case – but this does not make a consideration of issues surrounding the realism of the case *completely irrelevant*. Lack of realism comes in many flavors, one of which is devastating to any thought experiment: namely, incoherence. If a thought experiment is improbable, that is to be expected; if it is incoherent, it must be rejected.

The ticking bomb scenario does not, of course, initially appear to be incoherent. In fact, it seems anything but, particularly in a political climate where we *fear* cases very much like the one imagined in the TB case. What I hope to show in the following pages, however, is that the sorts of things presupposed by the ticking bomb case make it impossible to coherently imagine. Once we have a better grasp of things like the nature of effective interrogation, the experience of pain and the various reactions to it, we must modify the ticking bomb case in fundamental ways to make it even *intelligible*.

While our thought experiments may be as improbable as we like, they must be informed by the empirical reality of their constituent parts. This is so, quite simply, because a thought experiment will only *be about* a particular thing if it actually *corresponds* to that thing. I cannot conduct a thought experiment about circles, for example, if I describe them as bounded geometrical objects with three sides. Such a case would not be *improbable;* it would be utterly impossible: circles do not have three sides. This is part of the *essence* of what it means to be a 'circle.' To ask us to imagine a case of a circle with sides is simply to ask us to imagine something *that is not a circle*. The same problem emerges, I will argue, in the case of torture – in particular in the way that the ticking bomb case asks us to imagine successful interrogation, on the one hand, and pain, on the other.

There are two important points to make in relation to this one. First, the unintelligibility of a thought experiment need not be immediately *obvious*. Thought experiments regarding things that we *believe* we understand may be incoherent without us recognizing it. We might be asked to imagine house painters trying to paint a house a reddish green color in a single minute. Is it possible to do so? Initially, we might claim that it *is* possible, provided that the house is not too big, there are enough house painters, and so on. We will quickly see that the thought experiment is *incoherent*, however, when we discover that there *cannot* be a color that is reddish green. Red and green are at opposite points in the contrasts of colors. They cannot be combined to form a new color that might legitimately be called 'reddish green.' Here, the unintelligibility of the thought experiment does not immediately stand out. We are distracted by another aspect of the thought experiment: namely, the time constraint. Likewise, the case might appear intelligible because we have a good grasp of many aspects of color, painting, and so on. Once we understand more about the nature of color, however, this intelligibility disappears. The implausibility of the time-constrained painting is irrelevant to the intelligibility of the case; the nature of color, however, is anything but. As we can also see from these reflections, the *nature* of the elements of a thought experiment are not known *a priori*. This means that determining whether or not a thought experiment is intelligible will not be something one can determine *without examining empirical evidence*.

The second point to make is this: in some cases, thought experiments will contain what we *discover* to be incoherent elements. In fact, a thought experiment might well be designed to accomplish precisely this. I *am not* thus claiming that a thought experiment is illegitimate when what is *asked about* turns out to be unintelligible as imagined in the thought experiment. For example, if asked to imagine a reddish-green house, or a square circle, our thought experiment is not *automatically* illegitimate. After all, the point of the thought experiment might be to determine whether or not we think such a color (or shape) is possible. Once we realize that it is not possible, the thought experiment has served its purpose. We might put this as follows: any incoherence in a thought experiment is permissible only if it is the very thing the thought experiment is designed to 'test.' Thought experiments designed to test *multiple* intuitions are ill-conceived. The entire point of a well-designed thought experiment is to *isolate* a singular feature of a case in such a way that we will be able to assess our intuitions regarding that particular feature.

The ticking bomb scenario, quite obviously, is meant to test our intuitions about the moral permissibility of torture. To adequately isolate this intuition, it must be assumed that torture can be effective in a pre-determined span of time. This involves a number of additional assumptions about the predictability of pain infliction, pain response, motivational structure, as well as about what conditions need to obtain to carry out successful interrogation. By examining such assumptions, and better understanding the nature of both pain and interrogation, I will argue that we can expose the ticking bomb case for what it is: incoherent. I will also devote some significant time to articulating what makes the case merely implausible. I do this primarily because I aim to excavate the *multiple* problems faced by the TB case.

Never have such certainty

Perhaps the most obvious instance of unrealism in the ticking bomb case concerns the multiple levels of certainty we must assume to make the thought experiment work. The levels of certainty we must presume are as follows:

1. We know the person captured has knowledge that, if
acquired, will allow us to stop the detonation of the bomb
There are three particular issues that make certainty unlikely.

> *Issue 1:* how do we know the person is a terrorist? Is the intelligence reliable?
>
> *Issue 2:* how do we know the person has the required intelligence?
>
> *Issue 3:* how do we know the intelligence, once acquired, will still allow us to stop the bomb?

In any actual interrogation situation, as is well known, all of these issues must be faced. The failure of the United States military to face these issues led to filling Abu Ghraib and the detention center in Guantanamo Bay with persons who simply happened to be at the wrong place at the wrong time. In the view of some of those stationed as guards at Abu Ghraib, for example, up to 90% of the men, women, and children imprisoned there were completely innocent of any wrongdoing.[1] The same can be said of GITMO. Persons were rounded up in night raids, they were informed on for reward money, or under conditions of extreme duress, and, once incarcerated, there were strong incentives *not* to release them.

Even when we can be fairly certain that a person is a terrorist (multiple persons have informed on them; they have incriminating possessions; their name appears in intelligence documents, etc), it doesn't follow from this that we can be sure they know the particular things we would *like* to know. In most cases of interrogation, interrogators simply go fishing for information – who rented what room, what kind of car terrorist x drove, and to where. By cobbling together such bits of seemingly innocent information, the skilled interrogator can assemble actionable intelligence. But the process is hit or miss. One never knows, in advance, what one will get from a particular detainee – what crucial piece of information they may or may not have.

But even if we assume both that 1) the person interrogated is in fact a terrorist and that 2) he has information on a planned bomb attack, it is very unlikely that interrogation will make it possible to stop that attack. Let's assume that the terrorist talks. If he discloses the location of the bomb in plenty of time for a bomb squad to be assembled, to travel to the bomb's location, and to dismantle the bomb, it's unlikely that the bomb will still be there. Terrorist cells today operate by re-organizing when an agent fails to report back in a timely manner. Crucial information possessed by said agent is made irrelevant: plans are altered, locations changed, and so on.[2]

2. We know there is a bomb, and that it will in fact detonate
As we have already seen, the source of intelligence is crucial to its reliability. In recent years, the United States has used reward money in the

attempt to buy intelligence. This has produced any number of false leads – neighbors turning in neighbors against whom they hold a grudge, persons turning in mere acquaintances to help alleviate their abject poverty. Likewise, the use of coercive interrogation has produced a number of 'planned attacks' that led to escalations in the so-called 'terror threat level' in the Unites States, despite the fact that this 'intelligence' turned out to be without a base in reality.

But even if we *are* sure that there is a bomb, we certainly cannot be sure that it will work correctly – that its wiring is correct, that it will detonate, that the blast will be as large as expected. To be sure of this, as I have argued elsewhere,[3] would demand that we have actually seen the bomb constructed and placed where it would detonate. Of course, if we had seen this, there would be no *need* to torture.

3. Torture will work. We can trust the information we gather through torture

The most difficult piece of the ticking bomb scenario to accept, in my view, is that we know the torture will work. I will argue below that we have good reason to reject this. For the time being, however, note that the tortured terrorist does not have to withstand *indefinite* torture. She only has to endure torture until the bomb actually detonates – a time which, per hypothesis, is not that far off. If the pain becomes unbearable, the victim of torture can always reveal a *false* location of the bomb. This will lead to the bomb squad wasting its time, and will also lead to the tortured being relieved of the torture. If it *would not* lead to the cessation of torture, then the terrorist has no reason *whatsoever* to provide any kind of information, true or false. I will return to this point below (*Cannot presume it will work*).

There is an additional reason to be skeptical of anyone who claims that we have encountered a ticking bomb case. As Aaron Lercher has persuasively argued, if we *do* find ourselves in a situation which people have judged to be sufficiently similar to a ticking bomb case, we have good reason *in principle* to doubt this. As Lercher puts it:

> The people who make a judgment to torture will consistently have poor judgment, and make their judgments in situations that are conducive to poor judgment. Those in the position to make the decision cannot be relied on, not because they are bad people, but because the situation distorts their judgment. Unless there is an exceptionally good reason to believe witnesses' and participants' claims that torture was justified, we should not believe such claims. We should not accept such claims as moral knowledge. (72)[4]

In all of the above cases, we see things that simply cannot be known with the precision required to justify torture. As Schulz puts it, the "scenario asks us to believe, in other words, that the authorities have all the information that authorities dealing with a crisis *never* have" (*Phenomenon of Torture*, 262). As the case gets more and more realistic, the intuitions we have regarding the permissibility of torture begin to diverge more and more wildly.[5]

Cannot presume it will work

In the TB case, one is told that torture will work. The underlying assumption here, on the worst reading, is that torture will work on *anyone*. As we will see below (*Torture doesn't work*), there is good reason to dispute that torture works in a way that would justify its use, let alone the claim that it will work on anyone. If this is not the underlying assumption, the view here must be that there are at least some cases in which torture will *certainly* work, and that we can presume that, somehow, we know that this is one of those cases.

We need to disentangle two senses of 'working' here. One sense of 'working' is as follows: torture works if it will allow us to gather information from someone who is initially unwilling to give it. An alternative notion of torture 'working' requires more. Not only must torture be able to 'educe' information, but it must also be a way of getting this information that is uniquely effective. In this second sense, torture 'works' in the sense that its use is justified – it alone produces the information we require in a timely manner.

The TB case faces serious problems *regardless* of the sense of 'working' it employs. If the TB theorist presumes that torture works in the second sense, he has begged an important question: the entire issue is whether or not torture might work in a unique way that is sufficient to justify it. If it is not unique – if there are equally effective ways to acquire information – few would contend that torture was justified in the ticking bomb scenario. As I will argue below (*Torture doesn't work*), we have good reason to doubt that torture *ever* works in a respect that would justify its use.

Even if the TB theorist uses 'working' in the more restricted sense, that torture is capable of getting people to release information, the TB case's presupposition that this will happen is deeply problematic. One can never know, in advance, that torture will work. This is another respect in which the ticking bomb case is unrealistic. Even an expert torturer cannot be sure that her methods will be able to coax her victim into giving information. The difficulties surrounding applying torture to a particular person are legion: there is no singular method that will work on everyone, and not everyone will have a particular method that *will* work on them.

Cannot predict pain response

We have already considered, in some detail, the nature of pain (Chapter 3: *Pain*). It is anything but simple, and herein lies one of the irrealisms to which the ticking bomb scenario helps itself. Underlying the faith that torture works is a failure to comprehend the complexities of pain.

As we have seen, pain refers to a wide range of divergent phenomena, experienced at different degrees of intensity. While we all register pain in roughly the same way, we do *not* all tolerate pain in the same way. Patrick Wall makes this point in his useful *Pain: The Science of Suffering*:

> A very accurate test of pain threshold to electricity is to place electrodes on the skin of a volunteer and to slowly raise the strength of pulsed shocks. At a low level, the subject reports feeling an innocuous thump that turns into a sharp pricking sensation that is mildly unpleasant but, if augmented, would eventually become intolerable. Everyone who is free from disease has the same threshold for pain in this special sense. . . . We all have the same pain threshold. The variability appears when we perceive pain above the threshold level and when we approach what we can tolerate. (Wall, 60)

And here the variability is substantial and surprising. Under certain circumstances, pain is welcomed – particularly when this is regarded as a right of passage, or even as necessary to some type of salvation. Patrick Wall is right to point out that the image of the crucifixion, so central to Christianity, is one such image: Christ undergoes the most horrendous of executions as a noble sacrifice for the good of others.

The experience of pain is structured by our expectations. A dreaded shot can be as painful a thing as one might imagine; extremely painful ordeals can be undertaken with little ado when they are expected, or even revered, by the person who undergoes them.[6] We saw this, for example, in the cases of *S/M* and the *Ascetic*.

This has a special relevance to the idea of the terrorist who is subjected to torture. By its very definition, the term 'terrorist' evokes the notion of a person motivated by causes that he or she regards as having a value that transcends the value of the individual's life. This can be easily seen in the case of the suicide bomber (or another martyr) who decides to sacrifice her own life for what is regarded as a holy cause. If a person *expects* a great deal of pain (perhaps in a torturous interrogation), certainly the experience of this pain will be shaped by these previous expectations. As Wall's analysis reveals, the *meaning* of the pain one undergoes is crucial to the *way* one undergoes it. It is thus oversimplistic to simply assert that everyone will break under torture, and to defend this view by appeal to the immense pain involved. The significance of pain, after all, is far more important to the way one endures that pain than is the body's immediate reaction (sweat, increased heart-rate, and so on). It is with this in mind that we can understand how the early Christian martyrs could withstand their torture with such baffling bravery: to die for God was to find salvation.[7] Here, the meaning of pain makes that pain something to be celebrated rather than a force under which one must break. Should we not expect such a reaction from a well-trained ticking bomb terrorist? Isn't the use of the bomb, in the sorts of cases we're imagining, usually an act of holy war? Even if it is not, the sort of ideological dedication required to plan and execute such a horrendous terrorist act should give us pause when thinking about how the terrorist will respond to pain: he might regard it as justifying the attack, as religious sacrifice, or as necessary evil. Pain, in this respect, might motivate the very will it was meant to break.

But let us assume that we *can* predict that a person will undergo exactly the amount of pain that we want them to, and that they will experience this pain as the most dreadful thing imaginable. If we can imagine such a case (even though it is surely impossible), do we *then* have reason to suspect that the application of pain will produce the sort of intelligence that the ticking bomb case suggests? There is some scientific evidence to dispute even this.

> Ironically, the effects of stress as well as the neurological consequences of pain inhibit memory and executive function. This practically ensures that the individual subjected to these conditions will be unable to accurately remember the information for which he or she is coerced. [Moreover] Stress conditions have the effect, over a period of time, of reducing the independent individuality and increasing suggestibility, making the victim more receptive to the interrogator's demands for what information is wanted (which may not always be the truth). (149)[8]

The relation between pain and reliable memory, in fact, is well known in scientific investigations of memory. "Ribot's gradient, a phenomenon documented in numerous quantitative studies since the 1970s" postulates that "when there is trauma to the brain, the farther back the memory, the more likely it is to survive the trauma. The closer the memory is in time to trauma, the less likely it is to survive" (467). Given this, the use of brutality against a terrorist, even if it produces a genuine desire to talk, may also destroy his ability to remember the very thing that led us to brutality to begin with. It pays to examine empirical reality.

An even deeper irony here is that the effects of torture on memory have been documented even in those manuals that are used (perhaps inappropriately) to *justify* particular torture techniques. The KUBARK manual states explicitly that "psychologists and others who write about physical or psychological duress frequently object that under sufficient pressure subjects usually yield but that their ability to recall and communicate information accurately is as impaired as the will to resist" (84).[9]

Inadequate methodology

The problem with intuitions

The unrealistic quality of the ticking bomb scenario is not its major flaw. The vast majority of thought experiments are unrealistic. As mentioned above, the point of a thought experiment is to test our intuitions on particular cases. There are several problems with such 'experiments' on our intuitions that are worth mentioning.

First, intuitions seem to differ across cultures. Two examples of this have been recently exposed through the careful work of what are today called 'experimental philosophers.'[10] This suggests that the intuitions we have are often a product of different cultural heritages rather than the merits of the case. The relevance of this is straightforward: if the ticking bomb case is to gain any traction at all, it must generate the same sorts of intuitions in the majority of those who consider the case.[11] If there is no uniformity of intuition among those considering the case, the thought experiment will not have successfully demonstrated that there are cases where most *think* that the prohibition on torture ought to be overridden.

Perhaps surprisingly, though, there is no uniformity of intuitions even *within* so-called 'western' culture. The survey data on intuitions regarding the permissibility of torture is simply inconsistent.[12] Everything depends on the way the issue is framed, who does the framing, and the context in which the question is asked. This is the second major concern about the use of intuitions in cases like this: they are incredibly difficult to isolate and test in a way that corrects for these difficulties. The data that we have suggests some interesting patterns, to be sure. According to a poll conducted by the BBC in 2006, Germany, Australia, Canada, France, Italy, and the UK come down squarely against torture, with over 70% of the population claiming that torture is never acceptable. India, however, has only 23% advocating this position. In the US, 58% advocate absolute prohibition.[13]

Obviously, this is anything but a mandate for the use of torture even in ticking bomb cases. The difficulty underlying much of this, it seems, is that our intuitions can be trained in the best scenario, and manipulated in the worst.

Fritz Allhoff has recently attempted to test for intuitions in the ticking bomb case explicitly by sampling 1000 college students in the US and in Australia, trying to isolate their particular intuitions on whether and when torture is acceptable. Allhoff claims some important results: the assessment of torture depends (in part) on the guilt of the person to be tortured; a majority of persons are willing to torture when there is a sufficient good to be obtained through the use of torture.[14]

There is little doubt that this is important work, but it is not without significant methodological worries. There is an obvious age bias in the sample. College students are usually 18–22. This can spoil a sample very easily. The portion of the brain that carries out risk assessment, as is well-documented, is underdeveloped until the mid-20s. This might not matter at all when it comes to this case – but this is a question that ought to be considered: does the uniform age of the participants undermine the validity of the results? There is also an experience issue in the data. There is a lot of empirical data suggesting that experienced interrogators would utilize rapport-building rather than torture to extract information.[15]

The relative inexperience of those sampled needs to be addressed. Certainly watching 24 or the news does not make anyone an expert on torture – though it might well inform the way one's intuitions go when engaging in such thought experiments. Of course, we should also admit that a long career in the military might bias any sample in the opposite direction: the military of the US, for example, has had, until very recently, a long history (going back to George Washington) of opposing torture.

In any case, the question of experience/knowledge regarding the actual meaning of 'torture' cannot simply be ignored when attempting to gather information about the intuitions of persons and the *relevance* of those intuitions.[16]

To be clear, my contention here is not that the appeal to intuitions, such as the one we find in Allhoff's defense of the ticking bomb case, is irrelevant. Intuitions are a good place to begin to discuss particular issues. This is certainly one use of the ticking bomb scenario: it gives us a place to begin a discussion of the ethics of torture. The problem is that, more often than not, the ticking bomb scenario is used to *end* discussion by 'demonstrating' that torture must, in at least some cases, be acceptable. This is infelicitous, to say the least. Even if all of our intuitions agree (which they do not), it is not clear *why* they agree. Culture differences abound. Questions are framed differently, leading to different results. It *might* be the case that intuitions agree because we have a collectively correct sense of a particular case. Likewise, it might be the case that our intuitions are informed by latent racism and sexism.[17] These, however, are only two of many possibilities. This means, at a minimum, that we should be skeptical of any appeal to intuitions that is not supported by independent argument.

But we can't even be this confident in the case of the ticking bomb. Our intuitions *do not* agree. As an effort to show that the prohibition against torture cannot be absolute, the ticking bomb scenario does not succeed. Even in cases where it *looks* like we have some initial agreement (such as in Allhoff's recent work), there are significant issues surrounding what *explains* the seeming convergence, let alone what the scope of the convergence is.

Small (and unrepresentative) sample

There is another intuition that operates behind the scenes in the ticking bomb scenario. This is the intuition that torture *would work*. Most people probably think that torture will work in the ticking bomb scenario because they imagine *themselves* in this scenario. When I have been asked, in the past, whether or not I would talk under torture, I usually reply that I wouldn't allow it to get that far: I would begin talking before torture was even *mentioned*. I then follow this point by reminding my interlocutor that my own motivations should not be generalized to the case of the ticking bomb terrorist. My motivational structure, it seems scarcely necessary to state, should not be conflated with the motivational structure of someone who is willing to sacrifice his own life, as well as the lives of many others, for a particular cause. To assume that my own reactions to torture are an adequate sample of what *anyone's reaction* would be is to make a gross mistake about how general our own motivations are. If I were willing to sacrifice a thousand lives for some 'greater' cause, I might well be willing to undergo endless torture – or I might not. The point here is that it is an unforgivable methodological mistake to think that everyone will react to torture in the same way, or that the pain inflicted by torture will produce the same kinds of motivations in all people.

In addition to misunderstanding the difference between ourselves undergoing torture and someone who has dedicated herself to an identity-conferring cause undergoing that same torture, the ticking bomb case also misunderstands the relationship between our immediate reactions to the case and what we would *actually* do in such a case. Bob Brecher makes this point quite nicely:

> The first reason why the ticking bomb scenario remains a fantasy, and not a description of a rare but realistic possibility, is that it fails to distinguish what you or I *might* do in that imagined case and what you or I *could* do in an actual case. It fails to distinguish between individuals' possible visceral responses and any proper basis of public policy . . . [this failure] has been both disastrous and unnecessary. (22)

As Brecher goes on to explain,

> we cannot put ourselves in the position of a torturer, and for two reasons. First, there is the sort and the precision of the skills required; second, and far more importantly, there is the question of the depths to which the acquisition and practice of such skills requires the torturer to sink . . . Even if 'you' were there when the person 'you' knew to know where the bomb was, 'you' would not know what to do . . . The ticking bomb scenario requires us not to imagine what *we* would do, but to imagine what we would require *someone else* – a

professional torturer – to do on our behalf; and not, furthermore, as an act of supererogation or altruism, but as the practice of their profession . . . the institutionalization of the profession of torturer is a necessary condition of the example's even getting off the ground. (23–24)

This is a point that we will consider in some detail below (*Professional torturers: where policy and exception overlap*): the use of torture requires persons who *know what they are doing* – who have some type of mastery over this particular craft (though, as I will argue, the 'success' of even the highly trained is to be disputed).[18] The point to emphasize here is that, methodologically, the ticking bomb case cannot show what it purports to show. Even if we assume that the claims about our intuitions in this case are correct – and there's good reason to dispute even this – our intuitions in the case are irrelevant to whether or not torture should be carried out.

The irrelevance of our intuitions is twofold. First, because we are not motivationally identical to those who will undergo torture. Second, because we are not the ones who will be carrying out the torture. As Brecher points out above, the *real* question in the ticking bomb case is whether or not this case supports the maintenance of a class of torturers, trained by the state, and ready to react at a moment's notice to a threat like the (unrealistic) one hypothesized in the ticking bomb case. It seems obvious that our intuitions about *this* will differ even more widely than they already do.

Misunderstanding time's relation to interrogation

One of the central conditions of the ticking bomb case is that there is a limited amount of time to utilize torture. As Bob Brecher has argued, "if it is not known that time is (sufficiently) short, then it is not known that the case is a matter of necessity, and that there is therefore not time to try techniques such as 'talking the suspect down'" (35). This raises a fundamental issue about the ticking bomb case: can we 'time' torture? That is, do we have reason to suspect that torture can be successful in very constricted spans of time?

As we have seen, the brutal infliction of painful procedures has no guarantees (*Cannot predict pain response*). Using high levels of pain, even successfully, can have the effect of *deadening* pain receptors, producing unconsciousness, or even killing the person being tortured. This alone, I take it, is sufficient for demonstrating that the use of *physical* means of torture cannot guarantee the compliance of the person tortured. But there are additional reasons to worry about the use of physical torture in conducting an interrogation. This is captured in the CIA's *Human Resource Exploitation Training Manual*:

Intense pain is quite likely to produce false confessions, fabricated to avoid additional punishment. This results in a time-consuming delay while investigation is conducted and the admissions are proven untrue. During the respite, the subject can pull himself together and may even use the time to devise a more complex confession that takes still longer to disprove. (L-12)

Commenting on his own torture at Guantanamo Bay, Khalid Sheikh Mohammed admitted as much:

I gave a lot of false information in order to satisfy what I believed the interrogators wished to hear in order to make the ill-treatment stop . . . I'm sure that the false information I was forced to invent . . . wasted a lot of their time and led to several false red-alerts being placed in the US.[19]

It is a truism that those in pain will say anything to eliminate their pain. In the ticking bomb case, the use of physical torture magnifies this problem. The terrorist only needs to hold out until the bomb detonates. An obvious strategy to apply in a case such as this is to provide *false* information that will require action on the part of the interrogator. This would accomplish both the cessation of pain *and* the detonation of the ticking bomb.

But in fact, there is a deeper problem with the use of physical torture in these cases – its use can actually make it *less* likely that a suspect will cooperate, and hence less likely that the necessary intelligence will be gathered in time to save those threatened by the ticking bomb.

The torture situation is an external conflict, a contest between the subject and his tormentor. The pain which is being inflicted upon him [the interrogatee] from outside himself may actually intensify his will to resist. On the other hand, pain which he is inflicting on himself is more likely to sap his resistance. For example, if he is required to maintain rigid positions such as standing at attention or sitting in a stool for long periods of time, the immediate source of discomfort is not the 'questioner' but the subject himself. His conflict is then an internal struggle. As long as he maintains this position, he is attributing to the 'questioner' the ability to do something worse. But there is never a showdown where the 'questioner' demonstates this ability. After a period of time, the subject may exhaust his internal motivational strength. (CIA, *Human Resource Exploitation Training Manual*, L-12)

As this makes clear, the use of physical torture can actually *increase* the will of the interrogated to resist. There is thus good reason to resist the temptation to engage in physical torment in the interrogation situation. Doing so can increase and cement an adversarial relationship with the person being interrogated that is in fact the primary obstacle the interrogator faces. The *US Army Intelligence and Interrogation Handbook*, when discussing an interrogation technique known as 'Fear-Up (Harsh),' reinforces this point. "A good interrogator will implant in the source's mind that the interrogator himself is not the object to be feared, but is a possible way out of a trap" (75). The recommended form of interrogation – even when invoking what is called 'harsh' interrogation – attempts to preserve rapport between questioner and questioned. As we will see, this method of interrogation is, without question, the cornerstone of effective intelligence gathering.

In the ticking bomb case, then, the recourse to physical coercion and torture is undercut by the need for effective intelligence gathering. To engage in physical torture is to risk doing damage to the very *capacity* of the tortured to experience pain (and hence to undercut even the *chance* of torture being successful). It is also to risk increasing the adversarial relationship that provides a central motivation for *withholding* information – indeed, in all likelihood, this adversarial relationship is a central piece of the terrorist's understanding of his enemy. To torture him is to *justify* his actions (in his mind), and to reinforce, in all likelihood, all of the things that motivated him to plant a ticking bomb to begin with.

The situation gets even worse if one opts instead to engage in no-touch torture (the preferred kind in the twenty-first century, as we have seen). For no-touch torture to be effective, a substantial amount of time is required. The key to no-touch torture is twofold: first, one must control the environment of the tortured in such a way that the victim ceases to have any sense of autonomy or control; and, second, one must do this in a way that turns the victim *against himself.*

> The 'questioner' should be careful to manipulate the subject's environment to disrupt patterns, not to create them. Meals and sleep should be granted irregularly, in more than abundance or less than adequacy, on no discernible pattern. This is done to disorient the subject and destroy his capacity to resist. (L-3)

No ticking bomb scenario (properly so-called) can accommodate this approach to torture. There is simply insufficient time to break down the agency of the tortured – to eviscerate the autonomy of the tortured, which is the essential goal of torture.[20] What this reveals is that, regardless of the brutality of one's actions or the skill with which one carries them out, torture requires *time* – and a good deal of it. Indeed, the amount of time a successful interrogation will require cannot be predicted in advance. It is precisely this dimension of interrogation and torture that is overlooked – and deliberately so – in the ticking bomb scenario. As we noted above, it is the immediacy of an attack that makes torture 'necessary' in the ticking bomb scenario. But it is also this immediacy that makes it incredibly unlikely that torture will work.

As we have seen, one of the factors at play in the 'breaking' of a subject is that they have no control over their environment. They cannot determine, or even know, how long interrogation sessions will last, or even how many interrogations they might be subjected to over the coming days, weeks, or even years. This uncertainty helps to produce the sensation of utter dependence that is so sought-after by interrogators. When this uncertainty is removed, as it must be in the ticking bomb case, the manipulability of the suspect is significantly undermined.

In fact, to speak of manipulability as undermined is perhaps an understatement. Withstanding pain can be significantly enhanced by the awareness that the pain one suffers has a definitive stopping point. If there were no end to the pain of the dentist, few would bother to go. The gamble would simply be too great. There is an inverse relation between time allowed, on the one hand, and likelihood of withstanding torture, on the other. This places an interesting and subtle burden on those who would justify torture in ticking bomb scenarios: the more pressing the 'need' for torture, the less likely it will be to work.

Automatically excluding alternatives

One more obvious objection to be raised about the ticking bomb case is that alternatives to torture are ruled out *in principle*. Presumably, as we have noted, this is meant to isolate one's intuitions about torture. But it also systematically *misleads* the person asked to consider their intuitions. After all, the choice in scenarios more realistic than the ticking bomb scenario is *never* 'torture or do nothing.' Torture is stipulated to be necessary. The problem with this, of course, is that it stacks the deck in favor of torture to begin with. By stacking the deck, moreover, the ticking bomb scenario does not provide a good test case for our intuitions regarding the absolute prohibition of torture. A more reliable intuition pump, it seems to me, would ask about the permissibility of torture in relation to *other* means of action, rather than in relation to simply standing by and watching people die.

It is of course an empirical question whether or not posing the ticking bomb scenario in these terms would yield different results (not forgetting, of course, that there are already substantial difficulties with the diversity of results we have regarding such cases as they are stated). Asked to choose between, say, torture and canvassing the community for actionable leads concerning terrorists activities, it seems unlikely that anyone would choose torture. This points to an additional layer of unreality in the ticking bomb scenario: in the ticking bomb scenario, we are asked to imagine a case where what we do will determine a particular outcome. Either we torture, or a bomb is detonated killing thousands. With minimal education about intelligence gathering, there is another obvious

– and much more fruitful – way to spend the remaining time before the detonation of the bomb – one which seems to be obscured by the structure of the ticking bomb case: to mobilize all the forces at one's disposal to *find the bomb* – to mobilize law enforcement, civilians, and everyone else willing to help, to locate the device so that it can be dismantled.

Emptiness of term 'torture'

Because the ticking bomb case asks us to assume that torture will work, and that it will do so in a restricted time span, the meaning of the term 'torture' is anything but clear in this thought experiment. As Matthews points out, torture "functions like an unbound variable of predicate logic, bearing no relation to possible empirical instantiations" (96). It is simply an empty term, plugged into a thought experiment that is unconstrained even by the empirical *reality* of actual torture. In this respect, the term 'torture' might as well stand for 'dog' or 'cat,' as it resembles these mammals no less closely than it resembles actual torture practices.[21] It is presumably for this reason that the ticking bomb scenario is capable of justifying everything (if it can justify anything). As Matthews notes, similar arguments could be used "for the establishment of rape and torture camps, the deliberate spreading of terror, or *any* of the other purposes for which torture is used" (121). As with earlier objections to the ticking bomb scenario, we find a similar lesson to learn here: the intuitions we are appealing to in this case depend on a naïve understanding of what torture involves, and hence are inherently suspect.

Consequentialist arguments against torturing in the ticking bomb case

There are a number of consequentialist arguments against the use of torture. Most of these arguments, it seems to me, do not have direct relevance to the ticking bomb case. They are concerned with the negative consequences of enacting a *policy* of torture.[22] There are two consequentialist arguments, however, that *are* directly relevant to the TB case, despite the fact that they do not at first glance appear to be. These arguments stem from the short-sightedness of the thought experiment itself, which seems to assume that the negative consequences of torturing the attacker in the TB case will be the end of the price paid for torture. As we will see, this is a serious underestimation of how consequences may in fact play out.

TB as producing more terrorists

The first consequentialist argument against the TB case is that *any* case of torture will ultimately produce more terrorists, and this probability has been excluded from the calculations made in the TB scenario (which weighs one life against thousands). Once we calculate *future* terrorist attacks, the utilitarian calculations change dramatically. There is an obvious reply to this argument that is frequently invoked: we must distinguish between the *exceptional* case of torture (such as the one envisioned in the ticking bomb case) from torture that is engaged in regularly. Torture *as a policy*, the argument goes, would indeed have such results. Torture carried out only *exceptionally*, however, would not. One way to prevent exceptional instances of torture from producing *additional* terrorists would be to keep the *fact* of torture from becoming widely known. If this were possible, it can be argued, then the use of torture in a ticking bomb case need not have any such consequences.

This point, I think, must be conceded. *If* torture remains secret, the use of torture will not result in additional terrorists being recruited into terrorist organizations who are willing to engage in acts of extreme violence. While this point stands in principle, there are reasons to worry that, in practice, torture simply *cannot* remain secret. These reasons are as follows.

After a TB situation, there are four options for the tortured terrorist, none of which suggest an easy route to secrecy. The tortured person might 1) be jailed without trial, 2) be prosecuted within the criminal system, 3) be released, or 4) be executed. In each of these scenarios, the ability to maintain secrecy is something about which we should be seriously skeptical. Obviously, if either (2) or (3) occurred, secrecy is out of the question. Given access to a lawyer, testimony, or a prison population, word about the treatment of the tortured would spread with lightning speed.

Things do not fair much better in cases (1) and (4), though the process of discovery would certainly be slower. If the victim were placed in prison without trial, questions would inevitably arise about *why* the person was being detained, what conditions led to the detainment, and so on. Moreover, the International Committee of the Red Cross, Amnesty International, Human Rights Watch, and other NGOs would seek to clarify the condition of the prisoner, his treatment, and so on. Even when sworn to secrecy themselves (as in the case of the ICRC), information uncovered often tends to become public – sometimes sooner rather than later.[23] Even if the specific allegation of torture is not made public, allegations of abuse, or unlawful detention, might easily result from such detention practices.

The final option for the TB torturer, sadly, is probably the most likely: the tortured would simply be executed after successful dismantling of the bomb. This 'elimination of the evidence,' it is true, may well prevent accusations concerning torture from ever being justified. But justification is never the measure of what will be made public. It is possible that information about the torture, even if it is only suspected, would be leaked to the press (as in the Abu Ghraib photos, for example). This is precisely what happened, to cite only one example, in the Philippines. As William Schultz puts it: "Stories of torture and death inflicted upon the indigenous people by the American military had been passed on from one generation to the next until they had taken on 'mythical proportions'" (261).[24]

Actions, even carried out covertly, have consequences for the nations that execute them. These consequences are widespread and far-reaching. To torture, even in an isolated event (if that is possible), may well lead to an aggravated populace, or sect, that is more prepared than before to engage in violence against those who tortured.

But let us assume that this would not happen. Do we have reason to think that in this scenario no one would ever learn of the TB terrorist's torture? Likely TB terrorists are not simply isolated individuals, without families or contacts among other, similarly-minded people. The plan to detonate a device of the sort imagined in the ticking bomb case requires expertise and planning, making it extremely unlikely that anyone could carry out such a plan in complete isolation. This reminds us that, even if the TB torturer were killed and his torture were kept secret, we cannot think with any likelihood that rumors wouldn't circulate about his disappearance, or that media members wouldn't seek information. In some cases, the circulation of such speculation can be just as damaging as the release of actual information.

In societies with a free press (and, indeed, even in those without one), it is extraordinarily difficult to prevent extreme acts of violence from becoming public knowledge. Consider, for example, the 'top secret' interrogation techniques approved by the Bush administration. While the secrecy surrounding these policies was regarded as central to national security, news of their approval was reported as early as 2002.[25] As Mark Danner reported in an article in the *New Yorker* in April of 2009:

> News of the "black sites" first appeared prominently in the press – on the front page of *The Washington Post* – in December 2002. A year and a half later, after the publication and broadcast of the Abu Ghraib photographs – the one moment in the last half-dozen years when the torture story, thanks to the lurid images, became "televisual" – a great wave of leaks swept into public view hundreds of pages of "secret" documents about torture and the Bush administration's decision-making regarding it. There have been many important "revelations" since, but none of them has changed the essential fact: by no later than the summer of 2004, the American people had before them the basic narrative of how the elected and appointed officials of their government decided to torture prisoners and how they went about it.

The more recent leaking of the ICRC's report on Guantanamo Bay in 2009 is thus anything but an isolated incident. Again, Danner:

For though some of the details provided – and officially confirmed for the first time – in the ICRC report are new, and though the first-person accounts make chilling reading and have undoubted dramatic power, one can't help observing that the broader discussion of torture is by now in its essential outlines nearly five years old, and has become, in its predictably reenacted outrage and defiant denials from various parties, something like a shadow play.

It is a dangerous failure of foresight to exclude such results from our ticking bomb deliberations. As Danner makes us recognize, the consequences do not end when the torture does. In fact, given what we have so far been discussing, engaging in torture against a terrorist is only the beginning of the negative consequences likely to arise. William Schultz puts this point powerfully.

> Proponents of ticking bomb torture try to convince us that the calculation is straightforward: torture one terrorist; save 100 people. But that assumes that there are no further detrimental consequences once the victims of the bombing are saved – no retaliatory strikes, for example, by the torture victim's comrades to pay back the inhumanity done their brother. If that happens, the math may quickly change: 100 people today; 1,000 killed tomorrow . . . (261)

This is not the end of the consequentialist arguments available in regard to the ticking bomb scenario. One can argue that torture, even when used only in ticking bomb scenarios, tends to propel itself. After all, once one has engaged in torture, no clear boundaries exist any longer. Knowing whether or not one's situation *constitutes* a ticking bomb scenario, after all, is not clear cut. If torture is an option, many may well regard it as better to err on the side of safety.

One can also argue that torture tends to deteriorate the use of other investigative techniques, that it damages the reputation of the nation that employs it, and that it erodes the trust citizens place in their own government. These are, I think, plausible consequences of the use of torture. They are not, however, clearly applicable to the ticking bomb case. After all, it is certainly possible to imagine a solitary case of torture that does not lead to such results. The fact that these arguments might not apply to the ticking bomb thought experiment, however, hardly makes them irrelevant to assessing the use of torture generally. For this reason, I will devote considerable attention to them below (*Consequentialist arguments against torture policy*).

Professional torturers: where policy and exception overlap
As I pointed out earlier, "the institutionalization of the profession of torturer is a necessary condition of the ticking bomb example's even getting off the ground" (24). Such a professional class is a *prerequisite*

for adequate torture in the ticking bomb case. Recall that, in the ticking bomb case, we imagine someone who is an *expert* at torture – someone who will be able to extract the necessary information in an incredibly restricted amount of time. The idea of someone (like you or me), *never* having engaged in torture, and yet being competent to do this, is preposterous. Torture is a kind of *skill*, and to engage effectively in torture requires *training*. As will come as a surprise to no one, acquiring such skill will involve the existence of institutions in which one can become a torturer – as well as eventual victims upon which one can practice one's craft.[26] The addition of such institutions can have an effect on the entire mood of a culture – and a utilitarian cannot very well ignore such things.[27] To make sense of the ticking bomb scenario thus requires further envisioning that we have a trained torturer prepared to carry out the interrogation.

> The ticking bomb scenario requires a torturer desensitized to the infliction and endurance of suffering, trained to dehumanize the victims of torture, and who will obey orders without question. The training of this torturer involves deliberately inducing dispositions that are not only very likely to lead to crimes of obedience but that *have* led to crimes of obedience in the past. (287)[28]

This means that to consider, on consequentialist grounds, whether or not torture can be justified in the TB scenario, we must also consider whether or not we would be willing to house, even covertly, the means for training torturers.[29] This is not simply a calculation about what training programs ought to be available. It is also a calculation that includes the production of persons who will simply *obey*, and who have been trained to detach themselves fundamentally from any compassionate response they might otherwise have to their victims.

Of course, in the ticking bomb case, we stipulate that the order to torture is a justified one based on perfect knowledge. But this hardly entails that such persons will *only* receive such orders. Believing this would entail believing in a fairy tale. As Wolfendale argues, we cannot assume

> that torturers will only be given legitimate orders and will disobey illegal and immoral orders. We have every reason to doubt that military and political authorities will use torture only in cases that meet the ticking bomb criteria. As we have seen from current and past uses of torture, the training of torturers . . . is connected to the illegal and immoral use of torture on a vast scale. (287)

As this demonstrates, the utilitarian cannot simply think about the persons saved. In imagining an effective use of torture in the ticking bomb scenario, we must also include the consideration that promoting competent torturers will substantially increase the likelihood of acts of gross immorality carried out on command. The utilitarian, if she is to talk about torture, must talk about more realistic (and empirically-grounded) cases. This means chaining our thought experiments to reality – if only to make our thought experiments *coherent*. This does not mean we cannot consider the ticking bomb scenario (or, at any rate, coherent versions of it). It *does* mean that we must include the sorts of persons and institutions we would foster to make torture in such a case effective.

The arguments presented do much to show why allowing torture in exceptional circumstances may well lead to anything but its exceptional use: torture tends to expand. As Andrew Sullivan points out, "what the hundreds of abuse and torture incidents have shown is that, once you permit torture for someone somewhere, it has a habit of spreading" (323).[30] This is one of the central lessons of judicial torture in the Middle Ages. It very quickly overtook the courts of continental Europe, changing from one *possible* way of gathering evidence to one that was *de facto* required. But it is also a lesson of the present. Discussing the case of Israel, Eitan Felner writes

> From the moment that the Landau Commission [of Israel] stretched the concept of the 'ticking bomb' scenario to include cases where the danger to human life is not immediate, and sanctioned instead the use of force in cases of immediate need [as opposed to immediate *threat*], the exceptional case of the 'ticking bomb' became the paradigm for almost every GSS interrogation. (34)[31]

In the case of Israel, a willingness to recognize the use of physical force (though *not* the use of torture) in ticking bomb scenarios led to the massive use of such force – and, it appears, to the use of flat-out torturous techniques.[32] The same can be said of the United States under the Bush administration.

Of course, there is no *guarantee* that an isolated case of torture (in a ticking bomb scenario) will spread out to infect other areas of political and social life. This should not trouble a utilitarian, as utilitarians almost never traffic in necessities. What the history of torture *does* show, is that there is a marked tendency for one case of torture to become two, and two to become many. Any utilitarian analysis of torture must take this into account. Once we have done this, the results of our moral calculations are anything but clear.

Criticisms of torture

We have now explored the many difficulties with the ticking bomb scenario, as well as with the idea that such a scenario can be used to justify even isolated acts of torture. Obviously, many of the objections raised to the ticking bomb case also apply to the more general (institutional) use of torture. We will thus have some occasion to return to particular objections in what follows, and to expand these as appropriate to consider the ethical dimension of torture as a policy.

Torture doesn't work

In the preceding pages, I have frequently claimed that torture does not work. In this section, I would like to pay my argumentative dues. My way into the evidence for the ineffectiveness of torture, however, will be in reverse. To begin, I'd like to consider a common argument for the *effectiveness* of torture. A common criticism of the claim that torture doesn't work has been articulated as follows by Michael Ignatieff:

> As Posner and others have tartly pointed out, if torture and coercion were both as useless as critics pretend, why is there so much of it going on? While some abuse and outright torture can be attributed to the sadism of individuals, poor supervision, and so on, it must be the case that if experienced interrogators come to this conclusion, they do so on the basis of their experience. The argument that torture and coercion do not work is contradicted by the dire frequency with which both cases occur. (25–26)[33]

This argument raises several important questions while pointing out a phenomenon that requires explanation. That phenomenon, quite obviously, is the *pervasiveness* of torture. If it were so obvious that torture did not work, Ignatieff points out, it simply would not be used by states in the attempt to acquire actionable intelligence. Because it is used, then, it cannot be *obviously* useless. How then do we explain its frequent use?

One possibility, of course, is simply that people *believe* that it will work, and that they act in good faith on this belief. This is entirely compatible with the claim that torture does not *in fact* work. Ignatieff goes further, however, by claiming that 'experienced interrogators' have assessed the use of torture and, based on this experience, determined that torture *does* work. This makes it look, at least initially, like we should accept the claim that torture, at least in some cases, is effective. After all, in assessing the effectiveness of torture, aren't those who have carried it out in a better position to say whether or not it works?

Before exploring this in detail, it's worth noting that the decision to torture is *not* typically made by experienced interrogators. In this respect, the very foundation of Ignatieff's and Posner's (indirect) argument is deeply flawed. As we will see, most experienced interrogators do *not* advocate torture, nor do they claim that it works.[34] Moreover, "harsh approaches are typically the first choice of novice and untrained

interrogators but the last choice of experienced professional interrogators."[35] Appealing to those who *do* claim that torture works presumably involves appealing to those who make decisions regarding
interrogation policy. These persons, however, are seldom familiar with
actual interrogation.

> civilian authorities and military officers who make the strategic decisions about
> torture interrogation are rarely knowledgeable about interrogation, and those
> with the greatest knowledge – the experienced interrogators – are ranked too
> low in the military hierarchy to have a significant impact on decisions. (429)[36]

But let us assume, for the sake of argument, that Posner and Ignatieff
have access to testimony that is otherwise unavailable. Even if this is
the case, there is still good reason to suspect, perhaps surprisingly, that
the answer to the above question must be 'no' – even if torturers report
that torture works, there is good reason to disbelieve them. Those who
engage in torture on a regular basis have an additional incentive to regard
torture as an effective means of gathering information that will save lives.
The incentive here is a common one: to judge that torturing works, for a
torturer, would mean that one's actions had been at least arguably appropriate. To make the opposite judgment (that torture is ineffective) would
amount to incriminating oneself in one of the worst acts imaginable. To
say that torture doesn't work is to say that one (a torturer) is guilty of
serious moral failings. Few people have the courage, or the will, to admit
such things about themselves. It is incredibly difficult to face such cogni-
tive dissonance in a way that isn't self-serving.

Are there additional reasons why torture might be judged to work?
Darius Rejali provides one plausible account. As Rejali convincingly
argues, the secrecy surrounding torture is one of the primary problems
facing recognizing its ineffectiveness.

> Soldiers learn about torture not in schools, but through backroom apprentice-
> ships. Backroom apprenticeship proves to be a very powerful method of edu-
> cation, gradually transforming torture techniques in the course of a century.
> This method of transmission is difficult to detect, a quality torturers value in
> an age of increased international scrutiny of human rights abuses. (520)

The absence of university curricula involving torture helps to keep its
practice hidden from the academic eye – but it is certainly not the only
issue surrounding the continued illusion that it is an effective means of
intelligence gathering. As Rejali points out, "competitiveness also inhib-
its the accumulation of knowledge. Torturers do not give away their
trade secrets to their rival interrogators" (520). Part of the reason for
this, of course, is simply career ambition: one protects those techniques

one regards as most effective, if only to enable one to excel in the eyes of superiors.

This problem is compounded by the dearth of available evidence surrounding actual cases of torture. What is learned through torture is not subjected to analysis (or at least has not often been) because these lessons are documented only in texts that are inaccessible to scholars. The veil of 'top secret' hides us from the horror of torture, but it also prevents any analysis of the horror – and hence any ability to accumulate knowledge regarding its practice is significantly thwarted. While those in interrogation turn to scholars, scholars are left with little access to data. "The blind, thus, lead the blind: scholars cannot access classified documents, and governments read scholars instead of reading their own data" (Rejali, 522).

This alternative explanation of the faith in torture does much to dismantle the argument offered by theorists like Ignatieff and Posner – but there are additional responses that need to be made as well. The fact the practitioners of torture sometimes believe that it works should provide little comfort to anyone investigating the practice. It is entirely consistent to judge that torture works, having engaged in it routinely, and simply to be wrong. In fact, it is actually plausible that people are wrong rather frequently about the effectiveness of torture. This is so because the idea of torture 'working' is ill-defined. If 'working' consists merely in someone talking, then it seems easy enough to confirm that it works. After all, people being tortured will say many things – some true, and some not. Presumably, though, for torture to work it must enable operatives to acquire information that meets at least four initial conditions: 1) it must be true; 2) it must be current; 3) it must be actionable; 4) there are not alternative, equally efficient, means of gathering the intelligence.

The dominant problem in the information gained through torture is the propensity those undergoing torture have to say anything to end the pain. This is dramatically displayed in a famous case from the inquisition, widely quoted in the literature:

> She said, 'Señores, why will you not tell me what I have to say? Señor, put me on the ground – have I not said that I did it all?' She was told to talk. She said, 'I don't remember – take me away – I did what the witnesses say.' She was told to tell in detail what the witnesses said. She said, 'Señor, as I have told you, I do not know for certain. I have said that I did all that the witnesses say. Señores, it does not help me to say that I did it and I have admitted that what I have done has brought me to this suffering – Señor, you know the truth – Señores, for God's sake have mercy on me. Of Señor, take these things from my arms – Señor, please release me, they are killing me.' She was tied on the *potro* with the cords, she was admonished to tell the truth and the *garrotes* were ordered to be tightened. She said, 'Señor, do you not see how these people are killing me? I did it – for God's sake let me go.' (49)[37]

Quite obviously, it is not sufficient that one *speaks* when tortured. It is highly likely that this will happen. If the information given is false, however, this can hardly be considered an instance of torture 'working.'

But the truth of what a person says is not sufficient for showing that torture works. The information acquired must also be current information – not simply something that *used to be true*. This condition is related to the third one: for torture to 'work' the intelligence acquired must also be actionable – that is, one must be able to act on the information acquired in such a way that the action in question would make the torture worth the serious wrong committed to acquire the information.

The fourth condition concerns justification. Torture 'working' could not possibly be justified if there were other means of acquiring the same intelligence that did not involve the use of this dark method. Torture that works involves actionable, current, and true information that could not have been acquired by some other means in an equally (or near equally) effective way. By 'equally effective' we do not simply mean that said information could be acquired (after a terrorist attack has occurred, we have a great deal of information that is 'actionable,' though in a different sense). To be 'equally effective,' the alternative means of intelligence gathering must be such that it could *also* prevent what is putatively prevented by the use of torture.

Given these conditions, we should be skeptical of a practitioner's claim that torture is effective. This assertion looks incredibly difficult to assess. More likely than not, one is not simply looking at the data available, but basing one's judgment on a hunch about what the data 'must' mean. In assessing the effectiveness of torture, are we to believe that practitioners of torture have considered the available alternatives to intelligence-gathering (such as standard interrogation techniques, which *have* been shown to work in many cases), and have determined with sufficient assurance that these will be *ineffective* in this case? This seems possible, but doubtful.

As far as the first three conditions go, the only way to verify that all of these have been met (and in particular, the actionable condition) would be to act on the intelligence gathered through torture and actually prevent a particular attack. Do we have evidence that this has happened?

Members of the US Administration under President George W. Bush insist that there is. As former Vice President Dick Cheney told a CNN interviewer, in response to the question of whether or not he thought 'enhanced interrogation' had saved lives

> I think those programs were absolutely essential to the success we enjoyed of being able to collect the intelligence that let us defeat all further attempts to launch attacks against the United States since 9/11. I think that's a great success story.[38]

Of course, others with access to the same intelligence do not have the same confidence. President Barack Obama, responding to Cheney's interview, said simply "I fundamentally disagree with Dick Cheney."[39]

It is easy for many to simply take political sides: the Republicans trust Cheney (or, at any rate, the *view* Cheney is articulating), while the Democrats trust Obama. But such authority stand-offs do little to answer the question of whether or not there are *actual cases* where torture has been used successfully. Once again, we must remember that 'working' here does not *merely* mean acquiring information from a suspect through the use of torture. 'Working' means that this information *could not have been gained as effectively through other means*. So let us simply concede what seems hard to doubt: people subjected to torture did in fact sometimes reveal information. Did this information stop attacks? We might even concede this, though there's no proof of it. Could this information have been acquired in a way that *did not* involve the use of torture? Here is where things get difficult to determine. Judgments with the stamp of certainty seem here, as elsewhere, unavailable. The only thing we can do is go where the available evidence takes us. And where does the evidence take us? Given what we know, the cases of torture do not bear out the claim that torture works. As Rejali succinctly puts the point: "what is surprising is how *difficult* it is to find specific cases where torture produced information that was not known by other means" (496).

Torture was widely used in the French-Algerian war. There are no verified instances of torture working in ticking bomb cases in this theater. When asked whether or not torture was necessary to the victory, General Massu replied: "No, when I think about Algeria, it grieves me. We could have done things differently."[40] In one case where critical intelligence *was* acquired through torture (the safe house of the last leader of the FLN was revealed), this information was not new. "Informants had identified the FLN safe house months ago" (491).

One of the most oft-cited instances where torture supposedly worked was in the 1995 case of Abdul Hakim Murad in the Philippines. Murad was indeed tortured, and he did in fact talk. As mentioned above, however, this is far from sufficient for demonstrating that torture works in a sense that would justify its use. In Murad's case, the information he supplied was unnecessary.

> The police had also seized a huge chemical and bomb making factory, an Arabic manual for building powerful liquid bombs, dozens of fake passports, and a computer encrypted and in Arabic. When these files were decrypted, all the relevant information about the plots Murad later confessed to. They included objectives, flight schedules, and procedures, down to where to lay bombs and how to set the timer. (Rejali, 507)

Moreover, Murad seemed to be prepared to talk even without the use of torture. As Rejali explains, "It was Murad's imagination and personality, not actual torture, that got him talking, and, when he spoke, he told them what he probably concluded they already knew" (507–508).[41] Cases like this can be multiplied with ease: torture often does get persons to talk; when it does, the information uncovered is either already known or the person interrogated was already willing to talk.

One interesting and difficult case was reported in 2003 in Frankfurt, Germany. This case is often cited (much like the case of Abdul Hakim Murad) as an instance where torture works. *The Guardian* in the UK reported the story as follows:

> One morning last October [2002] . . . Wolfgang Daschner, deputy commissioner of the Frankfurt police, found himself with an agonising dilemma.
>
> His officers had arrested a man whom they were convinced was responsible for the kidnapping of 11-year-old Jakob von Metzler, son of a rich Frankfurt banker.
>
> For seven hours interrogators tried every trick in the book to get Magnus Gafgen to tell them where he was keeping the boy.
>
> Unknown to them, Jakob had already been murdered. But, as Gafgen sent the police off to search one false location after another, the fear grew that the boy's life might be slipping away in some hide-out.
>
> Mr Daschner decided that the time had come for a radical, but illegal, step. He instructed his subordinates to try to extract information "by means of the infliction of pain, under medical supervision and subject to prior warning."
>
> The warning alone proved enough. A terrified Gafgen told them where the boy was and confessed to the crime.[42]

In this case, only the *threat* of torture was used by German police officials. The threat of torture, however, counts as an instance of torture under international law (whether or not it actually is an instance of torture need not trouble us here). Does this case show that there is at least one case where torture has worked?

Once again, in the sense of 'working' we are currently using (the kind that would justify torture), the answer is no. First, the intelligence acquired from Gafgen was not actionable. It did not lead to the prevention of any harm, and in fact created complications for the prosecution of Gafgen. Certainly, finding the body of the victim was a good thing. There's no doubt of that. The aim of the threat, however, was to save the life of a child, and we cannot infer that torture would have worked to accomplish this if the conditions were different. Would Gafgen have revealed the location of the child if that child had been alive? Did Gafgen reveal the location because he had tired of the interrogation, or because he knew there was a strong case against him, or simply to avoid torture?

Of course, the threat did facilitate a confession within several hours of arrest. This poses an interesting problem, however. If Gafgen had been *innocent*, do we have reason to think that he *would not* have confessed falsely? If the use of coercion proved to be a central motivating factor for the confession, it seems to follow that his guilt was *not*, and hence that he would have confessed to the crime regardless of whether or not he had actually committed it. Moreover, there is little reason for thinking that conviction would have been unattainable without Gafgen's (deeply problematic) confession. After all, there had not been time to conduct an investigation. Likewise, Gafgen had only known for seven hours that the police were charging him with a crime. Many criminals require much more time to decide to plead guilty.

Every successful interrogation takes time. The use made of this time can be crucial to its outcome. The use of coercion has a very poor track record. Very often, procuring a confession (or intelligence) simply requires providing incentive and time to the subject being interrogated. As one 'legendary' NYPD interrogator has claimed, everyone wants to tell their story.[43] A good interrogator creates conditions where this is easy to do.[44]

> Most training materials and guides on law enforcement interrogation empha-size the need for one of the interrogators to develop rapport with the subject. Indeed, rapport is widely regarded as an essential foundation for most suc-cessful LE [law enforcement] interrogations. For example, a survey of 100 British detectives . . . found that nearly half (42%) believed that the previous interviewer's failure to establish satisfactory rapport with the suspect had con-tributed to the suspect's denial. (22)[45]

The US has had its fair share of torturous interrogations in recent years, despite having once been a champion of the UN Convention against Torture, as well as a role model to other nations. Detainees have included Abu Zubaydah, Khalid Sheikh Mohammed, Ibn al-Shaykh al-Libi, and Al-Qahtani. There is *no* evidence that any of these 'enhanced interroga-tions' produced any intelligence that was not also obtained (or easily obtainable) by other means. Of course, none of these cases demonstrate conclusively that there have been no successful cases of torture. What does seem clear, however, is that there is reason to be suspicious of any such case. Even if there are cases where torture has worked (in the sense of meeting conditions (1)–(3)), it will not be clear that it also meets con-dition (4), particularly given what we know about the history of torture.

Most trained interrogators reject the idea that force accomplishes anything that could not be accomplished in other ways. "Beyond the moral imperative, the competent interrogator avoids torture because it is counter-productive and unreliable. . . . In my two decades of experi-ence as an interrogator, I know of no competent interrogator that would resort to torture. Not one" (430).[46] This opinion is shared by "a substantial majority of law enforcement officials" (345).[47] It is also shared by experienced interrogators in the US Military. Twenty interrogators made this clear to Congress in July of 2006, claiming that

> [T]rained and experienced interrogators refute the assertion that so-called "coercive interrogation techniques" and torture are necessary to win the "War on Terror." Trained and experienced interrogators can, in fact, accomplish the intelligence gathering mission using only those techniques, developed and proven effective over decades, found in the Army Field Manual 34–52 (1992). You will also see that experienced interrogators find prisoner/detainee abuse and torture to be counter-productive to the intelligence gathering mission.[48]

In November of 2006, Jean Maria Arrigo, along with seven other psychologists and four trained interrogators, came to an identical conclusion as the result of a seminar investigating the psychological realities of torture:

> Torture interrogation does not yield reliable information. The popular belief that "torture works" conflicts with effective non-abusive methodologies of interrogation and with fundamental tenets of psychology. These were the conclusions reached at a meeting of recently retired, senior US Army interrogators and research psychologists who met to rethink the psychology of torture. (393)[49]

This is also one of the central lessons of Marine Major Sherwood F. Moran's famous report, "Suggestions for Japanese Interpreters Based on Work in the Field"[50]: force alienates the subject, and produces an incentive to remain silent. Above all, one should have "sympathetic common sense," and treat the interogatee with the respect all human beings deserve.[51] Empirical studies back this up in no uncertain terms.

> Research in both North America and in Asia (China) has shown that using coercive influence strategies causes targets (or sources, in the context of educing information) to feel disrespected, whereas persuasion strategies communicate respect . . . coercion creates a competitive dynamic that facilitates rejection of the other party's position where persuasion creates a cooperative dynamic that facilitates greater openness to the other party's position and productive conflict resolution. (25)[52]

As this indicates, torture is not simply ineffective, it actually makes things worse – not only because it produces an uncooperative dynamic, but also because it produces useless, distracting information – information that must be further investigated, and which thus can waste already limited resources.[53] Leaving this aside for the moment, do interrogators never-theless say that torture works (a claim that is central to Ignatieff's and Posner's argument for torture's effectiveness)? We've already seen some evidence that they do *not* say this.

Torture, whether hand-on or no-touch, has a poor empirical track record. Claims of 'success' cannot be verified. Instead, it appears that the claim that 'torture works' acts as an article of faith for those who endorse it. "The scientific community has never established that coercive interro-gation methods are an effective means of obtaining reliable information" (130).[54] In fact, the empirical record even suggests the opposite: "studies of the role of assault in promoting attitude change and in eliciting false confessions (even from US servicemen) revealed that it was ineffective. Belief change and compliance was more likely when physical abuse was minimal or absent" (33).[55] The most effective means of intelligence gathering, rather, involves rapport building with the interrogated, and, perhaps more importantly still, *public cooperation.*[56] As one CIA veteran noted, "what real CIA field officers know firsthand is that it is better to build a relationship of trust . . . than to extract quick confessions through tactics such as those used by the Nazis and the Soviets."[57]

Even when dealing with hostile persons, skilled interrogators contend that treating that hostile person *humanely* is a more reliable way to get crucial information. Indeed, the FBI reported gaining intelligence con-cerning Al Qaeda operations by using standard forms of interrogation with Abu Zubaydah.

> In those initial weeks of healing, before the white room and the chair and the light, Zubaydah seems to have talked freely with his captors, and during this time, according to news reports, FBI agents began to question him using "standard interview techniques," ensuring that he was bathed and his band-ages changed, urging improved medical care, and trying to "convince him they knew details of his activities." (They showed him, for example, a "box of blank audiotapes which they said contained recordings of his phone conversa-tions, but were actually empty.") According to this account, Abu Zubaydah, in the initial days before the white room, "began to provide intelligence insights into Al Qaeda."[58]

This manner of interrogation was cut off, however, by the CIA's insist-ence on the use of the new, 'enhanced' interrogation methods approved by President Bush. This was done because of a conviction that these 'enhanced' techniques would yield better intelligence – a conviction that appears groundless.

Convictions regarding the use of torture to extract information are held by many. Surprisingly, though, those holding such convictions do not usually seem to be experienced interrogators. As we have painfully learned from the actions of the United States in Iraq and Afghanistan, coercion leads to false accusations and false confessions. Indeed, such accusations were the "main source of intelligence" for the Bush administration's (false) claim that Iraq was in possession of secret weapons of mass destruction.[59] A faith in the force of torture, it appears, led a nation to war under false pretenses.

It appears that the argument offered by people like Posner and Ignatieff, then, fails to get off the ground. The problems with this argument are legion. The empirical facts are incorrect, and the inferences frankly suspect. The explanation of the continued use of torture is *not* that it has been appropriately demonstrated to be effective. In point of fact, nothing like this has happened.

Torture violates the dignity of persons

Pope Nicholas I, in 866, criticized torture as follows: "A confession must be spontaneous, not extracted by force. Will you not be ashamed if no proof emerges from the torture? Do you not recognize how iniquitous your procedure is?" (7).[60]

The thought of torturing the innocent is morally repugnant. For those who embrace the ticking bomb scenario, the violation of the dignity of the person tortured is hardly *irrelevant*. The claim, rather, is that such a violation is worth the moral cost. As we have seen, the ticking bomb case (as it is usually conceived) excludes the chance of error. When it *does not* exclude this possibility, there is some indication that there is a statistically significant difference between those willing to embrace torture and those not willing.[61]

But how do we manage to determine whether torture's use is *worth* the violation of agency (innocent or not) that it occasions? The crucial issue is whether or not we are to construe dignity as *absolutely* inviolable. This is not simply the issue of utilitarianism versus deontology – a debate that is likely worth less than is usually supposed. One might think that deontic concerns are the *usual* means of determining one's moral obligations, but also hold that our deontic obligations to particular persons can be overridden by similar obligations to *others*. The ticking bomb case might be read this way: our deontic obligations to the tortured are overridden by our deontic obligations to all of those who would otherwise be harmed.

Given this, the question of the violation of dignity in the current context need not turn on one's meta-ethical preferences. A moderate deontologist might well be able to approve of a ticking bomb case – securing and protecting the dignity of many agents exerts a greater moral obligation than protecting only one. The issue, rather, is whether or not we should view the dignity of agents as something that can, under *no* circumstances, be violated. This question is essentially the question of the ticking bomb case.[62]

The view that there are no exceptions to the respect for human dignity is a hotly contested one. It is also one, I think, for which it is difficult to produce persuasive, principled arguments. This is not because the view is *false*, but because it seems, in most instances, to mark a bedrock belief about the nature of morality. Persons can and do produce arguments in favor of this bedrock position, but these arguments seem no more certain than the principle they aim to support. In speaking about the inviolability of human dignity, many resort to the attempt to paint a picture of human dignity that might sway those with doubts.[63]

This problem is not unique to the deontological notion of dignity. In fact, it is a problem with every basic moral principle. Why are pleasure and happiness supposed to weigh more than everything else? Why are the consequences of an action given such weight? Why does my own character matter more than other things? Why is rationality the measure of morality? Why are my emotions to be weighed more than my reasons? In my view, there are no easy arguments to be had in favor of any of these particular views. To be clear: there *are* arguments to be had, but the arguments often serve only to restate the very thing one is attempting to demonstrate. When they do not do this, these arguments are often far more dubious than the principles themselves.

The appeal to dignity, however, does have a certain phenomenological force that appeals to other kinds of principles do not – or, more carefully, that they do not so obviously have. The idea of human dignity as inviolable has been captured by appeals to hearing the demands made on us by the moral law (Kant), by recognizing the 'face' of the Other as commanding us not to kill (Levinas), by appreciating the unique capacities of the human animal – the capacities which separate her from other animals (Aristotle, Plato, Marx). Despite all of these appeals, however, there is still room for doubt. One can still question whether or not dignity – despite all that it's worth – might admit of exceptions.

There are two dominant strategies that have been used to try to establish dignity, neither of which has been entirely successful. Both of these, perhaps not surprisingly, can be found in Kant. The first strategy[64] is the most recognizably Kantian: as agents, we must ('must' is here a logical notion) respect the capacities that allow us to pursue our individual wants and desires. A main capacity we have is to be autonomous. In respecting our autonomy and agency as something that we would not trade for anything, we also recognize that others possess this same capacity. By force of logic, we thus find that a commitment to our own agency requires us to be committed to the agency of others. Thus, from the recognition of our own dignity, we are drawn forcibly to the recognition of the dignity of others.

This argument has plenty of problems, and I won't defend it here.[65] I cite it only as one strategy used to defend the inviolability of agency. As is obvious, someone who does not already accept the conclusion of the argument is not likely to accept its premises. In this respect, the argument is fundamentally circular – something which is hardly surprising.

The second strategy for defending the inviolability of agency is a more straightforwardly phenomenological one. This, too, can be found in Kant's work. In his *Groundwork*, Kant claims that three central propositions constitute moral rationality: that an action must be done from duty to have moral worth,[66] that the moral worth of an action can be determined by its maxim,[67] and that "duty is the necessity of an action from respect for law."[68] An interesting feature of this third proposition, which Kant claims follows from the first two, is that it makes a direct appeal to our ability to *recognize* what demands are made on us by others. The very idea of duty, then, is linked to our recognition of those things that can legitimately ask something of us – namely, other human beings. On this view, the very idea and underlying logic of morality involves the recognition of the inviolability of human agency.

In one respect, this claim is simply question-begging: the claim amounts to saying that if you don't see the value of agency you are simply not seeing clearly. This is hardly an argument – but it is also not something to be dismissed out of hand. The idea of 'moral perception' might well have a place in our deliberations about morality that's just as important as any appeal to reason or freedom. If it is true that morality requires a recognition of those things that are the *locus* of morality (in Kant's thinking, this would be the human agent), which seems like a defensible point, *and* it is true that recognition is not strictly speaking a matter of applying rationality (also a defensible point), it would seem to follow that *any* defense of morality must ultimately have recourse to something other than argument – to a sort of 'moral primitive' that grounds and constitutes our moral deliberations. In this respect, the second strategy can be seen as akin to a transcendental argument rather than as a textbook case of question-begging: a recognition of the worth of human dignity is a condition for the possibility of moral thinking. Hence, to fail to recognize this dignity is to fail to think morally at all (one might nevertheless be reasoning *prudentially*, Kant acknowledges).[69]

As with the previous strategy, this one won't likely convince anyone who is not already leaning toward the inviolability of dignity. After all, one might contend, sacrificing some human beings might *also* involve a recognition of the worth of dignity – namely, of those to be saved by the sacrifice of one.

While I accept the inviolability of human dignity – and admit to being a moral absolutist in this sense – I also admit that no argument is likely to bring one from the opposite position to this one. It is far more likely that literature, art, and film might perform such a function: by particularizing human beings in living contexts, we can see the respect they are owed, and through this perception we can come to understand the phenomenological force of the 'face' of the Other (as Levinas would put it) – of the powerful commands others are entitled to make on us to respect them.[70]

Given the problematical nature of the appeal to dignity, then, I will confess that I do not think arguments stemming from this appeal have much chance of convincing persons who advocate torture. In my (not argued for) view, the advocacy of torture constitutes a failure of moral sight – and arguments are not designed to correct these kinds of failure.[71] Nevertheless, there are three points that need to be made here: first, something like a recognition of human dignity has become the hallmark of international law. It is the basis of the Universal Declaration of Human Rights, the Geneva Accords, and many other treaties besides. So, despite not being able to produce a free-standing proof of the inviolability of dignity, it seems to be a widely accepted notion. Second, the prior recognition of human dignity is able to explain the moral repugnance felt by those who witness torture, as well as among those who have learned of its use. Third, torture in the modern world seems to be coupled with the prior dehumanization of the subjects to be tortured – and this in fact is often part of the training would-be torturers undergo when learning their craft (see Chapter 7: *Situational variables that increase the likelihood of torture*). All of these things are evidence in favor of an antecedent recognition of the value of human dignity – and such widespread recognition, while hardly a proof of torture's unconditional wrongness, does provide some evidence for it.

Frequently in the literature on torture, the assault to dignity discussed involves only the dignity of the person tortured. Before leaving appeals to dignity behind, this is a misperception that ought to be corrected. To claim that torture only violates the dignity of the person tortured is to misunderstand the social nature of torture as a violation on *humanity* as such, as well as of the particular racial and ethnic dimensions of those who undergo torture. In his powerful indictment of torture in all its forms, Richard Matthews explodes the myth that damage is only done to *the person who is tortured*: "the individual is separated from the community and isolated. But the reverse holds as well. The community is separated and isolated from the individual. Both are thereby harmed" (51). Moreover, the family of those tortured undergo "parallel experiences" to the torture victim: "psychological terror and suffering on the part of the family; stress for the family as a result of the suffering inflicted on their loved one; confusion, anger, emotional isolation; difficulties in maintaining healthy relationships" (55). Torture involves the attempt to destroy a person's identity, and hence involves (at least a symbolic) violence against the constituent parts of this identity: one's gender, ethnicity, religion, and so on. In this respect, Matthews argues, torture is "simultaneously an assault on the entire culture" (57).

In certain respects, engaging in torture also damages the dignity of the person who tortures. As John Perry has argued. "part of the evil of the system of torture is what it does to the torturers. The torturer, too, undergoes a moral violation if he conceives of his victim as being without human dignity" (83).[72] As we will see (Chapter 7: *Damaged agency: the effects of torture on the torturer*), this same point has been made by those who have *inflicted* torture. They are often broken by what they have done, reduced from human agent to traumatized animal.

The assault on dignity found in torture does not end with the individual who is tortured. Indeed, as in a hate crime, the individual *as such* is merely the vehicle through which a larger population is assaulted. This feature of torture is one that is all too easy to ignore. The assault in torture arguably includes a racism and sexism that extends the damage of torture to an entire population – including the persons who are responsible for administering torture.

Consequentialist arguments against torture policy

The thought that torture, as a policy, can be carefully monitored – that it might operate, for example, through a system of warrants – strikes many as a devastatingly naïve idea. Torture tends to excess. Seeing why this is so will do much to demonstrate why the occasional proposals for the legalization of torture (with judicial oversight) are not well-founded. The view that the legalization of torture is the avenue nations ought to pursue has most famously been defended by Harvard Law Professor Alan Dershowitz:

> if torture is being or will be practiced, is it worse to close our eyes to it and tolerate its use by low-level law enforcement officials without accountability, or instead to bring it to the surface by requiring that a warrant of some kind be required as a precondition to the infliction of any type of torture under any circumstances? (257)[73]

The responses to Dershowitz's claim (here couched in a rhetorical question) have been extensive. Elsewhere, I have argued at length that Dershowitz's arguments are inadequate, and that he invents data where he ought to examine it.[74] Despite this critique, I have no doubt that Dershowitz has the best intentions in offering this sea change in policy. What requires our consideration here, however, is not what particular intentions lead to a proposal for a legalized torture policy; we are interested rather in whether or not there are good arguments *against* such views.

Torture cannot be controlled

The presupposition present in those who advocate legalized torture (such as Dershowitz) is that torture can be controlled, regulated, and effectively administered. This is precisely what Dershowitz believes can be accomplished through a policy requiring warrants: the "goal [of the advocacy of torture warrants] was, and remains, to reduce the use of torture to the smallest amount and degree possible, while creating public accountability for its rare use" (TR, 259).

Darius Rejali has forcefully called the assumptions underlying this view into question. As Rejali claims, "legalizing torture makes rogue operations inevitable, and one is likely to learn even less [about torture]" (529). By way of explanation, Rejali writes that "civil servants cannot exercise selective control once they have licensed armed men to exercise unlimited power over individuals" (529). Seeing why this is the case is important to understanding why the defense of torture as policy cannot work.

The strongest version of the view that torture will inevitably get out of control has been made by Richard Matthews. He puts the point as follows:

> It is not a risk but is inevitable. Torture attacks identity, and identity is social. When states torture, they attack not individuals but groups and communities . . . state torture is one tactic in a coercive assault on some community . . . [the harm of torture] spreads out across these entire groups in complicated ways. This spreading is intrinsic to torture and cannot be avoided. (202)

In my view, Matthews has not yet provided enough argument to support the claim of inevitability. Many will find it difficult to believe that any act of torture will inevitably produce multiple acts of torture. One only possible argument for this view might go as follows: torture is a practice. As such, anything that is to count as 'torture' must be built into particular institutions. If torture requires institutions, though, there cannot be a solitary act of torture (in much the way that one person cannot follow a rule only once).[75]

The problem with this argument, I think, is fairly obvious: it appeals to what look like *a priori* considerations to justify what must, in the end, be an empirical claim. It is true that state-run torture will *likely* get out of control – and it is presumably this kind of torture that Matthews has in mind in the above passage. But is it obvious that we cannot construct a counter-example? We need only imagine a state-sponsored torture program that is terminated almost immediately after its inception, and hence is not given enough time to get out of control. Insisting that this is not a case of torture (or state sponsored torture) seems dangerously like letting one's *a priori* commitments guide one's empirical findings.

At best, this points to the need for some additional elaboration about the kind of 'necessity' being appealed to in the above claim, and perhaps a comment on how empirical claims can involve necessity. At worst, the objection points to the need for Matthews to weaken his claim somewhat – to say that we are justified in thinking that state-sponsored torture is not controllable, rather than to say that loss of control is inevitable.[76] Moreover, there is empirical evidence for the weaker claim. Eitan Felner makes this point explicitly. "The Israeli case categorically proves the fallacy of believing – as some influential American opinion-makers do today – that it is possible to legitimize the use of torture to thwart terrorist attacks and at the same time restrict its use to exceptional cases" (29).[77]

There are multiple levels on which torture tends toward excess. Excess emerges at the hands of torturers, to be sure, but also at the level of the institutions that support the use of torture. Both modes of escalation beyond control are of immediate relevance in considering why torture as policy cannot accomplish its task – a task that endeavors to construct a rational, controlled extraction of information through the use of coercive techniques where no excess force is utilized by the agents engaging in the techniques.

Let us begin at the level of the torturer. Rejali (among others) has made a compelling case that torture at this level will not be exerted only at the most minimal level. The reason for this is *not* that torturers are particularly sadistic, or that they fail to have the appropriate amount of self-control. Torturers are seldom (if ever) sadists, and they are typically chosen because of their meritorious ability to maintain rational control over their emotional impulses.[78] The reason that control is lost at the level of the individual has to do with the *nature of torture itself*.

As we have seen, there is remarkable variability in the experience of pain from one individual to the next. The techniques for the infliction of pain cannot be trusted to apply uniformly across individuals. Some individuals will be able to tolerate a particular torment at a much higher level than others. These same individuals might also have a much lower tolerance for other forms of torture. The result of this, understandably enough, is that torturers tend to do two things in engaging in torture: First, they very quickly aim at high levels of pain (as they cannot know in advance what level of pain a person will be able to endure). Second, torturers engage in what Rejali calls a 'scattershot approach' (450). They try a variety of pain-inducing procedures in an effort to find what sorts of techniques will be most effective for a particular individual.

In addition to these features of torture as it is practiced, and indeed, as a result of these features, torturers "encounter three limits that neither they, nor the prisoner, can anticipate: death, unconsciousness, and physical danger" (450). The idea of the torturer exerting full restraint, and in total control of the situation, leads naturally to unanticipated results that are outside the realm of control. Is it possible to avoid such results? That seems unlikely, at least if we are honest about the way torture actually works.

> Maximal pain, scattershot approaches, inadvertent death, the delays inflicted by unconsciousness and physical damage are not accidental features of torture. They follow inevitably from rational responses to the realities of pain. Once the torture session starts, it necessarily devolves into an unrestrained hit-or-miss affair. (451)

Even a 'professional,' in the best sense of that word, cannot help but find himself going beyond what is actually required – sometimes with deadly results.

But there is reason to think that the term 'professional' can be used only loosely here. In the work of the torturer, the work itself tends toward escalation: regulations get ignored, and brutality increases with regularity. Indeed, escalation is in the very nature of torture. Rejali, once again, makes this point with clarity: "To think professionalism is a guard against causing excessive pain is an illusion. Instead torture breaks down professionalism. Professionals become less disciplined, more brutal, and less skilled while their organizations become more fragmented and corrupt" (454).

There is yet another respect in which, at the institutional level, torture tends to move outside the realm of control. This is not, perhaps, a *necessary* consequence of institutionalized torture. It is, however, a predictable one. As Ronald Crelinsten puts the point:

> Like many organizations, police or military units charged with 'protecting national security' must justify their expenditures, their manpower, their capital equipment. If the real world does not cooperate in supplying sufficient threats to national security, the definition of such threats is widened to maintain the supply of 'material.' (147)[79]

All of these demonstrate that the nature of torture is to *escalate* – that torture inherently *transgresses limits*.[80] We have seen this played out again and again in the use of torturous tactics at the level of policy. As Andrew Sullivan points out,

> What the hundreds of abuse and torture incidents have shown is that, once you permit torture for someone somewhere, it has a habit of spreading . Remember that torture was originally sanctioned in administration memos only for use against illegal combatants in rare cases. Within months of that decision, abuse and torture had become endemic throughout Iraq . . . what was originally supposed to be safe, sanctioned, and rare became endemic, disorganized and

brutal. The lesson is that it is impossible to quarantine torture in a hermetic box; it will inevitably contaminate the military as a whole. Once you have declared that some enemies are subhuman, you have told every soldier that every potential detainee he comes across might be exactly that kind of prisoner – and that anything can therefore be done to him . . . The only way to control torture is to ban it outright. Everywhere. Even then, in wartime, some 'bad apples' will always commit abuse. But at least we will have done all we can to constrain it. (323–324)[81]

To permit torture, then, is to permit what simply cannot be controlled. Leaving aside the training required for torturers (which we will consider in more detail in Chapter 7: *Becoming a torturer*), permitting torture also undermines the very skills that make torture, ultimately, unnecessary.

Undermines investigative skill

There are many consequences to the systematic use of torture. One that is seldom noted, however, is the way that the use of torture can actually undermine other investigative techniques. (It is likely that this is seldom noted because it is, at least *prima facie*, one of the lesser evils associated with torture). There are two significant problems with this phenomenon. First, the ability to detain and arrest criminals deteriorates as investigators increasingly rely on torture. Conviction rates rise in tandem with false arrests and coerced confessions. More innocent persons are imprisoned (or otherwise punished), while more of the guilty go free.

Secondly, and related to the first point, is that the reliance on torture by police investigators undermines the classical skills of solid detective work. The need to canvas a neighborhood, search out and analyze evidence, and so forth, is eclipsed by what can only be regarded as an easy way out: torturing is simply a quicker way to gain a conviction. "Lazy or overzealous police take advantage of a climate where judges and prosecutors look the other way when torture has clearly been used" (80).[82] With this, the culture of professional police work erodes as the presence and presumed 'need' for torture increases. Both of these consequences can be seen in particular cases – in the case of Japan, for example.[83] Summing up this problem in *Torture and Democracy*, Rejali writes:

> Coercive interrogation undermines other professional policing skills: Why do fingerprinting when you've got a bat? It is simply easier to turn to torture than to do the hard, time-consuming work of surveillance, interviewing, verification, and intelligence analysis . . .
>
> This phenomenon is not a new discovery. Investigators, judges, and secret services have know police torture leads to police de-skilling from decades of investigations . . . As professional skills decay, police rely more on interrogation to get information and, with it, increasing brutality. Torture is a shortcut

that soon becomes a well-travelled road. This creates 'a vicious cycle' in which the investigators are progressively deskilled. (456–457)

De-skilling, as a consequence of the systematic use of torture, thus leads with some regularity to more torture. This consequence results regardless of whether or not the policy permitting torture is officially sanctioned or unofficially ignored. This would not be a problem, perhaps, if torture actually worked. As we have seen, however, tortured is not something that can be relied upon.

Damages reputation of state and trust of citizens

It is hardly surprising that the trust of the person is eviscerated by the experience of torture. This evisceration is not simply a rational response to betrayal – the loss far exceeds such an understandable result. Jose Padilla, following his torture at the hands of US officials, for example, was fundamentally changed. According to an analysis based on the testimony of Mr. Padilla's lawyers, he

> has become profoundly suspicious, paranoid at times . . . His grimacing and eye blinking, often accompanied by a strange, tense spreading of his lips as though in an attempt to smile, has an eerie, psychotic feel to it . . . his presentation suggests not simply a reaction to fear and trauma, but really a disorganizing, psychotic reaction. (124)[84]

Mary R. Fabri, director of Marjorie Kovler Center for the Treatment of Survivors of Torture, remarks that "the destructive effect of torture on the human psyche and physique also undermines the moral fiber of a society – which must bear responsibility for what it has purportedly inflicted on its fellow human beings" (131).[85] The responsibility in question, of course, is not simply that one has inflicted unnecessary pain on another. The responsibility is for the violation of the dignity of persons – a dignity that is often claimed to be the very *meaning* of civilization. In this, the trust of the person tortured is utterly annihilated – but the loss of trust does not end here either. As it turns out, this is entirely predictable based on the effect torture has on the brain:

> Findings suggest that torture, like any other massive experience, dramatically alters the functional organization of the brain: an enlarged fear network is activated not only by trauma-related, but generally by highly arousing aversive cues. Similar to what is known from the neuroimaging studies with PTSD patients, the present data suggest that the medial and orbito-frontal cortical structures lose their ability to regulate the hyperresponsive fear structures, thus providing evidence for a dysfunctional interplay between amygdale and frontal cortex in the traumatized brain. (183–184)[86]

The negative effects of torture do not end with the paranoia of the victim – they expand to the very institutions that house and perpetuate it. Torture "leads to organizational decay; torturers tend to disobey orders and regulations" (500).[87] The tendency of torture to gravitate towards excess, and to stray across boundaries, coupled with a decreased ability to gather information effectively, ultimately aids in the destruction of a public trust already eroded by the ability to suspend the rule of law. Public cooperation is crucial to any intelligence operations. Such cooperation requires willingness on the part of the public to share information and to aid the authorities in apprehending those who act against the public interest. In a regime that tortures the very persons from whom it needs help – and this will likely happen, given the many respects in which torture cannot be controlled – the trust which cooperation requires is utterly destroyed, and with it the ability to cultivate informants.[88]

The damage to the reputation of a state caused by torture thus has at least three dimensions: first, the nation that employs torture loses moral standing in international relations. I don't presume that the exact effects of this can be predicted, but certainly it might manifest itself in increasingly difficult international relations, and difficulty in exerting influence over the operations of other nations over time. Second, the nation that employs torture loses the trust of those it tortures. Admittedly, of course, there are cases that do not follow this pattern. In some instances, such as in the case of Jose Padilla, a certain *trust* emerges from being tortured, and this trust is for the very people who are responsible for the torturing to begin with. The condition, known as Stockholm Syndrome, should not be taken as evidence of the maintenance of trust after torture. It is best regarded as a coping method to a profound *loss of trust* that occurs with 'the first blow.' Moreover, as in the case of Padilla, this trust in the administration that ordered torture was accompanied by a significant distrust of everyone else. This is a common response to torture: one loses trust, not only in the torturers, but in everyone encountered.

Third, trust is eroded even among those who do not undergo torture. The presumption that one has rights under the law – indeed, the very idea of the rule of law – is called into question by those this law does not protect. As Carlos Castresana argues, "torture affects the basic pillars of the legal structure of democratic States, its very essence . . . [accepting torture] compromises the safety and threatens the collapse of our whole legal system" (136).[89] Even if not literally true, this point has phenomenological relevance: citizens of a state where torture is permitted often *regard that state* as having little concern with human rights or humanitarian law. The damage done to the reputation of a government that tortures can take years to repair. And the negative consequences of this should not be underestimated: the reputation of a nation has much to do with its ability to influence the policies of other nations, as well as in international relations.

The trust lost on the part of citizens need not be limited to the government. Given the number of institutions involved in torture, torture, and those complicit in it, can fundamentally damage our ability to put our lives in the hands of any institution involved – the military, psychology, and medicine. As Steven Miles has shown, complicity in torture on the part of the medical profession has been extensive.[90] Miles documents the role of medical personnel in recent acts of human rights abuse – predominantly those abuses that have been carried out under the banner of military operations for the United States. Shocking events, such as the government classifying only "two of twenty-three self-hangings as attempted suicides" (105), are revealed for what they are: medical complicity in cover-up. Insofar as human rights abuses go unreported, or are facilitated, by medical personnel, these personnel have perpetuated the use of torture, and damaged whatever moral authority the medical profession might have. The silence of top medical personnel, in Miles' verdict, is "inexplicable and inexcusable" (152). Moreover, a "medical examiner who allows a false official statement that a homicide is death by natural causes to stand for months or years is arguably an accessory after the fact if that delay obstructs the apprehension, trial, or punishment of an assailant" (88). In the case of Abu Ghraib, medical personnel have violated their supreme responsibility: "The responsibility for prisoners' health and the healthfulness of their living conditions [which] falls squarely on medical personnel" (116).[91]

As Miles conclusively demonstrates, medical personnel were deeply involved in the 'torture lite' that occurred under the supervision of the American military: medical personnel monitored 'patients' to insure they could be tortured without dying; they used prior medical knowledge to devise torments for particular prisoners; and they used their expertise to cover-up evidence of torture, both on paper and on the bodies of those who were its victims. As Miles succinctly puts it, "[t]orturers need medical accomplices to keep prisoners alive as trauma is inflicted, to predict how severely detainees can be twisted, and to see that torture evaporates, leaving behind neither scars nor documentation" (167).

Miles' analysis is primarily about the US torture that has been carried out in recent years. This is hardly an exceptional occurrence. As Crelinsten and Schmid have noted,

> we find academics in the industrial, medical and psychological professions, *inventing and refining repression technology* which is exported to regimes using torture for social control. In 1984, for example, the US Commerce Department granted export licenses for 'specially designed implements of torture'. (3)[92]

We are not as far from the Nazi doctors as we would like to think.[93] As we continue to learn of these violations, our trust in the medical profession will surely erode.[94]

But even this is not the end of the damages caused by the use of torture. Jean Amery's account of his own torture, as we have seen, highlights the loss of trust that accompanies being subjected to this cruel practice.[95] Commenting on this feature of torture, Claudia Card distinguishes trust from trustworthiness, and argues that the erosion of trustworthiness can be even more destructive than the damage of trust:

> Empirical arguments that highlight torture's ineffectiveness and uncontainability should no doubt suffice to persuade even political realists that torture is ultimately not realistic. Yet those arguments skirt the moral heart of the matter. The best philosophical arguments highlight the betrayal of humanity in both tortured and torturer. Amery refers to the destruction of 'basic trust in the world.' Even if actual trust is not destroyed, torture may destroy trust*wor-thiness* in both tortured and torturer. Whether or not it does that it is at least partly an empirical matter (what does torture actually do?) and partly a philosophical one (what makes an agent worthy of trust?). But loss of trustworthiness is a cost that would negate the hoped-for gain of protecting a society or saving lives. It would mean the risk of letting some guilty (suspects who really are withholding vital information) go free, out of an insistence on standards of high evidence, *is* the cost worth bearing. For where is the value in a society or a life in which trustworthiness is lost? How could a nation defended by torture – *especially* so-called 'one-off' torture – be worthy of the trust of its citizens? What clandestine or hypocritical practices would such a government *not* be prepared to support in the name of self-defense? (13–14)[96]

In Card's view, engaging in torture – or even having leaders *willing* to engage in torture in rare cases – would damage our ability to find the citizens of our nation trustworthy. This, in turn, would significantly minimize the value of our society as well as the life we might live in it. Living under a regime that tortures – particularly when that regime tortures *its own citizens* – has devastating psychological effects. One need only think of those who lived in Soviet Russia under Stalin's purges, under Mao's cultural revolution, in Argentina's 'dirty war,' the Greek junta, the Brazilian torture and murder squads, or under Pol Pot's oppressive, genocidal regime. One can also look to the reaction of the French when the torture practices of the French-Algerian war came to light, or of the United States when the pictures of Abu Ghraib were released by the media. In all of these cases, the presence of torture sponsored by a nation – whether against its citizens or its enemies – stirred strong emotions in the public, even in those cases where expressing these emotions would have assured execution.

It is more difficult to see how having a leader willing to get her hands dirty by ordering torture would have the same effect on the quality of life in a nation. The mood after Truman's decision to use nuclear force on thousands of civilian Japanese was one of elation – it meant the end of the war, and a massive amount of American lives saved (at least arguably). Could we not imagine a similar reaction after the discovery of an instance of torture that had similar effects?

I think we could imagine such a reaction – but I nevertheless think Card's point stands. It *would* be an act of imagination, and no more. If it were announced tomorrow that a leader had authorized torture to avert a major threat, this announcement would be met with massive skepticism. Indeed, this is precisely what *has* happened in the United States in the recent past. Both (former) President George W. Bush and (former) Vice President Dick Cheney have made such announcements (or close enough[97]), and their claims have been met with disbelief. The absence of trust we have for our politicians, I would suggest, has been the result of many previous instances of legal exceptionalism – of politicians breaking the law in order to serve particular (perceived) interests, sometimes personal, and sometimes national. This has created a climate in which we simply do not trust what we are told. We expect the worst from our leaders.

It is not my charge to prove this point. This is only one possible explanation, after all. The more pressing issue is whether or not this helps us understand Card's central claim above: namely, that the loss of trustworthiness in one another and in our leaders would diminish our overall quality of life, and even call into question the value of our national identity. The answer to this, I think, is clear enough: our contentedness with politics in whatever nation we call home is affected by our ability to trust our leaders. Of course, this does not entail that we *ought* to trust our leaders. We might be better off, all things considered, to maintain an attitude of skepticism – if only because such skepticism demands a certain amount of transparency in political decision making. Nevertheless, I think it *is* fair to say that our lives *would* be enhanced if we had every reason to trust the actions of our military and those who command them. This, of course, is compatible with the sort of skepticism that asks for consistently transparent decision-making practices.

The next question is whether or not allowing torture, even only exceptionally, would increase or decrease the reasons we have to place trust in our government. Once again, I do not think much argument is required here: *any* decision that is made in secret that violates our treaty obligations, our domestic laws, and our values, and which becomes public, does incredible damage to the faith we are willing to put in those who lead us – and it is *very* difficult, particularly in constitutional democracies, to keep such things secret.[98] I thus think there is reason to accept

Card's claims – even when applied to the ticking bomb case: torture damages our trust in our nation, and this damage needs to be included in any consequentialist reasoning about the use of torture.

We shouldn't exaggerate the force of this point, though. If we have a case of torture that saved thousands, it might well be worth the cost to engage in that torture. This is not something that can be determined *a priori*. It seems unlikely that the sort of loss of trustworthiness of our leadership that such an event would occasion would *outweigh* the benefit of saving perhaps thousands of lives.

Card seems to suggest (at least on first reading) that the cost of loss of trustworthiness alone would not be worth engaging in even one instance of torture. I remain unconvinced on this point. In one respect, though, this is irrelevant. Torture does not occur in a controlled environment. There would not be *only one* consequence. Perhaps the other consequences of engaging in torture would be the result of a loss of trustworthiness, or perhaps Card is folding other consequences under this heading. Whatever the case may be, the sum total of negative consequences that would occasion *either* torture as policy or torture in the ticking bomb case speaks strongly against it.[99]

Additional issues with torture warrants and ticking bombs

Card's point that a society that allows torture would allow *anything*,[100] and hence would not be worthy of our trust, is a compelling one. It also suggests an independent argument against *any* justification of torture – and one that has been employed by a number of different people.[101] This *reductio* argument is captured by William F. Schulz in *Tainted Legacy: 9/11 and the Ruin of Human Rights* in discussing Alan Dershowitz's proposal for the use of torture warrants:

> Why ought correctional officers who argue that allowing dominant male prisoners to rape other prisoners helps preserve order among thugs and thus protects the lives of guards – why ought such officers not be allowed to seek 'warrants to tolerate prisoner rape' in particularly dangerous situations? The answer in all the cases is the same: because the act itself (brutalizing citizens, committing perjury, facilitating rape) is itself abhorrent and illegal. (265, *Phenomenon of Torture*)

Our abhorrence at the above suggestion represents our abhorrence regarding rape. The abhorrence is justified. If, however, we were to accept the idea of torture warrants (or the use of torture as a policy in other forms), the same logic would compel us to accept things like rape warrants, slavery warrants, and so on. The very idea of permissibility

– exceptional or not – is what is under investigation here. If there is *anything at all* that one regards as *absolutely* prohibited, then one has reason to reject the proposal for torture warrants, given that cases might be constructed (fictional or not) that would justify the prohibited action under certain circumstances.

The same basic *reductio* argument applies to the ticking bomb scenario. This *reductio* works, if it does, by noting that the logic of a ticking bomb case can work to justify *anything* at all, no matter how horrific. In this respect, the real force of the argument (as an intuition pump) is to determine whether or not we intuitively accept the idea of moral absolutes. I have already criticized this thought experiment in many ways. In the current context, there are two additional points I want to make: first, the thought experiment is not actually about torture. Second, we should worry that implicit racism and sexism might exist within the thought experiment, and color both its use and the responses people make to it.

There is nothing about the ticking bomb case that connects it to torture *uniquely.* If it works, it can justify *anything* at all, no matter how horrific. In this respect, the real force of the argument (as an intuition pump) is to determine whether or not we intuitively accept the idea of moral absolutes.

The ticking bomb argument is thus only *apparently* about torture. One can plug in any action to get the same results: if x will save thousands of people, x is permissible. In essence, if one accepts this kind of reasoning as intuitive, this *demonstrates that one has the intuition that any moral prohibition can be overridden.*

Of course, if one could demonstrate that there are absolutely no moral absolutes, it would of course follow that torture would be acceptable under certain circumstances (*any* action would be acceptable under certain circumstances, on this view). I do not claim to have offered a definitive refutation of this view. It might very well be true. But the primary point here is this one: the ticking bomb case only tests for intuitions about *this* particular question; it is not specific enough to be *about* torture. It might as well be about the permissibility of necrophilia, child molestation, or anything else.

But there is a deeper problem with the use of the ticking bomb case, and this concerns the immediate associations we bring to bear on thinking through the question of moral absolutes. In the torture case, there is evidence to suggest that we associate the terrorist with particular ethnic, religious, and racial stereotypes. For Americans, there is reason to suspect that we imagine the Middle Eastern extremist who wants us dead, and who would kill our families if he had the chance. Implicit racism and xenophobia work against us here, making the torture case – particularly after 9/11 – a bad measure of whether or not we accept that there are moral absolutes. Our insistence that we are *not* prejudiced by the way that we imagine the terrorist (Muslim, male, violent, oppressive, murderous, *other*) offers no real assurance that our thinking about a racialized terrorist has no effect on our intuitions.

> In the aftermath of 9/11, the figure of the 'terrorist' mobilizes collective fear in ways that recapitulate and consolidate previous ideologies of the national enemy. Yes. The terrorist is the contemporary enemy. The rhetoric, the attendant anxieties, and the diversionary strategies produced by the deployment of the figure of the terrorist are very similar to, and rely in very concrete ways on, the production of the [racialized] criminal as pervasive threat. (119)[102]

It thus seems to me that better tests of our intuitions regarding the existence of moral absolutes – if only to offer a control – would involve members of our own ethnic group. In addition, given the severity of the wrongness of torture – documented nearly endlessly – we ought to imagine the worst thing we can and ask when, if ever, engaging in that particular action might be justified. Is it morally permissible, for example, to rape and beat newborn babies in order to stop the ticking bomb?

One might object that newborn babies do not share the guilt of the terrorist in the ticking bomb case. This is a fair point, but its relevance is difficult to see, at least if what matters here is not hiding behind our own moral frailty (as many defenders of torture, such as Charles Krauthammer, claim). If we engage in torture because it is the *lesser* of two evils – and not because it is an acceptable thing to do – then it seems to be irrelevant whether or not the victim of torture is innocent. Torturing *anyone* is wrong, though we might concede that it is *more* wrong to torture the innocent. Is it so wrong to rape and beat the innocent baby that we should let thousands die? I hasten to remind the reader that persistent beating and raping *are techniques of torture*, and have been dubbed so by the International Criminal Court.[103]

Another peculiarity about an appeal to innocence regards what looks like a presupposition in such cases: namely, that torture should be *deserved* if it is to be carried out. Those who are guilty of certain crimes *did something* to be tortured, while the baby did not. Once again, the relevance of this is difficult to see. While it is true that engaging in crimes entails that we give up certain rights (the right to live outside of prison, for example), we *do not* regard the commission of crimes as sufficient to extinguish all rights. Even for those who think one can give up the right to life, no one thinks that it is acceptable to treat those on death row as 'rape dolls', or to force them to eat feces, or to have no right whatsoever to do with their property what they will after they have been executed. Indeed, it is a hallmark of law that certain things *cannot be done*. If we admit such limitations to law, it seems peculiar to make the guilt of a potential torture victim relevant to whether or not that person should be tortured. Indeed, such considerations seem likely motivated by the rather nasty need for revenge against those who violate our laws.

I thus think that the appeal to innocence is irrelevant to the current issue. That issue, of course, is whether or not there are absolute moral prohibitions. For those who say they would rape and beat a newborn in order to save, say, one thousand lives – and there are certainly some who would – I would pose some questions: how can you be sure you could bring yourself to do it? If you could not bring yourself to do it (which is, I hope, very likely), would you still contend that it is the right thing to do, and that you were simply too weak to carry it out? Would you then be willing to train yourself to be able to do it? To learn, systematically, to dehumanize babies (and everyone else) in the event that such a case emerged?

If the response to any of this involves an appeal to one's weakness in carrying out what one regards to be one's duty, it reeks of a certain 'don't be a sissy' mentality that has no place in moral deliberations. Indeed, such thinking is sexist to its core. The bravest thing to do might well be to allow one thousand people to die. As Rejali argues, "The conception of masculinity that informs the judgment, 'Yes, I would torture,' is based on deep doubts about the life one is living, about the values one is allegedly defending through torture, and ultimately, about one's own masculinity" (178).[104]

There are two general points I want to make about the case just described. First, I want to suggest something about the nature of our moral commitments that might seem (initially, at least) somewhat counter-intuitive. My suggestion is this: Our willingness to *assert* that something is the right thing to do might well be less important than what we *are* willing *to do;* what we are willing to do can *sometimes* reveal more about our moral commitments than any sentence we might utter. If this is correct, our visceral response to the above case is an important part of our assessment of its significance. Perhaps we *do not* have this visceral response to the terrorist in the ticking bomb case because of certain prejudices that sneak into the thought experiment – prejudices about race, ethnicity, and masculinity, and which stem from a residual hatred of those with whom we cannot identify. If our intuitions in this case are guided by such pre-conceptions, we would do best to set these intuitions aside.

The second point I want to make here is that, even if one would assent to the case above (having no particular visceral reaction), or if one rejects the view that our immediate moral reactions *matter* to our moral deliberations (which is not to say they are always definitive), then it seems one is committed to the view that the very idea of moral absolutes is problematic. And perhaps it is. But demonstrating this *is not the same* as demonstrating that torture is permissible.

How much evidence is there for the view that racist associations inform our thinking about the ticking bomb? In contemporary academic discourse surrounding torture, of course, such views are by no means explicitly expressed – but that does not mean such views aren't present, nor does it mean that we shouldn't worry about such views. The tone of the torture debate, as it has played out in the public sphere, may well infiltrate even the most high-minded thinking.

In the media, racism against Muslims has gone unchecked, and has been promulgated both implicitly and explicitly. On the explicit side of things, we have remarks from those on the far-right like Ann Coulter, who claimed that "we should invade [Arab and Muslim] countries, kill their leaders and convert them to Christianity."[105] Likewise, Michael Savage has claimed that "Arabs aren't really human and most Americans would just like to drop a nuclear bomb on them anyway."[106] These are hardly exceptional cases, even if they are generated by TV. Members of Congress have made claims just as extreme. In one instance, Texas Congressman Sam Johnson (R-TX) volunteered to drop nuclear weapons on Syria (this was at a church gathering!).[107] Tom Tancredo (R-CO) advocated (in 2005) a pre-emptive nuclear attack on Mecca. Reverend Jerry Falwell claimed that Mohammed was a terrorist on multiple occasions.[108] Reverend Pat Robertson, on CNN in 2002, said what amounted to the same thing.[109]

The expression of such views only represented an already felt prejudice; it did not *create* this prejudice (though it might have exacerbated it). Anti-Arab racism is hardly new – though it has increased since the 9/11 attacks, along with attempts to systematically study it. In the wake of September 11, 2001, American-Arab Anti-Discrimination Committee Research Institute reported 700 attacks on Arab or seemingly Arab persons, along with 800 cases of employment discrimination. While the period from 2003–2007 marked a decrease in hate crimes when compared to the immediate backlash after 9/11, the number of hate crimes is still more than it was in the 1990s.[110] Arab Americans have been the victims of death threats, vandalism, forced evictions, beatings, and more besides.

There is also ample evidence of systematic discrimination of those appearing to be from the Middle East, or appearing to be Muslim – and these have been on the rise.

> In 2006, CAIR [Council on American-Islamic Relations] processed a total of 2,467 civil rights complaints, compared to 1,972 in 2005 and 1,522 in 2004. This constitutes a 62 percent increase in the total number of complaints of anti-Muslim harassment, violence and discriminatory treatment from 2004. For the third straight year, the 2,467 reports also mark the highest number of Muslim civil rights complaints ever reported to CAIR in its thirteen-year history. (19)[111]

Polling data bears out an increasing islamophobia. The Pew Forum on Religion and Public Life Poll in 2004 reported that "almost 4 in 10

Americans have an unfavorable view of Islam, about the same number that has a favorable view" (ibid., 17). According to a Washington Post/ABC News poll, on the other hand, "the percentage of Americans who hold unfavorable views of Islam has risen over the last three years" (75).[112] In March of 2005, an ABC News poll reported that "43 percent think Islam does not teach respect for the beliefs of non-Muslims – up sharply from 22% [in 2002]" (18).[113] Opinions on increased violations of civil liberties of Muslim Americans also suggest a high level of suspicion of everything in the near East: A USA Today/Gallop poll "found that 53% of respondents favored 'requiring all Arabs, including those who are US citizens, to undergo special, more intensive security checks before boarding airplanes in the US . . . 46 percent favored 'requiring Arabs, including those who are US citizens, to carry a special ID'" (77).[114]

The attitudes toward Islam represent an astonishing ignorance of Islam, as well as of the Middle East in general. Whereas virtually any violent action carried out by a Muslim is characterized by the US media as a kind of religious violence, violent actions carried out by Christians seldom reference the religion of their perpetrators. The assumption, of course, is that Islam is intrinsically violent, despite the fact that the 1.2 billion Muslims in the world are no more violent than any other large religious population. When a Christian murders an abortion doctor, for example, the Christian is not identified as such – or, if he is, he is regarded as an *unrepresentative sample*. When a Muslim engages in violent action, on the other hand, the violence is regarded as endemic of the religion as such – despite the fact that *every* religion has its history written in blood. This provides us with ample reason to be cautious of *everyone's* intuitions when it comes to the ticking bomb scenario: our intuitions may well reflect our prejudices concerning the Middle East.[115]

Against torture

The ticking bomb case is typically seen as a motivating case for the exceptional use of torture. As I have shown, the ticking bomb case is confused through and through. Other arguments in favor of torture likewise fall flat. Arguments against torture in all forms, on the other hand – although not completely conclusive in some cases – provide us with a powerful reason for respecting a wisdom that has been embodied in law: torture is never to be used, under any circumstances, against any one.

Notes

1. These figures are given in reports by the Pentagon. They are also cited in numerous places in the literature. See, for example, Sullivan, p. 322, in Levinson (ed.), *Torture: A Collection*.

2. Michael Gross has made this same point in "Just and Jewish Warfare – Israeli Soldiers Seem to Disregard Rules of War," *Tikkun*, September 2001.

3. See "It's About Time: Defusing the Ticking Bomb Argument."

4. Aaron Lercher, "Torture and Moral Knowledge," *Review Journal of Political Philosophy*, 2008, Vol. 6, No. 1, pp. 67–74.

5. It is the empirical impossibility of assessing consequences that leads William Tindale to claim that we should follow Kant's advice in the notorious 'murderer at the door' thought experiment. The point of Kant's example, Tindale (rightly) contends, is *not* that the consequences are irrelevant, but that we have no control over them. See his "Tragic Choices: Reaffirming Absolutes in the Torture Debate," (2005) *International Journal of Applied Philosophy*, 19:2 209–222.

6. Darius Rejali provides one such example in *Torture and Modernity*, where Lady Sheil is quoted describing Sulayman Khan as having "danced to his place of execution in defiance of his tormentors and the agony of the burning candles" (12).

7. See Antonio Gallonio, *Tortures and Torments of the Christian Martyrs.*

8. Rona M. Fields, "The Neurobiological Consequences of Psychological Torture," in *The Trauma of Psychological Torture.*

9. This leads Steven Kleinman to remark that, "although criticized for its discussion of coercion, the KUBARK manual does not portray coercive methods as necessary – or even viable – means of effectively educing information" (133), "KUBARK Counterintelligence Interrogation Review: Observations of an Interrogator," in *Educing Information.*

10. See Jonathan Weinberg, Shaun Nichols, and Stephen Stich, "Normativity and Epistemic Intuitions" and E. Machery, Ron Mallon, Shaun Nichols, and Stephen Stich, "Semantics, Cross-Cultural Style," in *Experimental Philosophy*, ed. Joshua Knobe and Shaun Nichols.

11. As Michael Davis has pointed out, it must also be clear that the 'should' in 'Should we torture?' must be used in its moral, rather than in its prudential, sense. In the ticking bomb case, no such demonstration is forthcoming. See Michael Davis, "The Moral Justifiability of Torture and other Cruel, Inhuman, or Degrading Treatment."

12. For a discussion of this, see Chapter 2, Wisnewski and Emerick, *The Ethics of Torture.*

13. "One-third support torture," BBC News.

14. See Chapter 5 of his forthcoming *Terrorism, Ticking Time-Bombs, and Torture.*

15. See, for example, *Educing Information.*

16. Michael Davis has made a similar point. See Michael Davis, "The Moral Justifiability of Torture and other Cruel, Inhuman, or Degrading Treatment."

17. I will return to this worry very briefly in *Additional issues with torture warrants and ticking bombs.*

18. See *Torture doesn't work.*

19. Quoted in Danner, "US Torture: Voices from the Black Sites," *The New York Review of Books.*
20. See Chapter 4.
21. I've made a similar point in "It's about Time: Defusing the Ticking Bomb Argument".
22. These will be considered in Consquentialist Arguments against Torture Policy
23. This occurred in 2009, for example, when a report by the ICRC was leaked to the press, describing the conditions under which prisoners at Guantanamo Bay were detained, interrogated, and so on.
24. "Is the ticking bomb case plausible?" in *The Phenomenon of Torture*, originally from *Tainted Legacy: 9/11 and the Ruin of Human Rights.*
25. On December 26, 2002, Dana Priest and Barton Gellam reported the use of the 'top secret' 'stress and duress' tactics that the US had adopted in *The Washington Post*, "US Decries Abuse but Defends Interrogations."
26. These consideration lead Henry Shue to remark that "the moderate position on torture is an impractical abstraction – it is torture in dreamland" (237). It has also led him to give up his own view that torture might be justifiable in certain cases in favor of an absolutist position in regards to the prohibition against torture. See his "Torture in Dreamland: Disposing of the Ticking Bomb."
27. Rejali points out the existence of a professional class of torturers should be expected to result in that professional class vying for political power – something which would likely result in *more* arguments for torture's utility and worth. Once again, the point here is not that this would *necessarily* happen (that argument seems to me to be unavailable). The point, rather, is that these considerations must be included in any consequentialist analysis of the ticking bomb scenario.
28. Jessica Wolfendale, "Training Torturers: A Critique of the 'Ticking Bomb' Argument." A similar argument has been given by Jean Maria Arrigo in "A Utilitarian Argument against Torture Interrogation of Terrorists."
29. Fritz Allhoff has persuasively argued that the ticking bomb scenario *does not* rely solely on consequentialist reasoning (forthcoming). I do not mean to suggest that it does – but, as Allhoff would agree, consequentialist think is certainly *part* of the moral reasoning involved in the TB scenario.
30. Felner, "Torture and Terrorism," in *Torture: Does It Make Us Safer?*
31. Felner, ibid.
32. The evidence for this is extensive, including both the testimony of hundreds of detainees as well as official reports from the Israeli comptroller. See Felner, ibid.
33. In *Torture: Does It Make Us Safer?*
34. There are exceptions to this, of course. In *How to Break a Terrorist: The US Interrogators Who Used Brains, Not Brutality, To Take Down the Deadliest Man in Iraq*, Matthew Alexander offers an anecdote about a veteran interrogator who scoffs at the idea that one should use sympathy and rapport in interrogation. The veteran claims that the interrogator must "show [them]

who's boss." For Alexander, this represents a dangerous gambit, as "dehumanizing them is the first step down the slippery slope to torture," and that this had been explicitly warned against during his training as an interrogator (75). Alexander further notes that 'the old ways die hard,' though the reference of this is unclear. US military interrogation practices, at least one paper, have been humane for much of the US's history (excluding the Bush era). 'Old ways' may well refer to the habits of those with a certain faith in brutality, or to the overall ways of human beings throughout history.

35. "Rethinking The Psychology Of Torture: A Preliminary Report from Former Interrogators and Research Psychologists," Psychologists for Social Responsibility, www.psysr.org.

36. Ronnie Janoff-Bulman, "Erroneous Assumptions: Popular Belief in the Effectiveness of Torture Interrogation."

37. Quoted in Perry, *Torture: Religious Ethics and National Security.*

38. "Interview with Dick Cheney," *State of the Union With John King*, CNN, March 15, 2009.

39. "Obama on AIG Rage, Recession, Challenges," *60 Minutes*, March 22, 2009.

40. Cited in Rejali, 491.

41. For an interesting study of this case, see Stephanie Athey's "The terrorist we torture: the Tale of Abdul Hakim Murad" in *On Torture*.

42. "Germany Racked by torture controversy," John Cooper, February 28, 2003, *The Guardian*, available widely on the internet.

43. The interrogator is Jerry Giorgio. This is reported by Mark Bowden in "The Dark Art of Interrogation," in *The Atlantic Monthly*.

44. This point has been documented by a number of trained interrogators, and is cited in a number of studies of interrogation. See, for example, *Educing Information*.

45. Robert Coulam, "Approaches to Interrogation in the Struggle against Terrorism: Considerations of Cost and Benefit" in *Educing Information*.

46. R. Bennett, "Interrogator's request to professional psychologists" J. M. Arrigo (ed.), *Visible remedies for invisible settings and sources of torture* (American Psychological Association annual convention), New Orleans, LA, cited in Ronnie Janoff-Bulman, "Erroneous Assumptions: Popular Belief in the Effectiveness of Torture Interrogation."

47. Richard Goldstone, "Combating Terrorism: Zero Tolerance for Torture."

48. P. Bauer, "Statement on interrogation practices to the House Committee on the Armed Services," July 31, 2006.

49. Jean Maria Arrigo and Richard V. Wagner "Psychologists and Military Interrogators Rethink the Psychology of Torture."

50. This document is available at various sites on the internet. It is considered a classic in the interrogation literature.

51. Moran, 250, in *The Phenomenon of Torture*.

52. Randy Borum, "Approaching Truth: Behavioral Science Lessons on Educing Information from Human Sources," in *Educing Information*.

53. The CIA's bible of interrogation, *The Human Resource Exploitation Training Manual*, makes precisely this point (cited above).

54. Steven M. Kleinman, "KUBARK Counterintelligence Interrogation Review: Observations of an Interrogator" in *Educing Information*.

55. Borum, ibid.

56. Rejali: "The best source for information bar none is public cooperation" (458).

57. Cited in Rejali, 502–3.

58. Danner, ibid.

59. See 504, Rejali.

60. Quoted in Ross, "A History of Torture," in *Torture*.

61. See Allhoff, Chapter 5, forthcoming.

62. This is why, as I will suggest in Additional Issues with Torture Warrants and Ticking Bombs, the TB case isn't actually about *torture* at all – it's about whether or not we accept the idea of absolute moral prohibitions.

63. See, for example, Judith Butler, *Precarious Life*.

64. Kant makes this argument in a few places. See, for example, *Groundwork for the Metaphysics of Morals* and *Metaphysics of Morals*.

65. For an analysis of the argument, see both *The Ethics of Torture*, Chapter 3, and *Wittgenstein and Ethical Inquiry*, Chapter 2.

66. 4:397.

67. 4:400.

68. 4:400.

69. An example of an argument against torture that takes this line is Amihud Gilead's "Torture and Singularity."

70. This has been a central point of much feminist ethics: ethics only makes sense in *contexts*, and seeing these contexts is not a matter of simply articulating a few principles and then applying them.

71. For a defense of the idea of moral perception, see Wisnewski and Jacoby, "Failures of Sight: An Argument for Moral Perception."

72. *Torture: Religious Ethics and National Security*.

73. "Tortured Reasoning," in *Torture: A Collection*, ed. Levinson.

74. See my "Unwarranted Torture Warrants: A Critique of the Dershowitz Proposal."

75. The parenthetical reference is to Wittgenstein's *Philosophical Investigations* 199, of course.

76. Argumentative gaps in Matthews' book are infrequent occurrences, and should not distract any reader from what I take to be one of the finest books yet published on the question of torture.

77. "Torture and Terrorism: Painful Lessons from Israel" in *Torture*.

78. See, for example, Huggins et al., *Violence Workers*.

79. "In Their Own Words," in *The Phenomenon of Torture*.

80. John T. Parry argues that the continual possibility of escalation is part of the *definition* of torture (or, at any rate, that it ought to be). See his "Escalation and Necessity: Defining Torture at Home and Abroad" in *Torture*.

81. Sullivan, "The Abolition of Torture, in *Torture*, ed. Levinson.

82. Minky Worden, "Torture Spoken Here: Ending Global Torture," in *Torture: Does It Make Us Safer? Is It Ever OK?*

83. See Rejali, Chapter 2, *Torture and Democracy.*

84. Stuart Grassian, "Neuropsychiatric Effects of Solitary Confinement" in *The Trauma of Psychological Torture.*

85. Dr. Mary R. Fabri, "Treating Torture Victims," *Torture: Does It Make Us Safer? Is It Ever OK?*

86. Claudia Catani, Frank Neuner, Christian Wienbruch, Thomas Elbert, "The Tortured Brain" in *The Trauma of Psychological Torture.*

87. Rejali, *Torture and Democracy.*

88. Rejali, ibid.

89. "Torture as a Greater Evil" in *On Torture*, ed. Hilde.

90. Miles, *Oath Betrayed: Torture, Medical Complicity, and the War on Terror.*

91. That this duty is commonly acknowledged is evidenced by its presence in a number of ethical guidelines, not the least of which is the UN's Principles of Medical Ethics regarding the treatment of prisoners and detainees. According to this document, prison physicians "have a duty to provide [prisoners and detainees] with protection of their physical and mental health and treatment of disease" (116). Elsewhere, UN rules stipulate that physicians and clinicians have an obligation to insure such things as quantity and quality of food, hygiene of prisoners and cleanliness of the detaining facility.

92. "Introduction" *The Politics of Pain.* The reports cited above are from *Newsweek*, 2 November, 1984 and 26 November, 1984.

93. See Robert Jay Lifton, *The Nazi Doctors.*

94. It certainly does not help to assuage worries when respected psychologists come out in favor of using psychological expertise in interrogations, appealing to things like 'national security.' One such defense is made by Peter Suedfeld in "Torture, Interrogation, Security, and Psychology: Absolutistic versus Complex Thinking," *Analyses of Social Issues and Public policy*, Vol. 7, No. 1, 2007, 1–9. As the title (fallaciously) suggests, those who advocate absolutist positions engage in simplistic thinking. This is straightforwardly question-begging, and an instance of 'poisoning the well.' Suedfeld shows a remarkable lack of familiarity with the philosophical literature on torture, as well as the empirical literature on torture's effectiveness, despite his command of the psychological literature. I hope that this book stands as a refutation of the ridiculous claim that Suedfeld makes about absolutist positions. These accounts can be nuanced and thorough.

95. "Whoever has succumbed to torture can no longer feel at home in the world. The shame of destruction cannot be erased. Trust in the world, which already collapsed in part at the first blow, but in the end, under torture, fully, will not be regained" (40).

96. Claudia Card, "Ticking Bombs and Interrogations." For a reply to Card's overall position, see Clare Chambers, "Torture as an Evil: Response to Claudia Card, 'Ticking Bombs and Interrogation'."

97. These politicians have *not* claimed that they engaged in torture. The preferred locution is 'enhanced interrogation techniques.' Of course, the ICRC, as well as officials in Britain and Spain, have been more willing to call these techniques by their true name: torture.

98. I argued for this claim above. See *TB as producing more terrorists*.

99. As the reader will recall, I provided consequentialist arguments against the ticking bomb case in Consequentialist arguments against torturing in the ticking bomb case.

100. Discussed in *Misunderstanding time's relation to interrogation*.

101. I have suggested this line of argument in my review of Bagaric and Clarke's *Torture*, as well as in *The Ethics of Torture*.

102. Davis, *Abolition Democracy*.

103. For a discussion of the court's decisions regarding torture, see Cherie Booth, "Sexual Violence, Torture, and International Justice," in *Torture: Does It Make Us Safer? Is It Ever OK?*

104. "Torture Makes the Man," in *On Torture*, ed. Hilde.

105. *2003–2007 Report on Hate Crimes and Discrimination Against Arab Americans*, 89.

106. Ibid., 90.

107. Ibid., 92.

108. *Report on Hate Crimes and Discrimination Against Arab Americans: The Post-September 11 Backlash*, 129.

109. Ibid., 130.

110. *2003–2007 Report on Hate Crimes and Discrimination Against Arab Americans*, 10.

111. Parvez Ahmed, "Prejudice is real and exacts a heavy toll," *Islamophobia and Anti-Americanism*, ed. Mohamed Nimer.

112. Samer Shehata, "Popular media and opinion leaders are to Blame," *Islamophobia and Anti-Americanism*, ed. Mohamed Nimer.

113. Parvez Ahmed, "Prejudice is real and exacts a heavy toll," *Islamophobia and Anti-Americanism*, ed. Mohamed Nimer.

114. Samer Shehata, "Popular media and opinion leaders are to Blame," *Islamophobia and Anti-Americanism*, ed. Mohamed Nimer.

115. There is also ample reason to think that this sort of racism exists in nearly everyone. A series of interesting studies about our inchoate attitudes toward race have been conducted under the banner of the 'Implicit Assumption Project' by psychologists at Harvard and elsewhere. The results are startling. For more information on the project, and for articles outlining the result, see https://implicit.harvard.edu/implicit/

Chapter 7

The Psychology of Torture

Introduction

I have argued that the standard defenses of torture are inadequate. It has been my further contention that the wrongness of torture has been seriously underestimated. The previous chapters have tried to make the case for this claim by consistent appeal to the empirical literature on torture.

In this chapter, I want to elaborate on an additional moral casualty of torture: its *perpetrators*. This casualty, of course, does not compare to what those who are tortured undergo – and it is not universal. Some torturers go to their graves convinced they have done nothing wrong, or that, if they have, responsibility for this wrong lies elsewhere. The point of articulating this *additional* wrong-making feature of torture is not to diminish in any way the horrors of torture for those who undergo it. My aim, rather, is to demonstrate that the wrongness of torture is not limited to what it does to its victims; the animosity of torture extends beyond the agency it dominates.

What this suggests is borne out by the empirical literature. If torture were only perpetrated by the mentally deranged, it would not be so damaging to those who partake in it: if torture were the work of only moral monsters, we might be able to say that whatever effects it had on these moral monsters was of little concern. As we will see, however, torture can be done by anyone – it is not the province of only those who are exceptionally evil. Rather, the evil of torture proves to be *banal* (in Arendt's sense of that term) – it could be carried out by you or me, if the right circumstances presented themselves. In this respect, torture damages those who do it, both in the way it affects them, but also in what it *has them do*. Exploring this last point will lead us to investigate a substantial body of research in social psychology – research that, I will suggest, demonstrates that even the noblest among us can become torturers.

Becoming a torturer

We like to think of torturers as monsters – as somehow inhuman beasts who have given up living in a community of respect. In some cases, this turns out to be partially true – but in a surprising way. The view that monsters produce torture, I will argue, is false. Torture is done by ordinary people – by people just like you and me. But the act of torturing – of engaging in this fundamental violation of other human beings – has a way of transforming one into a broken person, often incapable of finding a happy, peaceful life in the world around you. In this sense, torture produces the inhuman; the inhuman does not produce torture.

To understand how ordinary people can engage in torture is to probe into an analysis of the origins of action generally. Traditionally, intentional actions have been explained in terms of the decisions one makes: I write a book because I made a decision to write a book; I order chocolate ice cream because I choose to order it; I help someone in distress because I see that they need it, and I make the decision to help. The standard analysis proceeds by attempting to explain *why* people make the decisions that they do. Once again, our explanation involves *the individual*: I decided to write a book because *I am the sort of person that enjoys philosophy*; I decided to have chocolate ice cream because *I am a sweets-lover*; I decided to help because *I am a helpful and generous person*. These kinds of explanations, then, aim to explicate actions in terms of the persons who carry them out: shy people behave shyly; outgoing people do outgoing things; violent people engage in violent actions; and so on.

But our intuitions about the source of our actions might well be wrong. Sometimes the most intuitively plausible view turns out to be flat-out false. There is a wide (and ever-growing) literature that suggests skepticism is the appropriate attitude when considering the abilities of our beliefs to have much effect at all on our everyday actions.[1] Much of what we believe seems, in certain respects, *irrelevant* to what we in fact do. There is a massive body of experimental literature that suggests that our actions are much more the product of minuscule situational factors than they are of our beliefs and desires at the conscious level. This suggests that things like engaging in helping behavior can be better predicted by examining the music playing in the background, or whether a person found change on the ground, than by whether or not that person has particular beliefs about the importance of helping.

Some specific experiments are worth discussing. The most famous experiments in this regard are those conducted by Stanley Milgram and Philip Zimbardo. Both sets of experiments speak to the power of varying situational stimuli to alter predicted courses of action among participants in psychological studies. In Milgram's famous experiments, it seems that the presence of an authority figure was a good indicator of whether or not a subject would engage in harming behavior. In Zimbardo's Stanford Prison Experiment, the random assignment of roles (as guard or prisoner) was sufficient to predict the kind of behavior the participant would engage in. (I will consider these in more detail below.)

These are not isolated experiments. It turns out that seminarians speaking on the Good Samaritan will stop to help a person in distress in more cases if they are told they are ahead of schedule (Darley and Batson 1973). It turns out that a person is *much* more likely to engage in helping behavior if they have just found a dime in a phone booth (Isen and Levin 1972). Likewise, the presence of pleasant or unpleasant sounds turn out to be good predictors for engaging in helping behavior – far better predictors than any information we have on various personality characteristics or belief sets (Matthews and Cannon 1975; Fried and Berkowitz 1979).

These experiments suggest a competing account of the origins of our actions. The two views of action (the traditional view and the one that challenges it) are summarized below.

> **Dispositional View:** our actions result from 'dispositions'; we do what we do because of the personality traits we have prior to our engagement in situations. This is the traditional explanation of actions. It can be traced back (at least) to Aristotle.
>
> **Situationist View:** our actions are more accurately predictable based on situational variables; we do what we do because of the situations we find ourselves in.

These two views represent two competing views of character, one that strikes us as intuitive, and which we employ regularly in our folk psychological explanations of actions, and another which seems to be indicated by numerous controlled experiments.

As mentioned above, Aristotle is a *locus classicus* for the dispositional view. Aristotle postulates that actions result from character traits which develop over time. One's propensity to engage in moral action, Aristotle contends, is a direct result of *who one is*. On this view, any action will be explained in terms of the antecedent character traits that one has developed through the process of habituation. Applied to torture, then, Aristotle provides one answer to the question 'Who tortures?': the person that has an immoral character, who has been habituated in such a way that this person consistently engages in immoral actions.[2]

The situationist alternative to this view removes character from the chain of explanation. Who tortures? Anyone will torture, if the situation is just right. One cannot predict, based on the character traits a particular person exhibits in one situation, how this person will behave in differing, novel situations. Rather, the fundamental determinants of action are often minuscule variables, infrequently noticed by the acting agents themselves, which shape one's response to that situation.

These alternatives are easily seen in the debate that emerged following the revelations of abuse at Abu Ghraib. Two competing narratives about the source of these abuses were constructed, the dominant of which was that promulgated by the Bush administration – a narrative that, in its very construction, limited culpability to those who had engaged in 'abuse.' The phrase 'a few bad apples' appeared regularly in the media, and predominantly on the FOX news network, in relation to the 'abuse'/'torture' that had taken place. In stunning clarity, then, we see what hangs on these alternative conceptions of the ultimate source of torturous actions: on the one hand, we have the moral security of the idea that torture is carried out by those with suspect characters (the bad apples); on the other hand, we have the situational recognition that the right circumstances can produce the worst sorts of action in anyone.

But speaking of 'situational recognition' here is perhaps premature. After all, for many, the 'bad apple' hypothesis is the only tenable one. For those who advocate this view, to alleviate responsibility by appeal to situational circumstances is simply too much to bear. This quip on behalf of the dispositional view, I think, suffers from two significant mistakes. First, it assumes that locating the explanation of an action in situational variables *in fact* alleviates responsibilities. It does no such thing. While recognizing the significant contributions of the situation to the actions one is likely to take, the situationist by no means thereby exculpates all wrong-doing. Quite the contrary. It is possible (and, indeed, absolutely customary) to be held responsible even for things one has done inadvertently (in cases of manslaughter, for example). So, there is no diminution of responsibility simply because situational factors played a part in the actions one undertakes. Recognizing that anyone might have engaged in such actions can in fact *maintain* culpability – after all, one no longer has one's dispositions as an excuse.

The second mistake present in the dispositional camp, at least as it has surfaced in the mainstream media, is to blithely ignore the mountain of empirical evidence that supports the situationist view. The force of situationist psychology is only felt when one recognizes just how much experimental data supports it.

The social psychological evidence

Two famous experiments: Milgram and Zimbardo

The most famous experiments supporting the situationist view are Stanley Milgram's studies on obedience to authority. In these studies, Milgram set out to determine the rate at which normal people would obey authority figures who gave them orders to commit grossly immoral actions. Milgram's guiding hypothesis was that *most* people would not carry out extreme acts of violence, and hence that such acts of violence, when they occurred, needed to be explained by other means than simply an appeal to authority. Milgram thought that something about the situation in Nazi Germany explained the atrocities that had been carried out there, and that such things would not be possible among Americans. His experiments revealed otherwise.

To test how often ordinary people might obey authority, Milgram set up an experiment with the following conditions: a volunteer would participate in what the volunteer thought was an experiment involving memory. He would be introduced to another 'volunteer' (in fact an actor working for the psychologists), who would be asked various questions to test his memory. When he got questions wrong, the subject (volunteer) would administer a shock – small at first, but with growing intensity for every question that was incorrectly answered. The shocks began at 15 volts and increased, in increments of 15, all the way to 450 volts. Increasing intensity was also designated by warnings posted above particular voltage levels (such as 'Danger – Severe Shock'). An authority figure would be present during the experiment, wearing a lab coat, and encouraging the subject to continue with the experiment despite any reservations about continuing (because the other 'volunteer' was screaming in pain, begging to stop the experiment, refusing to continue, and so on), the authority figure would reply by saying such things as 'The experiment must continue,' and 'Please continue.'

Two-thirds of those who volunteered for the experiment continued to shock the confederate (the actor who played the person being shocked) all the way to 450 volts. This occurred despite agonized screams, complaints of heart failure, and the refusal of the confederate to continue. While subjects were often visibly distressed by their actions, they nevertheless continued to administer shocks. Everyone who participated in the study shocked the confederate to some degree – but approximately 65% continued shocking until the experiment was over; they didn't once refuse to continue. They engaged in what they likely thought was torture, despite the fact that they knew it was wrong, they wanted to stop, and they had every right to stop. "This is, perhaps, the most fundamental lesson of our study: ordinary people, simply doing their jobs, and without any particular hostility on their part, can become agents in a terrible destructive process" (6).[3]

Of course, one might argue that this case suffered from participant selection problems: all participants were in New England, the scientists had the imprimatur of Yale about them, all candidates were motivated by pay (they each received $4). Perhaps, one might contend, some of these factors determined the selection of those who would participate, and perhaps the range of participants is what produced these outcomes. Milgram was aware of these criticisms, and set out to control for them.

Milgram's experiments have been widely replicated, and with shockingly consistent results (pun intended). In some variations, the number of participants willing to shock went as high as 90%. The implications of this are staggering: ordinary people, when confronted with authority, are willing to do things they know to be wrong.

The depth of the power situations hold over us can be seen even more clearly in an experiment carried out by the one-time high school classmate of Stanley Milgram, Philip Zimbardo, and is widely known as the Stanford Prison Experiment.

In August of 1971, Philip Zimbardo conducted an experiment designed to investigate the psychology of imprisonment. The experiment had surprising results – results that have since been much discussed in the media as well as in the academy. Zimbardo was primarily interested in the way that institutional roles led to 'de-identification' and suppression and forgetfulness of one's personal existence. The effects of de-personalization in institutional settings, Zimbardo rightly hypothesized, would result in anonymizing prisoners. What Zimbardo found, however, was much more shocking.

The set-up of the experiment was as follows: an advertisement was posted for subjects to take part in a two-week psychological experiment. Subjects would be paid $15 per day (remember, this is 1971) to take part in a prison simulation to be held at Stanford University. Of the many applicants, 21 were chosen. Those chosen each took personality tests (to avoid hiring those with authoritarian personalities, for example) and were screened for previous mental health conditions. No one with a prior arrest record was hired. Zimbardo's aim was, as he says, to "select young men who seemed to be normal, healthy, and average on all the psychological dimensions we measured" (32, *The Lucifer Effect*). Subjects were then randomly split into two groups: prisoners and guards. There were nine prisoners, nine guards, and three persons on stand-by in the event that one or more of the subjects would not be able to participate.

The simulated prison was constructed in the basement of an academic building on the Stanford campus. Offices were converted into three cells, each with three cellmates. The guards worked in eight-hour shifts, three per shift. The Palo Alto police were involved in the initial operations, as were the media. The police agreed to arrest the nine 'criminals.' After arrest and processing at the actual jail, prisoners were transferred to the simulated facility, where they were stripped down, given a number, and sprayed with what they were told was a de-lousing agent. They were then read the rules. There were 17 rules that all prisoners had to memorize. These included rules about obeying guards, not speaking during meals, never referring to others by name (always by number), and so on. In addition, each prisoner was required to wear a chain on his ankle (to provide a constant reminder of his detention). When violations of rules occurred, prisoners were forced to do push-ups, to stand in uncomfortable positions, or were sent to solitary confinement. All participants were made aware that they could quit the experiment at any time. Although the experiment was scheduled to last two weeks, it lasted only five days. It was shut down because things simply got out of hand.

What happened? To simply list the things that happened is perhaps inadequate, but nevertheless provides some indication of precisely how bad things got. In a period of five days, Stanford Prison was home to prisoner abuse, force-feeding, rioting, and mental breakdown. The participants in the study took on the roles they were randomly assigned. Despite the fact that everyone knew that the roles were randomly assigned – that they were no different than their counterparts – the roles simply took over; character seemed to be irrelevant. The participants "were not the proverbial 'bad apples' – rather, it was the 'bad barrel' of the Stanford Prison that was implicated in the transformations that had been demonstrated so vividly" (181).[4] Summing up the lessons to be learned from the experiment, Zimbardo remarks that

> This experiment has emerged as a powerful illustration of the potentially toxic impact of bad systems and bad situations in making good people behave in pathological ways that are alien to their nature. The narrative chronology . . . reveals the extent to which ordinary, normal, healthy young men succumbed to, or were seduced by, the social forces inherent in that behavioral context – as were the many of the other adults and professionals who came within its encompassing boundaries. The line between Good and Evil, once thought to be impermeable, proved instead to be quite permeable. (195)

If we take the situationist analysis seriously, a very different answer to the question 'Who tortures?' emerges. If situational variables are better predictors for actions than character traits, it seems than *anyone will torture. What predicts torture is not who one is, but where one is.*

> Any deed that any human being has ever committed, however horrible, is possible for any of us – under the right or wrong situational circumstances. That knowledge does not excuse evil; rather, it democratizes it, sharing its blame among ordinary actors rather than declaring it the province only of deviants and despots – of Them but not Us. (211)[5]

But the experimental data does not end here. In fact, this is only the beginning of the evidence that has been mounting in favor of the view that small, situational variables can have an immense impact on the kinds of actions persons will engage in. There is a wide (and ever-growing) literature that should lead us to be skeptical about the abilities of our beliefs and our character traits to have much effect at all on our everyday actions.[6]

As always in psychology, the range of empirical data cannot definitively prove that our character is irrelevant to action (a claim that would be too strong). But the data does suggest that, historically, we have placed far too much emphasis on the importance of character in guiding our actions – and that, in perhaps much of what we do, belief is an *after thought*.[7] Thus, our beliefs about torture might well have *no effect* on the way we conduct ourselves.

Situational variables that increase the likelihood of torture

Haritos-Fatouros interviewed 16 ex-torturers who had served in Greece during the rule of the military junta (1967–1974).[8] In his research – work which expanded on the work done by Milgram, discussed above – Haritos-Fatouros identified four learning mechanisms that were employed to train torturers, and which seem to be widely found in research on this kind of training. These four mechanisms were *overlearning*, *desensitization*, *role modeling*, and *reinforcement*.

These techniques were hardly unique to the experience in Greece.[9] They seem ubiquitous, and constitute four of the significant situational variables involved in the construction of torturers. They also each lead to what is widely referred to as *routinization* (a term coined by Herbert Kelman[10]) in the carrying-out of torture: "what is being done *to* someone transforms into what is being done: information gathering" (146).[11] The key to routinization is to gradually introduce the trainee to the context and acts of torture. This introduction involves desensitization in two ways: first, trainees are often *themselves* subjected to torture. This has the effect of inoculating them against viewing torture as entirely foreign. It also leads the trainee to become accustomed to the manner in which pain is inflicted. Second, trainees are gradually introduced to the procedure of subjecting others to torture.

> [Greek] servicemen were first brought into contact with prisoners by carrying food to them and 'occasionally' were ordered to 'give the prisoners some blows.' The next step was to place them as guards in the detention rooms where they watched others torturing prisoners; they would occasionally take part in the group floggings. Later they were asked to take part in the 'standing ordeal' during which time they had to beat the prisoner (on the legs mainly) every time he moved. (122)[12]

The same gradual introduction is reported to have occurred in many other contexts as well; it seems to be *de rigueur* in the construction of torturers.

> In almost every case, training will begin with physical and psychological abuse, even torture. From then on, the trainee is operating from a post-traumatic personality, which lays foundation for his accommodation to abusive authority and for his susceptibility to further personality change. (125)[13]

The repeated use of violence, gradually increasing over time, is a good predictor for future incidents of violence. As Zimbardo remarks, "some research on violence has demonstrated that if a person has never committed a violent act, it is difficult to predict whether he or she ever will. However, after the fourth or fifth violent act, the probability of recidivism is very high" (178).[14] In this way, training torturers by gradually increasing their exposure to violence, and thereby wearing down any initial reservations they may have about its use, helps to create persons who will be reliable torturers. The process of training is one that alters the world of the torturer fundamentally. The relationship of trust and empathy that we prize so highly in other human beings is turned into one of 'us' and 'them', where one's actions are directed against a dehumanized enemy the very presence of which is a threat to civilization.

> The very process of routinization of torture involves a kind of continuous and dynamic distortion of facts and events which, in the end, amounts to a construction of a new reality. This socially constructed reality . . . supplants conventional morality, substituting in its place the ideological dictates of the authority structure within which torture occurs. (Crelinston, 148)

When torture has reached the level of policy, as Herbert Kelman points out, the torture situation presents the actions of the potential torturer as representing a "transcendent mission" (131). The interests of one's fellow citizens, national security, the plight of a righteous people, and so on, have all been asserted as necessary to the use of harsh techniques that would otherwise obviously seem wrong. As Ariel Dorfman unforgettably puts it:

> Make no mistake: every regime that tortures does so in the name of salvation, some superior goal, some promise of paradise. Call it communism, call it the free market, call it the free world, call it the national interest, call it fascism, call it the leader, call it civilization, call it the service of God, call it the need for information, call it what you will. (9)[15]

Salvation is coupled with the prior dehumanization of the would-be victim. Moreover, the fact that one's actions are encouraged by superior officers, or even by official policy, dilutes any potential responsibility one might have. If the practice has become routine, this routinization "enables [torturers] to ignore the overall meaning of the tasks they are performing and eliminates the opportunity to raise moral questions" (Kelman, 131). Training enables what Ervin Staub has referred to as 'moral equilibration': "important moral values are replaced by other values that are treated as if they are moral values" (103).[16] Thus, moral questions are set aside. To the extent that they are *not* set aside, the morality of the torturer's action is often assessed on a scale conducive to *legitimating* that action. Rather than asking if one should be torturing, one asks if one is 'doing one's duty,' or 'protecting one's fellow citizens.'

The force of torturous activities being ordered from above (in the case where torture is a policy, official or otherwise) should not be underestimated. This helps to create a context in which torturing can be a measure of *success*. Moreover, we should not exaggerate the ability of persons to simply say 'no' to such orders, particularly given the training they have undergone. "The primary aim of actual military training," Jessica Wolfendale has forcefully argued, "is to cultivate the habits of unreflective obedience. Military training not only makes moral reflection harder, it aims to remove the capacity for such reflection altogether" (127–128).[17] As this suggests, "the process of being drawn into the web of torture starts considerably earlier than the moment in which a person finds himself by superior order faced with the choice to become a torturer or not" (17).[18]

The context within which one tortures also plays a significant role in the apparent legitimacy of the techniques one is using. This legitimacy stems not only from instances where torture is ordered. It also comes from the peer pressure exerted by a culture of torture. 'Fitting in' and 'performing well' are themselves situational variables that increase the likelihood that any particular person will engage in torture. "The torturer is in an institutional context, within a hierarchy in which others, his superiors and their superiors and their superiors, decide who is an enemy, what needs to be known, and what must be done to know it" (141).[19] The professionalization of torture also contributes to an agent's willingness to carry it out, as it "conveys the image of torture as a special profession dedicated to the service of the state" (30).[20] Finally, the presence of other figures of authority, as we have learned from Milgram, contributes to a certain veneer of legitimacy.

> An additional element of the torture situation that contributes to its perceived legitimacy is the participation of medical professionals, who often play an active role by evaluating victims' physical capacity to go through the process, by making sure that the torture does not go beyond the point of causing the victim to die, and by performing other functions. (132)[21]

As we see in Milgram's work, authority figures issuing orders have a significant effect on the understanding an agent has of his or her own actions. The same applies in the context of state torture: "*authorization* helps to define the situation in such a way that standard moral principles do not apply . . . [the torturer] feels absolved of the responsibility to make personal moral choices" (28–29).[22] This is exacerbated by the propensity in much military training to try to reduce the capacity of servicepersons to think critically about the orders they are given. In certain respects, the extreme hierarchy of military culture encourages the view that responsibility is traced up the line of command for orders given. The soldiers' only responsibility is to *perform his duties*, where these duties are understood to involve obedience to his superior's demands.

The displacement of responsibility is further encouraged by the frequent insularity of those persons who engage in torturous interrogation: they are an 'elite' in whatever military operation is being carried out, not subject to the same rules that others are subject to. This kind of insularity is promoted in myriad ways. Torturers are often commanded to keep their activities a secret from family and friends. Specialized units that engage in torture are frequently provided with a set of guidelines that they are to follow (often different from the guidelines of others). But even these guidelines, it often turns out, offer no incentive to comply, as there is frequently little oversight regarding the actual methods employed: what matters is the end result, not how one gets there.

This latter fact can be seen, for example, in police units (such as those in Los Angeles,[23] Chicago,[24] and in Brazil,[25] to name only a few examples) that have engaged in torture. "Group anonymity encouraged the elite squad's insularity and supported violence workers' bonding, dependence on one another, and separation from outsiders" (185).[26] Such insularity can also be seen in the interrogation techniques employed by the CIA, which has, since its inception, been reluctant to share results with other intelligence agencies in the United States. The use of secrecy, as well as the presupposition that one is not subject to those rules that govern other governmental bodies, provides a rather unsubtle means of displacing one's responsibility for the actions in which one engages.

As we've seen, one of the tactics used to successfully make a torturer lies in successfully dehumanizing one's victims. As the Stanford Prison Experiment and Milgram's Obedience study make clear, however, this is not *necessary* to induce people to torture. Nevertheless, the successful dehumanization of a group of people makes the transition to torture even easier than it would otherwise be. By removing a group of people from the realm of the 'human' (by 'Othering' them), we no longer have to acknowledge any of the demands that they make on us. This is carried out by the systematic use of epithets when speaking of the enemy, by the use of continual ideological training, and by engaging in routine acts demeaning the very existence of the enemy.[27] "The targets of torture are defined as enemies of the state who constitute a serious threats to the state's security and survival. For that, as well as for other reasons, such as their ethnicity or ideology, they are placed outside the protection of the state" (28).[28] The aim of such training, of course, is to destroy any kind of moral objection that might exist on the part of the perpetrator – the enemy is an *animal*, after all, and not worthy of even moderate restraint.

Interestingly, even in the Milgram experiments, such dehumanization sometimes occurred – but it occurred *after* the shocks had been delivered. As Milgram remarks,

> many subjects harshly devalue the victim *as a consequence* of acting against him. Such comments as 'He was so stupid and stubborn he deserved to get shocked,' were common. Once having acted against the victim, these subjects found it necessary to view him as an unworthy individual, whose punishment was made inevitable by his own deficiencies of intellect and character. (10)

In nations that torture, such dehumanization is an integral part of a torturer's training. As we can see, however, continuous torture actually *increases* (or, at any rate, can increase) the extent of this dehumanization.

If the situationist view is right, the 'bad apple' explanation of torturers cannot be correct. Analysis of particular instances of torture seems to bear this out: "the violence workers were quite ordinary, showing no evidence of premorbid personalities that would have predisposed them to such careers . . . The most rational torturers, according to our Brazilian interviewees, were those without 'character disorders'" (240–241).[29] Zimbardo has offered an extensive analysis of the Abu Ghraib case that bears out this point: the perpetrators of torture at Abu Ghraib were not particularly immoral. They were, in many respects, ordinary men and women who found themselves in a world without structure and with an absence of consequences for their actions ("they witnessed perpetrators literally 'getting away with murder'"[30]). This is not an excuse; it is simply an observation. Had any of us been put in such a situation, it is likely that we would have engaged in the same kinds of behavior.[31] No one is innocent; everyone is capable of the worst forms of abuse.

Damaged agency: the effects of torture on the torturer

We have spent time exploring two related questions: 'who tortures?' and 'what damage is done to the victim?' A third question must now be posed: what damage does torture do to the person who tortures?

Many former torturers, as well as those who have engaged in routine violence against others, often suffer from a type of Post-Traumatic Stress Disorder that emerges from engaging in actions like torture and assassination. Military personnel are frequently diagnosed with various mental health conditions after (and sometimes during) their service. They cannot live with what they have done once they recognize its severity.

> [The] reason for the high level of psychiatric illness among military personnel is that many personnel find the deliberate killing of another human being extremely traumatic, so much so that in past wars there is evidence that a significant number of military personnel either did not fire their weapons or deliberately missed . . . new training methods were developed prior to the Vietnam War that specifically aimed at overcoming the psychological resistance to killing. (135)[32]

In some cases, former torturers have actually sought out their victims to ask for forgiveness.[33] In other cases, torturers isolate themselves in their suffering, no longer able to recognize themselves in the actions they have carried out. This is an extremely common narrative among those unable to cope with the violence they have inflicted: they never thought they could do such things. Recognizing that they *can* and *could* do such things creates a psychological fissure that is deeply distressing to the former perpetrator of torture.

Killing has a way of staying with people. As Claude Anshin Thomas writes regarding his experience in Vietnam,

> My job in Vietnam was to kill people. By the time I was first injured in combat (two or three months into my tour), I had already been directly responsible for the deaths of several hundred people. And today, each day, I can still see many of their faces. (20)[34]

Thomas' story is a powerful one, both honest and surprising, and representative of the kinds of trauma faced by those who have become, even for a short period, devoid of the sympathy that constitutes our humanity. Upon returning from Vietnam, Thomas notes that he was "unable to socialize or reintegrate back into [his] own culture" (27). "There was no 'after the war'" for him, and his experience, in this respect, is hardly unique (29). Torturers frequently report similar reactions: they are haunted by what they have done – by the gruesome violation of the human community – so much so, in fact, that they have difficulty returning to that community. This process begins even before one has become a full-blown torturer:

> When we learn how the torturer-trainee is broken in, our knowledge of posttraumatic stress allows us to predict the trainee's condition by the end of his initiation, and introduction to the next phases of his training. We know he will struggle to manage recurrent intrusive imagery or body sensations, and that he will balance that with both voluntary and unconscious numbing of his normal responses. He will suffer damage to his attachments to himself and others.

Neurologically and emotionally he will be irritable and hyper-responsive. His psychological needs and defenses are likely to become more primitive. If the abuse is repeated, his suffering denied, and his chances for restoration of self are blocked, then his initial dissociative responses may become lasting mechanisms. In that very likely case, his memory may become selective, his susceptibility to trance will increase, his perceptions will be distorted, and the meaning he attaches to his life may dramatically alter . . .

And so what we see is that regardless of his psychological state as he enters training, the recruit will evolve . . . to an increasing identification with his trainer's world view. (126)[35]

Of course, not everyone who tortures falls prey to psychiatric issues. In fact, many torturers persist in the belief that they have done nothing wrong – or that the wrongs they had done were ones for which they should not justifiably bear responsibility. This is the view we find, for example, among many of the Brazilian torturers interviewed by Zimbardo and colleagues in *Violence Workers*. It is also the view we find in Hannah Arendt's account of Adolph Eichman, architect of the Nazi's 'final solution.'[36]

This does not entail, however, that participating in the infliction of torture has no consequences for those who torture. One consequence faced by Brazilian torturers – despite the frequent self-certainty that they were guilty of no serious wrongs – was to be forced to live in an environment where anyone could be tortured, where the rule of law had faltered. "In the end, a culture of fear – which the violence workers had helped to nurture and sustain – came to victimize them as well" (16).[37]

This same culture of fear came to dominate the psyches of the highest members of the former Soviet Union, particularly during the reign of Stalin. To live in a society where the rule of law has been sequestered away as a relic of the past – as something that cannot be used at the expense of an elusive 'national security' – is to live in a society where one's personal security has been deeply compromised. The fact that one has participated in fostering this environment does little to diminish the effect of living *in* such an environment. Stalin himself, for example, constantly feared for his own life – as did everyone in his (frequently changing) regime.

Conclusion

The aim of this chapter has by no means been to excuse the acts of torturers. The aim, rather, has been to demonstrate a painful fact about human agents: we are all susceptible to the worst kinds of action. Hopefully, as we learn not to demonize those who torture, we will also learn to pay attention to the substantial moral dangers the world presents to us.

Damage caused by torture extends both to the perpetrators of torture and to any society that houses and trains torturers. I will now turn my attention to a case study of a nation that has recently engaged in torture and highlight some of the many variables that made this practice both possible and likely. The nation in question is the United States during the presidency of George W. Bush.

Notes

1. Here is a representative sample of some of the literature: Asch, 1955; Milgram, 1963; Darley and Latane, 1968, 1970; Isen and Levin, 1972; Darley and Batson, 1973; Zimbardo, Banks and Haney, 1973; Matthews and Cannon, 1975; Batson et al., 1978; Fried and Berkowitz, 1979; for impressive overviews of the relevant literature, see Doris, 2002; as well as Zimbardo, 2007.

2. In certain respects, torturers *do* undergo habituation through training, as we will see below. Training, however, occurs in institutional contexts that predict particular kinds of outcomes. This is rather different from what Aristotle had in mind by 'habituation.'

3. Stanley Milgram, *Obedience to Authority*.

4. Zimbardo, *The Lucifer Effect*.

5. Zimbardo, *The Lucifer Effect*.

6. A representative sample of some of the literature is listed in note 1.

7. For an interesting account of how the data in neuroscience supports this view, see Wegner, *The Illusion of Conscious Will*.

8. This research is excerpted in *The Phenomenon of Torture*, pp. 120–123. It is also in *The Politics of Pain*, edited by Crelinston and Schmid.

9. Federico Allodi has also done research in this vein, with findings consistent with those presented here. See his "Somoza's National Guard," in *The Politics of Pain*.

10. See Herbert C. Kelman, "The Social Context of Torture: Policy Process and Authority Structure," in *The Politics of Pain*.

11. Crelinsten, "In their own words," in *The Politics of Pain*.

12. Martha K. Huggins, Mika Haritos-Fatouros, and Philip G. Zimbardo. *Violence Workers: Police Torturers and Murderers Reconstruct Brazilian Atrocities*. Berkeley and Los Angeles, CA: University of California Press, 2002.

13. Grolston, in *Phenomenon of Torture*.

14. Huggins, Haritos-Fatouros, and Zimbardo, *Violence workers*.

15. Ariel Dorfman, "The Price we Pay for Paradise is Torture," *The Australian*, May 10, 2004. A similar point is made in Herbert C. Kelman, "The Social Context of Torture: Policy Process and Authority Structure," in *The Politics of Pain*, pp. 27–28.

16. Ervin Staub, "Torture: Psychological and Cultural Origins," in *The Politics of Pain*. See also *The Roots of Evil*.

17. Wolfendale, *Torture and the Military Profession*. A similar point has been made by Wolfgang Heinz in "The Military, Torture and Human Rights: Experiences from Argentina, Brazil, Chile and Uruguay," in *The Politics of Pain*.

18. Pieter H. Kooijmans, "Torturers and their masters," in *The Politics of Pain*.

19. Crelinston, "In Their Own Words," in *Phenomenon of Torture*.

20. Herbert C. Kelman, "The Social Context of Torture: Policy Process and Authority Structure," in *The Politics of Pain*.

21. Herbert C. Kelman, "The policy context of torture: A social psychological analysis."

22. Herbert C. Kelman, "The Social Context of Torture: Policy Process and Authority Structure," in *The Politics of Pain*.

23. The Huntington Park Police Department of Los Angeles has an ugly history involving brutality that often amounts to torture. See, for example, "Huntington Park Department Leads Southeast in Police Brutality Claims," July 6, 1986, *Los Angeles Times*, Dec. 19, 1986, "Cops Accused of Torturing Teenager," *Mohave Daily Mirror*, Dec. 19, 1986, "Claims Filed for Alleged Torture by 'Stun Guns' Huntington Beach Police Accused of Cruel Tactics," Dec. 26, *Los Angeles Times*.

24. See John Conroy, *Unspeakable Acts, Ordinary People*.

25. See *Violence Workers*.

26. See *Violence Workers*.

27. It is for this reason that interrogators are often trained to *avoid* using such epithets. See Matthew Alexander, *How to Break a Terrorist*.

28. Herbert C. Kelman, "The Social Context of Torture: Policy Process and Authority Structure," in *The Politics of Pain*.

29. Huggins et al., *Violence Workers*.

30. Zimbardo, *The Lucifer Effect*, 409.

31. The second half of Zimbardo's *The Lucifer Effect* is dedicated to the analysis of the Abu Ghraib case.

32. Wolfendale, *Torture and the Military Profession*.

33. See *A Miracle, A Universe*.

34. Thomas, *At Hell's Gate: A Soldier's Journey from War to Peace*.

35. Grolston, in *Phenomenon of Torture*.

36. See Arendt, *Eichman in Jerusalem*.

37. *Violence Workers*.

Chapter 8

The Politics of Torture: Orwellian Themes in the Bush League

The face of an administration: the Bush League

If there is one lesson to learn from the Bush Presidency, it is that no law – whether domestic statute or international treaty – can resist systematic misinterpretation. This, in my view, points to a problem with language that is quite general, and which haunted the philosophers of ancient Greece: the ability to reason – to articulate one's views systematically in *logos* – is insufficient. One must also have the capacity to comprehend *through* the language one employs.

This might seem like an obvious point; it is no less deep for its obviousness. The use of argument and the toolbox of reason must be kept fundamentally distinct from what the Greeks called 'nous' – a term that is sometimes translated as 'reason,' but is better understood as 'comprehension.' The best arguments in the world can dwell on the surface of language, never quite mastering what lies beneath. It is this that is captured in the wisdom of appealing to the 'spirit, if not the word' of a text.

The Bush administration was remarkably successful in inverting this principle. It was true to the *word* of the law, while it utterly ignored the *spirit*. In the memoranda that surround the Bush involvement with torture ('enhanced interrogation'), we see consistent argument without comprehension – rationality without reasonableness – and the kind of sophistry that disgraced an entire class of professionals in Plato's eyes.

It is here, I think, that the tools of philosophy are most readily applied to questions of policy – to show that policies are not justified, or that the arguments behind them do not stand up to scrutiny. That is what I hope to do in this section of the current chapter. I want to look closely and carefully at the arguments surrounding several key Bush administration decisions. I examine these as a case study, in essence, of the way that legal reasoning can be manipulated toward virtually any view, and hence as an argument for the continued necessity of philosophical analysis (construed broadly).

Geneva among the Bush League

The US torture scandal, most agree, started with the deliberations of a few lawyers and aides, working in concert with President Bush, Secretary of Defense Rumsfeld, and Vice President Cheney, and determined to remove the constraints imposed by US adherence to the Geneva Convention – in particular, the third Convention, which deals with the treatment of prisoners of war during times of armed conflict, and even more particularly, Common Article Three. Common Article Three of the convention (so-called because it appears in all four of the Geneva Conventions) strictly forbids:

> (a) violence to life and person, in particular murder of all kinds, mutilation, cruel treatment and torture; (b) taking of hostages; (c) outrages upon personal dignity, in particular, humiliating and degrading treatment; (d) the passing of sentences and the carrying out of executions without previous judgment pronounced by a regularly constituted court affording all the judicial guarantees which are recognized as indispensable by civilized peoples.

The consistent argument of the administration revolved around the idea that the US was in a 'new kind of war,' and that the restraints imposed by the convention no longer made sense. (They were 'quaint,' as Alberto Gonzales once remarked). The difficulty constructed by the Bush administration is a purely theoretical one, and is fairly easy to see: 'terrorists' are not civilians in the strict sense of the word; they are combatants. Initially, this would make it appear as though they were entitled to those specific conditions laid out in Geneva for Prisoners of War. The problem with this is relatively straightforward as well, provided one wants to see a problem: the conditions required to be construed as a combatant under Geneva III are not met by 'terrorists.' That list of conditions is given in Article 4:

> A. Prisoners of war, in the sense of the present Convention, are persons belonging to one of the following categories, who have fallen into the power of the enemy:
> (1) Members of the armed forces of a Party to the conflict, as well as members of militias or volunteer corps forming part of such armed forces.
> (2) Members of other militias and members of other volunteer corps, including those of organized resistance movements, belonging to a Party to the conflict and operating in or outside their own territory, even if this territory is occupied, provided that such militias or volunteer corps, including such organized resistance movements, fulfill the following conditions: (a) that of being commanded by a person responsible for his subordinates; (b) that of having a fixed distinctive sign recognizable at a distance; (c)

that of carrying arms openly; (d) that of conducting their operations in accordance with the laws and customs of war.

Obviously, 'terrorists' do not meet most of these conditions, and in certain cases, they will meet none of them. Weapons will be hidden, there will be no determinate command structure across 'cells', and no discernible uniforms will be worn. This state of affairs led the Bush League to designate 'terrorists' and 'suspected terrorists' as 'enemy combatants' – or at least that is the official story. More likely, it was the desire to get around Geneva, habeas corpus, and other legal constraints that motivated seeing this particular situation as a 'problem' to begin with. (I will present much more evidence for this below.)

There are at least two major difficulties with the Bush League's understanding of Geneva and its applicability to persons captured during hostilities. First, the Bush League seems to simply misread the distinctions in the Geneva Conventions. Geneva III, it is true, deals with Prisoners of War, while Geneva IV deals with civilians. However, as Joseph Margulies argues

> One mistake commonly made is to assume that, if the combatant does not qualify as a POW, then he has no rights under the Geneva Conventions. This is clearly not correct. Geneva IV (the Civilian Convention) applies broadly to all people 'who, at a given moment and *in any manner whatsoever*, find themselves' in enemy hands. The Civilian Convention protects these people – even if they have violated the laws of war and are therefore 'unlawful combatants' – from 'acts of violence or threats thereof' ('Civilian' is a term of art in the Convention, and is not limited to those people who were not engaged in hostilities) . . . there is no gap between Conventions III and IV, no fissure into which prisoners may fall, unprotected by the law. (Margulies, 54–55)[1]

The second problem with the inapplicability argument, of course, is that it had been made too many times by *others* in various situations – by the Viet Cong and by North Korea, for example. This argument had *always* been set aside and criticized by the US administration. Historically speaking, the 'problem' identified by the Bush administration was only a constructed problem – that is, it only emerged as a 'problem' when one wanted to problematize the Geneva Convention generally. Under similar circumstances, the US had done precisely the opposite: it had ignored quaint theoretical questions and simply *made Geneva work* to fit novel situations.

> Vietnam was in many respects an unconventional conflict. Many of the combatants – particularly the irregular units of the Viet Cong – did not wear uniforms or carry their arms openly, as required by the POW convention. In fact,

the Viet Cong often made a concerted effort to appear indistinguishable from innocent civilians . . . [they] terrorized civilians, kidnapping and assassinating public officials miles from any battlefield . . . [Nevertheless] the US detention policy in Vietnam was based on unwavering commitment to the letter and spirit of the Geneva Conventions. To implement this policy, the military constructed a novel legal framework, drafting regulations that adapted and applied the Conventions to an unconventional conflict. But the legal framework was intended to serve the policy preference – a policy that made humane treatment of prisoners its highest priority. (Margulies, 78–80)[2]

Indeed, the principles of Common Article Three had become part of military culture. They had been insisted on even before there were any Conventions in place. During the Civil War, President Lincoln claimed

Military necessity does not admit of cruelty – that is, the infliction of suffering for the sake of suffering or for revenge, nor of maiming or wounding except in fight, nor of torture to extort confessions . . . in general, military necessity does not include any act of hostility which makes the return to peace unnecessarily difficult. (Article 16, Instructions for the Government of Armies of the United States in the Field, originally prepared as General Orders #100, Adjutant General's Office, 1863; cited in Sands, *Torture Team*)

This has been reaffirmed on multiple occasions: in the US signing of the Geneva Conventions in 1949, the signing of Protocol I in 1977, in the implementation of the Conventions in the Field (even before ratification, in the Korean War, the military was instructed to act *as if* Geneva applied), in the US Army Field Manual, in military training, and in the diplomatic reactions to other nations who have claimed, for various reasons, that they were 'beyond' the Conventions.

So, US common law, military culture, and US international treaty obligations demanded that the US adhere to Geneva. This was precisely the advice Bush received from military leaders (as opposed to civilian lawyers). Indeed, Secretary of State Colin Powell was strongly opposed to any deviation from Geneva. As he argued in a memo to the Counsel to President dated January 6, 2002, suspending Geneva would have significant negative repercussions (the bullets are in the original memo):

- It will reverse over a century of U.S. policy and practice in supporting the Geneva Conventions and undermine the protections of the law of war for our troops, both in this specific conflict and in general.
- It has a high cost in terms of negative international reaction, with immediate adverse consequences for our conduct of foreign policy.
- It will undermine public support among critical allies, making military cooperation more difficult to sustain.

- Europeans and other will likely have legal problems with extradition or other forms of cooperation in law enforcement, including bringing terrorists to justice.
- It may provoke some individual foreign prosecutors to investigate and prosecute our officials and troops.
- It will make us more vulnerable to domestic and international legal challenge and deprive us of important legal options. (*The Torture Papers*, 123)

William H. Taft similarly argued that it would be a mistake to abandon Geneva in regard to the so-called 'war on terror.' In a memo dated February 2, 2002, Taft argues as follows:

> The President should know that a decision that the Conventions do apply is consistent with the plain language of the Conventions and the unvaried practice of the United States in introducing its forces into conflict over fifty years. It is consistent with the advice of DOS lawyers and, as far as is known, the position of every other party to the Conventions. It is consistent with UN Security Council Resolution 1193 affirming that "All parties to the conflict (in Afghanistan) are bound to comply with their obligations under international humanitarian law and in particular the Geneva Conventions . . . ." It is not inconsistent with the DOJ opinion that the Conventions generally do not apply to our world-wide effort to combat terrorism and to bring al Qaeda members to justice.
>
> From a policy standpoint, a decision that the Conventions apply provides the best legal basis for treating the al Qaeda and Taliban detainees in the way we intend to treat them. It demonstrates that the United States bases its conduct not just on its policy preferences but on its international legal obligations. Agreement by all lawyers that the War Crimes Act does not apply to our conduct means that the risk of prosecution under that statute is negligible. Any small benefit from reducing it further will be purchased at the expense of the men and women in our armed forces that we send into combat. A decision that the Conventions do not apply to the conflict in Afghanistan in which our armed forces are engaged deprives our troops there of any claim to the protection of the Convention in the event they are captured and weakens the protections accorded by the Conventions to our troops in future conflicts. (*The Torture Papers*, 129)

These are firm rejections of the initial arguments of the Office of Legal Counsel that the Geneva Conventions do not apply. Both Powell and Taft leave open the possibility that the Conventions might not apply in particular cases. They insist, however, that a decision to view Geneva as inapplicable *across the board* will have significant ill effects, and that such a decision is *against the spirit* of the Conventions. Taft's memo is particularly forceful in this regard: the recommendations to regard

Geneva as inapplicable is against "the plain language of the Convention and the unvaried practice of the United States in introducing its forces into conflict over fifty years."

Nevertheless, President Bush rejected all of these arguments, as well as the tradition of the US military, and insisted that Geneva would not apply to al Qaeda. Bush's announcement states:

> I hereby reaffirm the order previously issued by the Secretary of Defense to the United States Armed Forced requiring that the detainees be treated humanely and, to the extent appropriate and consistent with military necessity, in a manner consistent with the principles of Geneva. (Memo, February 7, 2002, *The Torture Papers*, 135)

As we are now painfully aware, the first sentence is killed by caveat: detainees will be treated humanely, it says, but than asserts that this will be the case *unless we need to treat them inhumanely*. Geneva will be followed, the memo says, *unless we need to set it aside*. This claim offers in its beginning a message of propaganda to silence critics (we will treat humanely). The message is then reversed in the caveats that follow.

It is in the confines of the Geneva deliberations that we also see the first instances of a rather disturbing view of the power of the executive branch. This view, which we will look at in detail below (The Constitution, US Law, and the Unitary Executive, Again), maintains that the President stands outside of all law insofar as his actions involve him acting as the Commander-in-Chief of the US. On this reading, the President has constitutional authority to do *anything at all* so long as he does so under the banner of leading the military. This includes suspending treaties, changing policies, denying civil liberties, and much more besides. Although this was not the argument provided for not utilizing Geneva against 'enemy combatants,' it remained a part of deliberations. Even if Geneva *did* apply, the argument went, the President had the constitutional authority to disregard it. It is this view of the power of the President, we will see, that resurfaces again and again in the defense of torture.

The torture memo: a Bush League document

The standard definition of 'torture' is provided by the 1984 United Nations Convention Against Torture. That definition, laid out in Article 1 and widely cited in legal literature on torture, runs as follows:

> the term "torture" means any act by which severe pain or suffering, whether physical or mental, is intentionally inflicted on a person for such purposes as obtaining from him or a third person information or a confession, punishing him for an act he or a third person has committed or is suspected of having

committed, or intimidating or coercing him or a third person, or for any reason based on discrimination of any kind, when such pain or suffering is inflicted by or at the instigation of or with the consent or acquiescence of a public official or other person acting in an official capacity. It does not include pain or suffering arising only from, inherent in or incidental to lawful sanctions.

A second definition of torture can be found in the United States Code, Section 2340:

> [Torture is an] act committed by a person acting under the color of law specifically intended to inflict severe physical or mental pain or suffering (other than pain or suffering incidental to lawful sanctions) upon another person within his custody or physical control.

These are the two primary definitions (understandably) relied on by the authors of the infamous 'torture memo' of August, 2002. The analysis provided regarding the legality of torture, given these definitions, is at times laughable, but always at least marginally frightening. From two documents that outright forbid torture *under any circumstances whatsoever*, we get an analysis that essentially permits anything the President of the US might order. As we will see, the torture memo virtually defines torture out of existence. And if that is not sufficient, it makes litigation based on torture incredibly difficult to justify.

Importantly, it should be remembered that this 'memo' had, in effect, the weight of law. According to the US Constitution, the President of the US has the right (and, indeed, obligation) to interpret both domestic laws and international treaties. For this very reason, the President is served by an Office of Legal Counsel (OLC), as well as by a cadre of lawyers working with and under the Department of Defense and the Justice Department. These lawyers essentially interpret the law to and for the President. They are meant to be the best legal minds of the land. The torture memo, then, is not some frivolous exercise in academic jurisprudence; it is an understanding of how the President ought to interpret what he is obligated to do given the torture statutes and the international obligations of the US. Moreover, it is the legal basis of policy decisions the President might make – and this is anything but academic.

Jay S. Bybee (and unnamed co-author John Yoo), both of the Office of Legal Counsel, claim that

> physical pain amounting to torture must be equivalent in intensity to the pain accompanying serious physical injury, such as organ failure, impairment of bodily function, or even death. For purely mental pain or suffering to amount to torture under section 2340, it must result in significant psychological harm of significant duration, e.g., lasting for months or even years . . . we conclude

that the statute, taken as a whole, makes plain that it prohibits only extreme acts. (317)

Already, in the second paragraph of the Bybee memo, we find a very strange sort of legal reasoning: Bybee is relying on a *medical* definition of pain that involves 'serious physical injury' to define a *legal* concept. Even those entirely unfamiliar with both philosophy of language and jurisprudence can see why this move is deeply problematic: a medical definition defines a concept in a *medically useful way*. When we speak of 'serious injury,' and the 'severe pain' which accompanies it, we define 'severe pain' with a specific set of contrasts in mind. In a medical context, the contrast class here would be (for example) injuries that would be treated only *after* a more serious injury had been dealt with. Thus, the most 'serious' injury would be the one that would result in imminent death (a gun shot wound to the chest, for example). This would trump another injury, even if the other injury was just as painful (a gun shot wound to the knee). To hijack this use of the phrase 'serious injury' as a *criterion* for 'severe pain' is to snatch a term from the context in which it makes perfectly good semantic sense, only to place it in a new context where its justification is wholly absent.

In fact, the exact *point* of the medical definition in question is even more restricted. As Joseph Margulies notes,

> the authors import this language from a different statute, a 2000 law on the availability of public health benefits to cover emergency medical conditions. It is simply bizarre that Bybee and Yoo would try to define 'severe pain' without reference to the context in which these words were used – a statute intended to fulfill our obligations under an an international treaty meant to prevent torture – and it is even more strange that they should believe the words would have the same meaning in the torture statute as they do in a statute intended to address the problem of scarce medical resources. (91)[3]

The *legal* context does not require anywhere near so high a standard for 'serious injury.' A gun shot wound to the knee, or the arm, or the finger, would certainly count as a serious injury, even if it was relatively late in the emergency room treatment queue. Moreover, the point of the definition of torture in terms of severe pain is to distinguish it from minor pain that might well belong to the lawful execution of punishment. In other words, a torture statute cannot very well define torture as the infliction of *any* pain whatsoever, as many lawful punishments are known to cause certain levels of distress and pain. Incarceration itself can cause a good deal of psychological anguish; handcuffs may well cause a minimal level of discomfort to those who wear them. In law, we must distinguish such unfortunate (but minor) pain from the variety of pain that is unnecessary, and, indeed, far more severe. As we can see, the contrast class is simply distinct. 'Severe pain' and 'serious injury' are those that go well beyond the kinds of injuries one might obtain during the normal process of carrying out a sentence. In the legal case, then, the bar is set much lower for the amount of pain necessary for an action to count as 'torture.'

Where this line is, of course, is an important and troubling question – but one we do not need to address here. The point is that Bybee's memo makes it impossible for the line to be anywhere except bordering on death – and this seems to stack the deck in favor of a permissive interrogational approach that, to many, all ready looks remarkably like torture.

But the analysis of the torture statutes provided by the Bybee memo gets much worse. Consider again what the memo has to say about what constitutes 'psychological torture.'

> For purely mental pain or suffering to amount to torture under section 2340, it must result in significant psychological harm of significant duration, e.g., lasting for months or even years . . . (317)

Imagine that you have been detained and subjected to grueling interrogation. Your treatment has included the following: interrogations lasting 20 hours for 10 consecutive days (sleep 'management'); simulated suffocation; public humiliation; slapping. Now imagine that you want to prosecute those who interrogated you for engaging in psychological torture.

According to the Bybee/Yoo analysis, you have no case. In order to *prove* that actual torture has taken place, it must be the case that you have experienced psychological harm – not merely during your interrogation – but for a 'significant duration.' This means that you cannot bring charges against your captors until your harm has existed for 'months, or even years.' Justice will have to wait until you suffer long enough.

Of course, Bybee might well respond that he was only providing the criteria by which we could *know* whether or not someone had undergone psychological torture. If this is so, though, the standard seems unduly high. After all, it would be far simpler to count as evidence of psychological torture the use of particular techniques that are spelled out in the *Geneva Conventions* and elsewhere. To claim that we must wait months (or years) before we can know that someone has been tortured would prevent the rights of the tortured to prompt justice – and would frankly ask too much of the prosecutor.

The notion of 'intent' plays a crucial role in the Bush memos. Consider:

> The statute requires that severe pain and suffering must be inflicted with specific intent . . . in order for a defendant to have acted with specific intent, he

must expressly intend to achieve the forbidden act . . . (defining specific intent as 'the intent to accomplish the precise criminal act that one is later charged with') . . . the infliction of such pain must be the defendant's precise objective . . . if the defendant acted knowing that severe pain or suffering was reasonably likely to result from his actions, but no more, he would have acted only with general intent. (319)

In regard to psychological torture, the memo holds the following:

The statute requires that the defendant specifically intend to inflict severe mental pain or suffering. Because the statute requires this mental state with respect to the infliction of severe mental pain, and because it expressly defines severe mental pain in terms of prolonged mental harm, that mental state must be present with respect to prolonged mental harm. (323)

An obvious problem with this sort of definition is that it seems to make torture *impossible* if one is involved in interrogation. For an act to count as torture, an agent must *intend* to *engage in torture*. So, if an interrogator has been assigned to 'extract intelligence' from a 'source,' the intent of this soldier can be presumed to be to extract said intelligence. Only in cases where an interrogator demonstrably intended to *cause prolonged mental harm* could said interrogator be convicted of violating the statute in question. This, in essence, means that only the mentally disturbed (and out of control) interrogator would ever face possible conviction.

As I hope is obvious, this standard leaves something to be desired. It makes it *logically impossible* for an interrogator, working an interrogation, to commit torture. In essence, torture is defined out of existence in the interrogation setting. So long as the interrogator intends to extract information, then no crime has been committed. Even if an interrogator does the most horribly demented things to a subject, knowing full well that this will result in 'prolonged mental harm,' the interrogator (by the reasoning of the memo) is *still* not guilty of torture. The interrogator must specifically intend the prolonged mental harm, on the Bybee/Yoo view. It is not enough merely to engage knowingly in actions that will result in such harm.

The situation is the same in regard to physical torture. Unless an interrogator *specifically intends* to cause 'severe pain' (where 'severe pain,' the reader will recall, is meant to reach the level of organ failure or death), then no torture has occurred. This leaves open the possibility that the actions of an interrogator *do reach this level*, but that the action is nevertheless not torture. To be torture, Bybee and Yoo claim, the pain must both be *specifically intended*, and it must *actually occur*.

Once again, torture for the interrogator seems virtually impossible. The interrogator, *qua* interrogator, can always claim that she is interested in extracting information, and that all of her actions had that specific intent: the removal of fingernails, the use of electroshock, the mock executions[4] – each aims to get information. Even though it was obvious such things would result in severe pain, this was only a known consequence, not the intended action. Hence, this cannot count as torture.

I find this reasoning to be *prima facie* implausible. It is the worst kind of rhetorical flourish that analyzes a crime into non-existent, provided it is a crime carried out by the right kinds of criminals. While it is certainly the case that intent figures importantly in many of our laws, it is beyond a stretch to claim that it should play such a prominent role in our torture legislation. Indeed, the very point of torture policy is to prevent certain kinds of treatment – it is *not* to prohibit certain kinds of *intending*.

Of course, the language of intention is undeniably present in the statute. It is there, obviously, to insure that *surgery* cannot legally count as torture. In a case such as this, the aim of the action is obviously to save the life of the patient (say), and not to simply engage in what would otherwise be torturous activity. The distinction between specific intent and general intent, moreover, is a standard legal distinction. Black's Law Dictionary defines specific intent as "the intent to accomplish the precise criminal act that one is later charged with. In common-law these crimes included robbery, assault, larceny, burglary, forgery, false pretenses, embezzlement, solicitation and conspiracy." A general-intent crime is defined as "the state of mind required for the commission of certain common-law crimes, not requiring a specific intent or imposing strict liability . . . General intent crimes usually take the form of recklessness or negligence" (*Black's Law Dictionary* [ed 7], St. Paul, MN: West Group, 1999). As David Luban points out, however, the use to which Bybee/Yoo put the language of 'specific intent' is deeply problematic.

> But why does the Bybee Memo belabor this point for two densely-written, single-spaced pages, reiterating again and again that knowingly inflicting severe pain is not torture unless inflicting pain is the 'precise objective'? After all, the memo is written for interrogators, not people who inflict pain as a mere by-product of their job, such as periodontists or heart surgeons. In interrogation, if you knowingly inflict pain, it's because you're trying to inflict pain. This is one context where specific intent and knowledge empirically coincide. (59)[5]

The authors of the torture memo have helped themselves to what is often called the doctrine of double effect. This doctrine maintains that an action may be morally permissible even if it results in significant *foreseeable* harm, provided that the resulting harm was unintended by the agent who engaged in the action. This is precisely the sort of reasoning that Bybee and Yoo are employing in the torture memo: provided that an interrogator does not *intend* to cause harm, that agent may permissibly engage in actions that will forseeably result in such harms, if these arise during the course of 'good faith' interrogation.

Luban's response to this, I think, is definitive – and it manages to sidestep the troubling issue of whether or not the doctrine of double effect is in fact a legitimate principle.[6] What Luban's point here effectively shows is that the doctrine of double effect (DDE) will apply *only* when there is a meaningful distinction between *knowingly* engaging in an action which will result in harm and having harm as the intent of one's knowing act. Although some would dispute that there are *any* cases where this distinction is meaningful, we need not settle this here for Luban's point to stand: in the case of interrogation, no such distinction can be made. As Luban concisely and bluntly puts it, "In interrogation, if you knowingly inflict pain, it's because you are trying to inflict pain" (59).[7]

Some additional analysis of 'intent'

One might retort that one's specific aim is in fact information extraction, and hence the analogy with the doctor case is much more powerful than Luban's analysis lets on. I doubt very much that this is true, but it is worth a more thorough investigation. Let's imagine someone responding to what we have been arguing as follows: the heart surgeon knowingly harms the patient by cutting him open. If there was another less intrusive way to get access to the heart, the doctor would surely use it. But there isn't any other available means. The only way to reach the desired (and morally permissible end) is to cut open the patient's chest. The doctor, however, is not *intending* to cause harm to the patient by cutting open his chest. By analogy, the argument might continue, the interrogator, when he engages in sleep deprivation, does not intend to harm the interogatee. If there were another way to extract the information, the interrogator would certainly use it. He places no intrinsic value in the methods employed.

It is easy to get carried away on the seas of language here, to borrow one of Wittgenstein's best known images. The idea of 'intent' here is fluid, its boundaries unclear. To sort out whether or not the analogy holds, we'll need to look in detail at several key points of comparison. First, let's deal with some obvious disanalogies.

1. The good to be achieved in the two cases is anything but parallel. The good in the torture case is meant to be the good of *others* rather than the good of the person being interrogated.
2. The patient in our example is presumably *consenting* to the heart surgery. If the patient did not consent, the cases might be much more analogous. They would also both (arguably) constitute morally problematic actions.

3. The claim that 'there is no other way' to engage in interrogation is demonstrably false. The dominant model of interrogation over the past fifty years in the US has involved rapport building.
4. Related to (2), the patient might opt out of the surgery without retaliation. This option is not available to the interrogatee.

No analogy is perfect. Indeed, if we had a perfect analogy, we would not be dealing with distinct analogues at all. Any two things that are the same in every respect are, in fact, not *two* things at all. It should thus come as no surprise that such significant disanalogies exist. The real problem for the analogy, in my view, is the haphazard use of 'intent' that is being made use of. It is anything but precise. Indeed, the current haphazard use might allow me to impute to myself any number of intentions at this particular moment: I *intend to* communicate (it is incidental that I am writing a sentence); I intend to write a sentence (it is incidental that I am using a computer); I intend to use a computer (it is incidental that it is in my office); I intend to work in my office (it is incidental that it is a weekday); I intend to meet deadlines; I intend to finish this chapter; I intend to go home at 5 pm.

This list could easily go on. What is it, exactly, that I am doing at this very moment (the moment of composing this sentence)? There is not an adequate answer to this question. The reason for this is, straightforwardly, that the notion of 'intention' lacks any unified and distinct sense. Thus, unless we *give it a sense*, it will remain pointless to inquire into *the* meaning of 'intent,' as there is no single meaning to this most amorphous of legal concepts. Consider the following example of 'intent,' provided by J. L. Austin:

> I needed money to play the ponies, so I dipped into the till. Of course, I *intended* (all the time) to put it back as soon as I had collected my winnings. That was my intention: I took it with the intention of putting it back. But was that my *purpose* in taking it? Did I take it for the purpose of, or on purpose to, put it back? Plainly not. (275)[8]

As this example makes plain, an 'intention' is not always identical to a 'purpose.' Of course, sometimes these two concepts *do* overlap. Austin (and we) need not deny that such overlap exists. What will not do, however, is to presume that 'purpose' and 'intention' are *identical* in every context, legal or otherwise. If we were to maintain this view, the purpose of an interrogator might well be 'to follow orders,' even if in doing so the interrogator *intentionally* inflicted profound pain on a subject.

I am not suggesting here that 'to intentionally x' is the same as 'to intend to do x.' As Austin has beautifully and exhaustively shown, there are several instances where these concepts do not overlap. I *am* suggesting that the purpose of an act should not be presumed to be the legal meaning of 'to intend to x.' I might intend to extract information, but do this for the purpose of getting a promotion, or of saving lives, or anything else. Thus, even if we state that the purpose of an interrogation is to obtain actionable intelligence, it doesn't follow that this is the intention.

I do not presume that there is a strict meaning to the notion of legal intention. One view, though, might run as follows: 'one intends to x (in the legal sense) if it is the case that said person intentionally did x.' Here, we can parse 'intentionally did x' as 'was the direct (as opposed to 'indirect') causal agent in the execution of x.' This would entail that the intentional infliction of painful interrogation techniques, even if the intent (purpose) was the extraction of information, would still count as 'specific intent' in the legal sense of the phrase. Insofar as one was the direct cause of said pain, and knowingly engaged in that action, one can be said to have intended the pain.

This view admittedly has a messy consequence: namely, that we must say that the heart surgeon intentionally harms the patient. I do not think this is a particularly problematic result, however. If the doctor did *not* intentionally harm the patient (in the sense given to this phrase above), then only a lesser case could be brought against the doctor in the event that the patient did not consent (or revoked consent) – the doctor could be charged only with *malpractice* rather than *battery*. This strikes me as deeply implausible. There is a fundamental difference between engaging in surgery on a subject *with the consent of that subject*, and engaging in surgery *against the will* of said subject. What makes the surgeon's intended harm acceptable is that the patient has *been informed, and will agree, to the very harm said patient will undergo*. In the event that excess harm occurs, to which the subject did not consent, malpractice litigation applies (a harm occurred, or a procedure was undertaken, to which no consent was given).

I do not mean to suggest that this sketch of a view has been adequately defended. It is only a sketch. The point of this sketch is to show how many alternative conceptions of 'intention' are available to the strict one given in the Bybee memo (which presumes that 'strict intent' and 'purpose' are identical).

Meet the new memo, same as the old memo . . .

It might well be claimed that the preceding analysis is correct, but that this was largely acknowledged by the Bush League. After all, the original memo was criticized by the administration itself (and was suspended in March 2004), and the torture prohibition was re-affirmed. But things are not as straightforward as they might initially seem. Despite the creation of a new memo outlining the Administration's policy on torture, this memo largely duplicates the position of the initial memo, despite some (fairly extensive) cosmetic revisions.

The December 2004 Memo explicitly supersedes the Bybee/Yoo memo. Many of the problems with the Bybee/Yoo memo are corrected by the new memo (for example, the analysis of 'specific intent' is far more plausible). But none of these changes had any significant effect on the *policy* of the United States in conducting its military affairs. This is spelled out quite explicitly in the beginning of the document:

> This memorandum supercedes the August 2002 Memorandum in its entirety. Because this discussion in that memorandum concerning the President's Commander-in-Chief power and potential defenses to liability was – and remains – unnecessary, it has been eliminated from the analysis that follows. Consideration of the bounds of any such authority would be inconsistent with the President's unequivocal directive that the United States personnel do not engage in torture. (362)[9]

Although this might initially appear a perfectly reasonable claim, it is important to see that it leaves intact the view that the President has the authority to order anything he so chooses. In this respect, it leaves the view of the President's Commander-in-Chief powers entirely untouched. So, while it might be the case that the President has ordered that no one engages in torture (more on this in a moment), this in no way entails that ordering torture is outside of the President's constitutional rights. As Commander-in-Chief, the President can order anything he likes. To forbid him to do so, the Bush League maintains, would be unconstitutional. Moreover, As Margulies points out:

> in a footnote, the authors make the point of saying they reviewed the prior opinions addressing 'issues involving treatment of detainees' – including the torture memo – and found that none of the earlier conclusions 'would be different under the standards set forth in this memorandum.' Substantively, in other words, the new memo changes nothing. (108)

The significance of Bush's order that no one engage in torture is thus by no means straightforward. After all, the administration has consistently perverted the meaning of the term 'torture,' making it into something arcane, and totally ignoring the use to which the term has been put within US legislation and policy. Thus, it is by no means clear what it means to say that the President has 'banned torture,' particularly given the behavior of the Bush administration *after* this memo.

John Yoo's memo of March 14, 2004 (declassified April, 2008) to William Haynes Re: *Military Interrogation of Alien Unlawful*

Combatants Held Outside the United States actually restates the views put forth in the Bybee/Yoo 2002 memo, despite the fact that this memo was denounced the year before. Regarding the much criticized analysis of 'severe pain,' Yoo's 2004 analysis is virtually identical to that offered in 2002:

> Significantly, the phrase "severe pain," appears in statutes defining an emergency medical condition for the purpose of providing health benefits. *See, e.g.*, 8 U.S.C. § 1369 (2000); 42 U.S.C § l395w-22 (2000); *id.* §1395x (2000); *id.* § 1395dd (2000); *id* § 1396b (2000); *id* § 1396u-2 (2000). These statutes define an emergency condition as one "manifesting itself by,' acute symptoms of sufficient severity (including *severe pain)* such that a prudent lay person, who possesses an average knowledge of health and medicine, could reasonably expect the absence of 'immediate medical attention to result in placing the health of the individual . . . (i) in serious jeopardy, (ii) serious impairment to bodily functions, or (iii) serious dysfunction of any bodily organ or part." *Id.* § 1395w-22(d)(3)(B) (emphasis added). Although these statutes address a substantially different subject from section 2340, they are nonetheless helpful for understanding what constitutes severe physical pain. They treat severe pain as an indicator of ailments that are likely to result in permanent and serious physical damage in the absence of immediate medical treatment. Such damage must rise to the level of death, organ failure, or the permanent, impairment of a significant body function. These statutes suggest that to constitute torture "severe pain" must rise to a similarly high level – the level that would ordinarily be associated with a physical condition or injury sufficiently serious that it would result in death, organ failure, or serious impairment of body functions. (38–39)

The claims of the Bush administration that the US does not torture, and that the errors of 2002 had been corrected in later legal opinions, simply don't stand up. In relation to the US's obligations under the UN Convention Against Torture (as well as customary international law), the 2004 Yoo memo is similarly familiar:

> Thus, if interrogation methods were inconsistent with the United States' obligations under CAT, but were justified by necessity or self-defense, we would view these actions still as consistent ultimately with international law. Although these actions might violate *CAT*, they would still be in service of the more fundamental principle of self-defense that cannot be extinguished by CAT or any other treaty. Further, if the President ordered that conduct, such an order would amount to a suspension or termination of the Convention. In so doing, the President's order and the resulting conduct would not be a violation of international law because the United States would no longer be bound by the treaty. (58)[10]

I will not multiply examples from the Yoo memo here. These two sufficiently demonstrate that Bush's proclamation was anything but definitive. While these words were spoken, memoranda were being written to
thwart the very thing to which lip service was being paid.

But the evidence of course does not end there. On October 16, 2006,
Bush signed into law the Military Commissions Act of 2006. This act
provides immunity to CIA interrogators who have "engaged in activity
characterized as torture."[11] On March 8, 2008, Bush also vetoed a bill
that would forbid members of the CIA to engage in what the administration euphemistically called 'enhanced interrogation techniques.' The
bill, essentially, aimed to extend the torture ban to cover the actions of
the CIA – including waterboarding. In explanation, Bush remarked that
"Because the danger remains, we need to ensure our intelligence officials
have all they need to stop the terrorists."[12] He went on to say, without
any evidence whatsoever, that "this is no time for Congress to abandon
practices that have a proven track record of keeping America safe."[13]

In an interview with ABC-TV in 2008, Bush also acknowledged that
top officials had met to discuss 'enhanced' interrogation on a number
of occasions. These officials included: Secretary of State Colin Powell,
Secretary of Defense Donald Rumsfeld, Vice President Dick Cheney, and
a litany of the usual suspect lawyers: David Addington, John Ashcroft,
Alberto Gonzales, William Haynes, and so on (it is not clear how many
of this group were present at any particular meeting).[14] Bush remarked "I
told the country we did that. And I told them it was legal. We had legal
opinions that enabled us to do that . . . I didn't have any problems at all
trying to find out what Khalid Sheikh Mohammed knew."[15]

Of course, the Bush League has routinely insisted that waterboarding is
not torture. But the definition of torture, frankly, is not up to the League.
As Tony Norman has wryly remarked, "Bush is the first American president in history to claim a measure of omnipotence as one of the functions
of his office."[16] Indeed, waterboarding cannot simply be deemed 'not
torture' without comment, particularly since the US has a legal history
of regarding it as torture. Waterboarding, a practice that "has been
prosecuted as torture in US Military Courts since the Spanish-American
War,"[17] has repeatedly been defended by Bush, as well as by key members
in his administration – but this defense hardly makes it innocuous.

Apparently, participants in deliberations about interrogation policies
were hand-picked. "State Department officials and military lawyers were
intentionally excluded from these deliberations."[18] Moreover, as more
information has been made available from sites of 'enhanced' interrogation, we have come to see just how harshly persons – often later let
go without *any criminal charges being filed* – are in fact treated. This is
nowhere more clear than in the case of Detainee 063, at Guantanamo
Bay, Mohammad al-Qahtani. Al Qahtani was subjected to 160 days of

isolation, 48 of 54 consecutive days of 18 to 20-hour interrogations, threats to his family, insults on his dignity and his religion, being subjected to unwanted female contact during Ramadan (when this would be particularly offensive), having fake menstrual blood smeared on him, and much more besides.[19] The Pentagon has defended this interrogation, calling it professional, and insisting that it was neither cruel nor inhuman.[20]

The Constitution, US law, and the unitary executive, again

Perhaps the most disturbing section of the torture memo centers on the so-called 'War Time Powers' of the President. Much of the argument of the Bush league revolves around what has come to be called 'the unitary executive.' In the avalanche of memoranda following 9/11, this view cashes out as follows:

> Even if an interrogation method arguably were to violate Section 2340A, the statute would be unconstituitional if it impermissibly encroached on the President's constitutional power to conduct a military campaign. As Commander-in-Chief, the President has the constitutional authority to order interrogations of enemy combatants to gain intelligence information concerning the military plans of the enemy . . . Any effort to apply Section 2340A in a manner that interferes with the President's direction of such core war matters as the detention and interrogation of enemy combatants thus would be unconstitutional. (Section V, 'Torture Memo,' 344)

This claim – one that re-emerges in several different documents – acts as an executive magic bullet. It is also a bullet that seems to be lethal to the separation of powers.[21] The claims made above translate the 'Commander-in-Chief' power into a virtual super power – making the President capable of ordering absolutely anything, and without the possibility of oversight. This came out clearly in challenges posed by the decision in *Rasul v. Bush*.

The position of the Bush League entails that any objections to torture cannot get off the ground. *Any* attempt to limit the authority of the President will count, on this view, as violating the President's constitutional authority. This, if correct, entails that *no law* can prevent a President from ordering torture.

Is there any basis for thinking that this is *in fact* what the US Constitution requires? The Supreme Court does not seem to think so. As Justice Souter wryly noted, the President "is not Commander-in-Chief of the country, only of the military" (*Hamdi v. Rumsfeld*). Indeed, the Supreme Court has consistently rebuked the administration for its strained reading of the Constitution. Decisions in several cases have systematically scaled back the powers claimed for the executive branch of the US Government in the torture memo and elsewhere. Here is what the text of the Constitution actually says:

> The President shall be Commander in Chief of the Army and Navy of the United States, and of the Militia of the several States, when called into the actual Service of the United States (Article 2, Section 1)

To get from this to the 'Unitary Executive,' understood as I've laid it out here, is a work of magic. It relies on selective reading, and acute ignorance. The view that Bush overstepped his bounds has been borne out by four Supreme Court decisions.

Rasul v. Bush (2004)

The Supreme Court ruled that non-US Citizens held in Guantanamo had the right to challenge their detention, despite the fact that the facilities were under the *de jure* jurisdiction of another nation (Cuba).

Hamdi v. Rumsfeld (2004)

The Supreme Court ruled that US citizens detained as terrorist suspects had the right to challenge their detention by the US Government.

Hamdan v. Rumsfeld (2006)

The Supreme Court rules that military commissions lack "the power to proceed because its structures and procedures violate both the Uniform Code of Military Justice and the four Geneva Conventions signed in 1949."[22] It was also maintained that Common Article Three of the Geneva Convention applied to members of al Qaeda.

Boumediene v. Bush (2008)

The Supreme Court rules that detainees at Guantanamo have the right to a writ of habeas corpus. As Justice Kennedy puts it in the majority opinion:

> We hold these petitioners do have the habeas corpus privilege. Congress has enacted a statute, the Detainee Treatment Act of 2005 (DTA), 119 Stat. 2739, that provides certain procedures for review of the detainees' status. We hold that those procedures are not an adequate and effective substitute for habeas corpus. Therefore §7 of the Military Commissions Act of 2006 (MCA), 28 U. S. C. A. §2241(e) (Supp. 2007), operates as an unconstitutional suspension of the writ. (1–2)

It is useful to see how each of these decisions rebukes the Bush League's attempt to secure greater and greater executive power. In the table below, each decision is correlated with the policy it effectively ruled unconstitutional. Beneath the name of each case, I have also indicated what basic legal concept it reiterates is not subject to executive suspension.

Supreme Court Decision	Bush Policy Countered
Rasul v. Bush (habeas)	View that foreign nationals do not have a right to a hearing in the US court system regarding their detention in Guantanamo Bay
Hamdam v. Rumsfeld (Geneva)	View that common article 3 of the Geneva Convention does not apply to members of al Qaeda
Hamdi v Rumsfled (2004) (habeas)	View that terrorist suspects did not have the right to challenge their detention
Boumediene v. Bush (2008) (habeas)	View that detainees at Guantanamo do not have the right to writs of habeas corpus

In response to these rulings, the Bush League has once again attempted to find its way around Supreme Court decisions. Rather than pursuing the ways this has happened – ways that follow the patterns set out here, and ample evidence of which is available from other sources[23] – it will be worth having a closer look at the specific parts of the US Constitution that the Bush lawyers were anxious to explain away. Three Amendments that were particularly troublesome were the fifth, eighth, and fourteenth Amendments. These Amendments state the following:

Amendment 5. No person shall be held to answer for a capital, or otherwise infamous crime, unless on a presentment or indictment of a Grand Jury, except in cases arising in the land or naval forces, or in the Militia, when in actual service in time of War or public danger; nor shall any person be subject for the same offense to be twice put in jeopardy of life or limb; nor shall be compelled in any criminal case to be a witness against himself, nor be deprived of life, liberty, or property, without due process of law; nor shall private property be taken for public use, without just compensation.

Amendment 8. Excessive bail shall not be required, nor excessive fines imposed, nor cruel and unusual punishments inflicted.

Amendment 14. 1. All persons born or naturalized in the United States, and subject to the jurisdiction thereof, are citizens of the United States and of the

State wherein they reside. No State shall make or enforce any law which shall abridge the privileges or immunities of citizens of the United States; nor shall any State deprive any person of life, liberty, or property, without due process of law; nor deny to any person within its jurisdiction the equal protection of the laws.

In one way or another, each of the above Amendments stands in the way of pro-torture policies such as those advocated by the Bush League. The readings of these Amendments offered by the Bush League are instances of what I call 'pragmatic manipulations' of language. The motivation to avoid straightforward readings of these Amendments is clear in the torture memo itself. One of the subheadings of that documents is entitled "Interpretation to Avoid Constitutional Problems." The very *aim* of the policy analysis presented is to provide some kind of account of torture ("enhanced interrogation techniques") that would lie outside the purview of the US constitution. The strategy of the Bush League was twofold: first, it claimed that all torture legislation has been ratified so as to interpret 'torture' as it was interpreted by the eighth Amendment. So far, so good. But the administration then argued that the eighth Amendment regarded the concept of 'cruel and unusual' as geographically bound to the United States. This meant, according to the Bush lawyers, that the US *only* had obligations not to torture within the geographical boundaries of the US, and that, outside of these boundaries, it was under no obligation to do anything in particular. Moreover, as a host of memos had all ready argued (and as we've all ready seen), the attempt to restrict the actions of the President would *itself* be unconstitutional given the status of the President as Commander-in-Chief.

We won't bother to reject the Unitary Executive view again; the Supreme Court has done that for us. It is worth noting, though, that this argument is as specious as they come. As Margulies has pointed out, "linking the Torture Convention to the 8th Amendment [initially] meant that both would be given the same substantive scope. Unfortunately, the Administration's lawyers have transformed this substantive understanding into a geographic loophole . . . this is just bad lawyering" (179).

A second prong of the strategy of the Bush league was to eliminate concerns about due process, as enshrined in the fifth and fourteenth Amendments of the US Constitution. The arguments here were as follows: in a time of war, the President can suspend the Habeas Statute, so the fifth Amendment's due process clause simply does not apply. There is a 'new paradigm' of war that requires new modes of intelligence gathering, and hence the suspension of habeas corpus is justified. In regard to the fourteenth Amendment, which guarantees protection to *all* persons (not just citizens) within the jurisdiction of the United States, the Bush league argued that the detention facilities it operated were outside of US jurisdiction (Guantanamo is in Cuba, for example). Hence, the protections of this Amendment do not cover those 'detainees' being interrogated in such facilities.

The Supreme Court, of course, disagreed. Once again, the idea that the US did not have 'jurisdiction' at Guantanamo seemed like a rhetorician's flourish and no more. The Administration relied on a strange clause in the US lease with Cuba, made in 1903, which claimed that Cuba maintained 'sovereignty' over Guantanamo during the tenure of its lease to the US. The idea of a maintained sovereignty proved too vacuous for the majority of the Justices to accept.[24] As Justice Souter put it during oral argument in *Rasul v. Bush*:

> in bringing people from Afghanistan or wherever they were brought to Guantanamo, we are doing in functional terms exactly what we would do if we brought them to the District of Columbia, in a functional sense, leaving aside the metaphysics of ultimate sovereignty. If the metaphysics of ultimate sovereignty do not preclude us from doing what we have been doing for the last 100 years, why is it a bar to the exercise of judicial jurisdiction under the Habeas Statute?" (175)[25]

Why indeed. The lawyers of the Bush League attempted to dismantle international law, the protection of basic human rights, and the value of due process – arguably one of the central themes of the US Constitution[26] – by reading clauses of that Constitution without regard for the document as a whole. This kind of selective misreading was in turn motivated by a basic disrespect for those legal processes that were, in essence, put in place to prevent tyrannical detentions in the first place.[27]

Additional objections based on these Amendments were likewise quickly argued away: torture could not be used in order to get someone to implicate themselves in criminal activity, according to the fifth Amendment. But if those being interrogated were not involved in criminal proceedings, there would be no constitutional issues to worry about. The eighth Amendment says no *punishment* can be cruel and unusual. A 'punishment' is what results after one has been convicted of a crime. In the case of the interrogation of detainees, though, there was not even a trial – so torturing said detainees could not count as a 'punishment' of any sort whatsoever. In a memo dated March, 2003 (declassified in April 2008), John Yoo argues

> A second constitutional provision that might be thought relevant to interrogations is the Eighth Amendment. The Eighth· Amendment, however, applies solely to those persons upon whom criminal sanctions have been imposed. As the Supreme Court has explained, the Cruel and Unusual Punishments Clause "was designed to protect those convicted of crimes." *Ingraham v. Wright*, 430

U.S. 651, 664 (1977). As a result, "Eighth Amendment scrutiny is appropriate only after the State has complied with the constitutional guarantees traditionally associated with criminal prosecutions." *Id.* at 671 *nAO*. The Eighth Amendment thus has no application to those individuals who have not been punished as part of a criminal proceeding, irrespective of the fact that they have been detained by·the government. (p. 10)

My aim in rehearsing these kinds of arguments is to display the abuse of language and reason that has come to the service of torture and the will to utilize it.

Political motivation and the Orwellian game

What motivated this analysis of the evidence? What led lawyers like Yoo and Bybee to look for ways to *justify* the 'new techniques' when so much data – as well as military culture – was set against practicing this kind of coercive interrogation?

Some keys to solving this riddle are actually present in the Bybee memo itself. What seems to be behind the memo is a commitment to a particular outcome. This seems clear in the dedication to claim absolute power for the executive branch. Likewise, some of the lawyers involved in getting new interrogation techniques approved have said, forthrightly, that the *aim* of particular memoranda was to remove the constraints of Geneva.[28] The standard chain of legal checks and balances, it appears, was simply ignored.[29]

It is possible, of course, that Bybee, Yoo, and other lawyers simply made mistakes in their legal reasoning. Perhaps they had the best of intentions. I submit, however, that this prospect is no happier than its alternative, for if these lawyers made such egregious errors, they should not have been in a *position* to make them.

The eventual approval of 'enhanced interrogation techniques' by then Secretary of Defense Donald Rumsfeld came when Rumsfeld signed a memo by William J. Haynes, and which recommended 18 interrogation techniques that were not present in the Army's *Field Manual*. The etiology of this particular memo, as well as the reason Rumsfeld signed it, and the President approved of this decision over the objections of lifetime military Secretary of State Colin Powell, is a subject of much contention. Why would an administration approve of techniques that went against military culture, that violated international law and the treaty obligations of the US?

The answer to this, perhaps, can only be speculative. Certainly there were a number of factors at play. Some of these factors, though, are as dismaying as one can possibly imagine. It appears that network television, for example, actually played a role in the decision making that led to the 18 techniques laid out in the Haynes memo. Apparently, the television character Jack Bauer of the show 24, known for his use of torturous interrogation, "gave people lots of ideas."[30] In the most tragic and stupid way, we see life imitating art.

It also appears that the process of checks and balances – the very backbone of solid decision making and analysis – was intentionally thwarted by the powers that be, and in particular by William J. Haynes, II, the General Counsel to then Secretary of Defense Donald Rumsfeld. The memo that first outlined the 'new techniques' was authored by Haynes, signed by Rumsfeld, and ultimately acted as the paper justification for the detainee abuse at GITMO.

Haynes' memo, though, is only one piece of paper. There is substantial evidence that the memo itself was merely the articulation of a policy decision that had already been made.[31] Rumsfeld allegedly gave the go-ahead to begin applying a new interrogation plan to General Miller, the person in charge at GITMO, *prior* to signing this memo. In addition, the analysis of interrogation provided by Yoo and Bybee had all ready been completed – and had, as we have seen, made it nearly impossible for anyone other than the Marquis de Sade to actually commit an act of torture. All of this, it should also be remembered, occurred in a climate where the applicability of the Geneva Conventions had been outright denied by the Commander-in-Chief of the US Military, President George W. Bush.

Inhumane treatment, it seems, was simply in the air. The goal of Haynes' eventual memo was not to *suggest* a policy but to make it official. In order to do this, Haynes apparently anticipated resistance from other lawyers normally involved in the analysis of such questions. This, it seems, would explain why the Haynes memo was *not subjected to peer review.* In fact, the normal procedure of allowing differing departments to provide legal opinion on a memo of this magnitude (one that recommended, essentially, changing the practices of the US Military since the Civil War) was simply bypassed. As Phillipe Sands reports, the Chairmen of the Joint Chiefs of Staff never even *saw* the memo. Likewise, military lawyers were simply not given time and opportunity to carry out the detailed analysis such a policy change would require. Sands nicely sums up the situation – one that predictably would have disastrous consequences: "First it was decided that the Geneva Conventions did not apply, so there were no rules. Then the military lawyers were cut out and the decision was put in the hands of Jim Haynes, with the help of other political appointees at the Justice Department" (106; see also 178).

The primary players in the torture scandal were Bush League folks and their political appointees. Despite appearances, this is not a story without heroes – heroes within the establishment who did everything in their power to stop the advent of techniques "tantamount to being considered torture."[32] These include Alberto Mora, then General Counsel of the Navy, and the Army's General Counsel Steve Morello. It also includes those deeply within the Bush administration, like Colin Powell. Despite a pension for cynicism, I cannot help but be heartened by the attempts of many in the US military to prevent war crimes.

I have not lost faith in the rule of law. The Supreme Court has rebuked the Bush administration's policies regarding habeas corpus and the Geneva Conventions. The view of the unitary executive has been sternly criticized by the highest court of the land. This is indeed the US system at work – even if the work is slow, and justice long in the coming.

At the time of writing, the Bush administration has now gone from the halls of power – with Obama having ordered the end of harsh interrogation, and the closing of CIA black sites along with Guantanamo Bay – only two questions remain.

1) How long will it take to repair the damage to international law and universal human rights caused by the United States?
2) When will those responsible for violating the Geneva Convention, as well as the Universal Declaration of Human Rights, be brought to justice? When – if ever – will we find ourselves seeing the trial of these war criminals – and that *just is* the definition of someone who violates Geneva, or conspires to violate it; when will we see the trial of Donald Rumsfeld, Dick Cheney, David Addington, John Yoo, Jay Bybee, Doug Feith, and even George W. Bush?

While I am realistic about the prospects of such a trial, I remain convinced that justice requires it – and that such a trial would do an immense amount of work in repairing the damage done to international law during the Bush administration.

Notes

1. As Margulies notes, Geneva IV does have one exception: "it does not protect nationals of a co-belligerent" (note 43, page 277).
2. This is not to deny that there were abuses of prisoners in Vietnam. The point here is about the stated policies of the United States during these two, similar conflicts with an enemy that didn't seem to meet the requirements of Geneva. It is also worth mentioning that the North Vietnamese explicitly denied that US forces had a right to be treated according to Geneva, as the actions of the US were 'illegal.' There was thus no reciprocity in the US application of the code.
3. *Guantánamo and the Abuse of Presidential Power.*
4. These are among the examples of torture provided in the Bybee memo. Note once again, however, that committing such act *is insufficient* for torture according to said memo. One must also *intend* to torture.

5. David Luban, "Liberalism, Torture, and the Ticking Bomb," in *The Torture Debate in America.*

6. There are many cases where the doctrine seems to apply nicely. In euthanasia, for example, a doctor might administer a lethal amount of pain killer, with the foreseeable result that the patient will die. The doctor only intends to ease the pain of the patient. The intention is *not* to end the patient's life. It just so happens, though, that achieving the intended result involves the death of the patient. Why the doctor's actions are here morally permissible seems to be nicely explained by the doctrine of double effect. Similar kinds of arguments can be made in regard to abortion and affirmative action.

   I am not convinced that the doctrine of double effect has any kind of justificatory significance. Indeed, there are plenty of other cases that make DDE look atrociously inappropriate (suicide bombing, so-called 'collateral damage,' etc). It seems virtually impossible, without appeal to alternative principles, to determine when the DDE applies *appropriately*. If this is right, then the DDE offers no justification of a course of action. To justify such a course of action, we would need some *additional* principle, which just demonstrates that the DDE is impotent if it aims at more than articulating a previous set of moral intuitions.

7. Andrew Fiala has made a similar point about torture: "[Torture] is difficult to justify by using double effect. Indeed, torture intends the harm it causes as a means through which it aims to bring about its end," (172), "Waterboarding, Torture, and Violence: Normative Definitions and the Burden of Proof," *Review Journal of Political Philosophy*, 2008, Vol. 6, No. 1, pp. 153–173.

8. J. L. Austin, "Three Ways of Spilling Ink," in *Philosophical Papers;* see also "A Plea for Excuses" in the same volume.

9. *The Torture Debate in America.*

10. It is worth noting that this memo explicitly ignores the 'one year clause' of the Geneva conventions, which stipulates that any party which quits the treaty must allow one year before the convention ceases to apply.

11. P. 42, *The Washington Monthly*, January/February/March, 2008.

12. Steven Lee Meyes, Mark Mazzetti, "Veto of Bill on C.I.A. Tactics Affirms Bush's Legacy", *New York Times*, March 9, 2008, A1.

13. Ibid.

14. Dahlia Lithwick, "Getting Away with Torture; Legal Maneuvering has shielded those responsible for conditions at Guantanamo Bay," *Newsweek*, New York: May 5, 2008. Vol 151, Iss. 18.

15. Helen Thomas, "Bush Admits he Approved Torture," *Seattle Post, Intelligences*, May 2, 2008. P. B5. This was widely reported.

16. Tony Norman, "Making Torture the American Way," *Pittsburgh Post-Gazette*, March 11, 2008, A2.

17. Dan Eggen and Paul Kane, "On Day 2, Democrats See Change in Mukasey; Nominee Endorses President's Positions," *The Washington Post*, Oct. 19, 2007, p. A1.

18. Dan Eggen, "Bush Approved Meetings on Interrogation Techniques; President's Comments to ABC News Prove Top-Level Involvement in Allowing Harsh Coercion," *Washington Post*, April 12, 2008. A3.

19. See Sands, *Torture Team*.

20. See p. 86, p. 247, and p. 258, Joseph Margulies, *Guantánamo and the Abuse of Presidential Power*.

21. This is precisely the worry Justice Breyer raised during oral arguments in *Hamdan v. Rumsfeld*, where it looks as though the President was attempting to become the judiciary as well as the executive. See 279–284, *Terrorism and the Constitution: The Post 9/11 Cases*.

22. Supreme Court Decision, p. 2, delivered by Justice Stevens.

23. See Sands, Margulies, etc.

24. The Justices dissenting were Scalia, Thomas, and Rehnquist.

25. *Terrorism and the Constitution*.

26. See Ely.

27. If this was indeed the meaning of the text as the framers (and others) saw it, Scalia's dissent should be incredibly surprising to us.

28. See Phillipe Sands. Doug Feith reportedly made this specific claim to Sands.

29. See 92, Sands.

30. 62, Sands, in interview with Diane Beaver.

31. This is the argument made in Phillipe Sands' *Torture Team*.

32. This is attributed to Alberto Mora, General Counsel to the US Navy, quoted in *Torture Team*, Phillipe Sands.

Chapter 9

Hope Amid Pessimism: Concluding Reflections on Ending Torture

Introduction

The final chapter of this book is not really a chapter. In some respects, it is the confessional ruminations that must follow the completion of a long project – a confessional that admits what one has done and how it has gone wrong. The confession is as much about closure as it is about recognition – a recognition that congratulations *are not* in order; that one has not done enough, and perhaps never will.

I have spent hundreds of pages trying to understand the human animal – the only one that tortures – *homo torquere, homo tormentum*. I have considered the psychology, the history, the politics, and the morality of torture. I have leveled dozens of pages of argument against the permissibility of torture in *any* case. With the book now complete, I cannot help but see all that is wrong with it – all that it has missed or not argued clearly enough. Worse still, I feel the force of argument's limitations. In this respect, my confession occasions a humiliating admission: arguments will not end torture. Perhaps nothing will.

I want to spend these final pages articulating why argument is impotent against torture, as it is against *any* grossly immoral practice. I hope the reader will indulge what is less than argument in what follows, appreciating that any argument for the impotence of argument would be too ironic to bear.

An anecdote

I once knew a young man who was vehemently opposed to abortion. He was 19, and was quite familiar with many of the arguments available in the philosophical literature. He quite enjoyed talking about the wrongs of taking life, whether in the context of the death penalty, war, or abortion. His pacifism was consistent, and he was convinced that his pacifism entailed the moral bankruptcy of elective abortion. His arguments were fairly good – at least as good as such arguments can be. An interesting thing happened, however, when the young man in question became a father-to-be. His live-in girlfriend at the time (also 19) became pregnant, and the man immediately changed his mind about the merits of abortion.

There are many ways to describe this change of heart, and the correct way to describe it is perhaps impossible to determine. One way to describe it, of course, is that the young man was simply a hypocrite – he did not have the courage of his convictions. When push came to proverbial shove, he abandoned his moral principles and took what seemed like the 'easy way' out.

But there is, I think, an equally plausible way of describing the case. When the seriousness of unwanted pregnancy was brought home to him, the arguments he had previously used seemed of little consequence. Importantly, he *did not* come to see these arguments as containing logical errors (at least not at that point). Rather, the way he *saw* and understood abortion was shaped by confronting it existentially. It is true that his previous conviction faded from view almost immediately, but this says more about the strength of the conviction than it does about the character of the young man (or so I opine). His was what I would like to call a 'paper conviction' – a doctrine that one maintains in conversations, but which has little force in the flow of everyday life.

One frightening thing about our paper convictions (and I assume we all have them) is that we do not know *what* convictions we have matter to us existentially (rather than merely propositionally). When I was only 19, I thought, quite vehemently, that abortion was wrong (and, indeed, it *might* be wrong). But my seemingly solid conviction melted into air when I saw the absolute horror on my partner's face at the thought of having a child, when I looked around our one-room apartment and our abject poverty, and when I thought about what it might mean to the rest of our lives. In a flash, the clump of cells that would turn into a child, under the right conditions, didn't seem nearly as significant as it once had. I realized at that point that the conviction I had maintained until that point had been a fragile, ungrounded thing: it was something I liked to argue about, but not something that I *saw* with any kind of moral clarity or strength.

This autobiographical example provides occasion to explore what it means to *have* a moral conviction, as well as the way we maintain moral convictions. This distinction, I think, is of use in thinking about what is sometimes called 'moral perception,'[1] and in thinking about why wrong doings often persist despite all of our assertions that they are wrong.[2] The distinction to be drawn is one between our paper convictions (the things we're willing to say and to offer arguments about) and our existential convictions (those strong evaluations that orient the very way we think and live through particular issues). Our existential convictions (or our 'strong evaluations,' to use Charles Taylor's apt category)[3] constitute the moral framework within which arguments can be made *at all*. They inform the way we *see* the moral issues we are considering. In this respect, they are much more important to living the moral life – and much more 'authentically' a part of our vision of the good than are the sentences we are willing to utter and defend.

Of course, our paper and existential convictions sometimes overlap. They are not, after all, mutually exclusive. Nevertheless, the ways these convictions function in our lives are quite distinct. A propositional conviction functions primarily in discourse. It constitutes a 'belief' in one of the traditional senses of this term: when asked 'Do you believe x?,' we will reply 'Yes.' The belief in question here *just is* the propositional content that one is willing to assent to in the flow of conversation.

An existential conviction, on the other hand, need not ever function in discourse (though it might). In some cases, persons are actually *unable* to say what it is about some situation or action that they find morally problematic or morally obligatory – they simply *do* find it so. Such inarticulacy is sometimes mistaken for an absence of arguments for a view, or even the absence of thought about a view – but it need not be so. Many things that we are convinced of existentially are simply too basic to admit of articulation, at least if this articulation aims at completeness. More often, our existential convictions, if they come to language at all, are simply paraphrased rather than asserted: 'He shouldn't do that *because it's wrong*" we say, not concerning ourselves with the fact that what we mean by 'it shouldn't be done' *just is* 'it is wrong.'

As we can see, the role of argument in relation to these respective convictions marks a fundamental difference between them. One can be 'argued into' a paper conviction, regardless of one's existential commitments. The 'rationality' of one's paper convictions, in turn, governs the way these convictions function in discourse – they must be consistent, be defensible in our practice of reason-giving, and intelligible when articulated. The logic of an existential conviction, on the other hand, is not the logic of propositional logic: our strong evaluations often resist articulation and do not always fair well in the practice of justification.

There is no simple explanation for the ways in which our articulate, rational convictions (our 'paper' convictions) influence or are influenced by our evaluative, existential commitments. Our paper convictions can conflict with our existential ones: we might abhor viscerally and existentially the suffering inflicted by factory farming, or abject poverty, and yet assert that 'animals have no rights,' or that 'the poor can always work their way out of poverty.' Our paper convictions can come to *alter* our existential ones: our 'rational' conviction that animals do not have rights might lead us simply to *not see* their plight; our view that members of another group are 'genetically inferior' or 'barbaric' might lead to our inability to actually *see* the face of those human beings we judge to be inferior. Likewise, our existential convictions can dethrone our rational ones: we might reject every argument offered for slavery, or the inferiority of some race, simply in virtue of a *somatic*, existential recognition that these views (and the arguments that support them) are simply missing something, even if we can't yet say what it is. (This, I think, was what finally happened when my partner and I, at 19, became pregnant: the existential force of our dilemma revealed the utter vacuity of all those sentences, uttered over all those years, that regarded elective abortion as 'immoral'.)

It is a fascinating feature of the human condition that such things can come apart. That they *can* come apart, Kant reminds us, is why we are susceptible to morality at all. If we were strictly rational beings, there would be no need for an appeal to duties: we would follow the cold, impersonal demands of rationality without any difficulty. I, for one, am *glad* we are not completely rational. Argument, it seems to me, allows us to see only what is 'rational.' It thus relegates the irrational to the irrelevant. In the case of our immediate, ethical relations to one another, the results of this can be devastating.

Why arguments for torture will persist, and why law will not end torture

The power of argument has never been sufficient to end an oppressive and abusive practice. The enactment of laws, likewise, cannot *by itself* eliminate those things it recognizes as criminal. This is not to say that argument is useless. It isn't. If I believed it to be worthless, the many hours I have spent thinking (and writing) about torture would be difficult for me to explain. My aim here is thus *not* to undermine all that has come before; it is, rather, to articulate why even the best set of arguments is unlikely to end torture.

In J.M. Coetzee's brilliant novella, *The Lives of Animals*, the protagonist (Elizabeth Costello) articulates her own skepticism about argument as follows:

> "For, seen from the outside, from a being alien to it, reason is simply a vast tautology. Of course reason will validate reason as the first principle of the universe – what else should it do? Dethrone itself? Reasoning systems, as systems of totality, do not have that power. If there were a position from which reason could attack and dethrone itself, reason would already have occupied that position; otherwise it would not be total." (25)

Coetzee, through the voice of Elizabeth Costello, calls into question the very thing that has so often been used to speak in our names: the universality of reason. Costello sees that this 'universality' is vacuous – or at least can be. The 'universality' of reason masks the significant *particular* affinities we bear to other beings like us – the whimper of the dog who has been beaten; the suffering of the chimp who has lost a child. These particular, affective connections between *individuals* is replaced with an abstraction of equivalence: detached rational subjects share the capacity *to be detached*, and with it the capacity to *ignore* particularity – particularly the singularity of suffering. Suffering is *always* particular, and it always has a face. Reason, by contrast, is the faceless abstract. It is the essence of argument to have no face, and the nature of suffering to require one.

This critique of rationality is hardly new, but its lack of novelty does not track lack of importance. 'Argument,' construed as the universal language of detached subjects capable of looking objectively at the facts, applying principles to those facts, and generating results through logical processes, has often served – even if inappropriately – as a means of eliminating differences that make all the difference. The particularity of crimes against women becomes masked by standards that apply to 'all reasonable persons,' where 'persons' happen to be ungendered objects – which is to say, as so many feminists are right to remind us, *presumptively male*. The particularity of the Arab is masked by the generalized and abstract being of an 'extremist' whose humanity and capacity for love and honor – indeed, his capacity for rationality itself – are defined out of existence. The particularity of the suffering of the tortured is masked by the rational calculation of costs and benefits, the weighing of numbers. The number is abstract, objective; the face of the tortured is anything but. There is no universality in the face to hide behind – no argument that speaks powerfully enough to warrant a lack of response.

Like other tools, argument has significant limitations. It is not an equalizer, capable of defeating all resistance and bias. As we all know, rationality cannot help but to reason with and through bias – and it is for this reason that rationality's blindness is not an asset, but a liability. In *Precarious Lives*, Judith Butler puts this point powerfully in thinking through the way a supposedly universal rationality systematically excludes those deemed to exist outside of its bounds: "To what extent have Arab peoples, predominantly practitioners of Islam, fallen outside the 'human' as it has been naturalized in its 'Western' mold by the contemporary workings of humanism?" (32).

Argument is and remains only as reliable as the sight of those who employ it. The arguments for torture are *rational*, to some extent, but this is the kind of rationality one finds in arguments employed to justify eugenics, degradation, and oppression – it is the rationality of the market and the slave-owner, only protecting what is 'rightfully' his; it is the rationality of efficient execution, where carefully thought-out humaneness is deployed in an arena of inhumanity. It is the rationality of the Bush administration, imploring us to wage war to save the women of Islam from its barbaric men. Bush *the feminist* represents the perversity masked by the worst kinds of argument: military actions in the Middle

East are justified to advance the feminist cause, despite the fact that medical aid is withheld from organizations that are willing to protect the reproductive rights of the same women in whose name (purportedly) we draw blood.[4]

The power of law – objective, blind, universal – presents us with precisely the same problem. This is evidenced in the absence of international laws protecting women *as* women – the very *universality* of law acts as an obstacle to its *aim*. Catherine MacKinnon puts this point forcefully when considering the relationship between laws against torture when compared to laws surrounding domestic abuse.

> the accounts of [abused women], all the same things happen that happen in Amnesty International reports and accounts of torture – except they happen in homes in Nebraska or in pornography studios in Los Angeles rather than prison cells in Chile or detention centers in Turkey. But the social and legal responses to torture are not the same at all. Torture is not considered personal. Torture is not attributed to one sick individual at a time and dismissed as exceptional, or if it is, that maneuver is dismissed as a cover-up by the human rights community. Torture victims are not generally asked how many were there with them, as if it is not important if it happened only to you or you and a few others like you. With torture, an increase is not dismissed as just an increase in reporting, as if a constant level of such abuse is acceptable. Billions of dollars are not made selling as entertainment pictures of what is regarded as torture, nor is torture as such generally regarded as sexual entertainment. Never is a victim of torture asked, did you really want it? (21)[5]

To emphasize law's universality is to ignore the fact that universality by its nature *excludes* that which defies universalization – or, rather, that which is not regarded as the universal. In the case of torture and domestic abuse, torture is regarded as what *men* do to one another in the contexts of state violence. When men do this to women, however, and the context is in the home (even if political institutions *do* support such abuse by refusing to enact sufficient measures against it), the violence is only 'domestic abuse,' and hence fails to ascend to the level of a crime against humanity. Thoughts like this lead Catherine Mackinnon to pose the question explicitly: in the context of law, are women human?

Law's impotence exists in another respect as well. Criminal law is *backward-looking*. It creates incentives to *avoid* particular courses of action, but it does not (and probably cannot) remove the motivation to engage in what it criminalizes. The point here is not to belittle the importance and power of law. Laws act as a line in the sand – as something that one can appeal to when our actions and our ideals conflict with one another, or with the actions and the ideals of others.

But the history of law, like the history of argument, tells a fascinating story of the impotence of law to change the minds of those it aims to stop. This history is written in the drunken revelry of prohibition-era party-goers, in the mandatory sentences of drug users, and on the bodies of the lynched. If there is to be an end to torture, I fear, it will not be found in the creation of additional laws or in the deployment of additional arguments.

Where will we look for the end of torture? It will not be in the universal and the abstract. It will be, rather, in our ability to see, in concrete particularity, the suffering that torture involves – a suffering that cannot be represented in the axioms of a propositional logic; a suffering that is as immediate as the stare that implores us to do no more.

Abstraction, I think, is the ally of torture. The faceless are those who must be susceptible to torture – whether they are made faceless by the cool application of moral principles, or by the systematic 'Othering' of its victims as 'barbaric,' 'extremist,' 'monsterous,' 'Muslim.' Torture involves action against an abstraction. Ending torture will be impossible without refusing the abstraction of argument in favor of *moral sight*. There will be no end to torture until we force ourselves to see the face of the concrete humanity before us – and recognize both its irreplacability as well as the legitimate demands this irreplacability makes of us.

This, I think, is what Levinas got so wonderfully right: the particularity of ethical demands is obscured by our compulsion to be slaves to abstract rationality. The human, in this sense, is always the face before us – making demands on us; the immediacy of the human, and the vulnerability we embody, is hidden behind our rational application of abstract principles. Argument, in this sense, should not be allowed to operate unchecked; abstract arguments cannot replace primordial recognition.

To think that seeing the limits of argument amounts to giving up on the notion of 'objectivity,' it seems to me, is to operate with a misunderstanding of the very nature of the objective. The objective is not simply that which can be demonstrated by argument; it is also that which is *real*. To yearn for epistemic objectivity at the expense of ontological objectivity (to borrow a distinction from John Searle)[6], is to misunderstand what ethics is *about*. The abstract ethical principle may be one that we can defend with argument, but it should not therefore be regarded as somehow more real than the suffering we encounter. There is nothing more real than suffering, save perhaps the obligation we have to respond to the demands this suffering makes on us.

This, then, is the limitation of argument: it does not see suffering with sufficient clarity. Suffering is excluded both by the nature of argument and by its situated employment. It excludes suffering by nature because argument is essentially propositional; suffering does not bear this structure, and so cannot be captured by the machinations of argument. But argument excludes suffering in a much more nefarious way as well: it operates, as it must, from contexts that are influenced deeply by the particular biases of those who employ it. This can be seen with stunning, horrific clarity in the use of argument to justify the most brutal forms of human action.

In the lecture 'Society Must be Defended,' Foucault argues that, "in a normalizing society, race or racism is the precondition that makes killing possible." He goes on to explain that the term 'killing' is to be understood as broadly as possible: "When I say 'killing,' I obviously do not mean simply murder as such, but also every form of indirect murder: the fact of exposing someone to death, increasing the risk of death for some people, or, quite simply, political death, expulsion, rejection, and so on" (256). Racism, as a precondition for political violence, allows the State to act against the members of other States, as well as its own members. The actions the state carries out are *rational* ones, given the biases from which it operates, acting like axiomatic constraints on what plausible inferences can and cannot be made.

Foucault's point is that the enemy to be killed must be regarded as fundamentally *unlike us* – as fundamentally 'Other.' We have seen this, for example, in the training of torturers: the implicit, perhaps natural, reluctance to kill other human beings poses a *problem* for the torture trainee, and this problem is overcome by a regiment that serves to distinguish *us* from *them*. To a lesser extent, we can see this even in the history of torture: it is the heretic that can be tortured, albeit only by the devout; it is the criminal who can be put to the *question*, but only after this has been ordered by the manifestation of the law itself: the judge. Here, argument devises a regiment that accomplishes a particular goal: the elimination of the face of the 'Other.'

The 'Othering' of victims of extreme violence has something to teach us about the defenses of torture. To what extent are the defenses of extreme violence predicated on the failure to recognize ourselves in the face of the 'Other'? To what extent does any systematic use of torture – or any defense of such use, for that matter – emerge based on a fundamental misconception of the humanity of our victims – a fundamental inability to see them concretely?

The genocidal campaigns of the twentieth century are marked by Othering at every turn: there are enemies of the revolution, or of the party; there are 'barbaric' Arabs and 'beastly' Jews; 'vicious' Muslims and 'foolish' Christians; haters of freedom and lovers of infidelity. There are the Good and the Evil. Until we stop allowing ourselves to ignore the very real humanity of other persons, torture will not end. It will not so long as we ignore the particular for the abstract, and as long as we allow our abstract ruminations to be guided by a prior racism, sexism, and xenophobia.

These considerations present us with a pessimistic view of the elimination of torture – but we should be specific about the arena in which this pessimism exists. The above reflections provide us with reasons for skepticism that torture will be eliminated by law, or by the powerful arguments against it. They provide reasons for skepticism about eliminating the ordering of torture by our politicians, intelligence agencies, and military personnel. As I have suggested, this pessimism is grounded in recognizing a pervasive moral blindness. By 'Othering' our enemies, we make torture possible. We make it possible to set aside all of those paper convictions that we, as a nation, claim to be committed to. Our treaties and our laws, repeated in speeches and policy decisions, cannot stand up to our prejudices. Paper convictions burn up in the heat of conflict.

In many cases, of course, our existential convictions can come to our rescue: the face of our victims can remind us of their humanity and its worth. It is much easier to order torture than it is to carry out – one does not have to face the inhumanity that one engages in; one does not have to hear the screams of one's victim, or see the torment written on their bodies and faces. Sitting behind a desk with the similarly minded makes the decision to torture easier than the requirement to carry it out – a requirement that is often met with reluctance in new torturers. Paper convictions are set aside in a way that existential ones cannot be – in a way that is immediate and often leaves no psychological scars on those who have set the convictions aside.

My skepticism about argument and law, then, is a skepticism about our paper convictions being strong enough to stand up to the felt need for 'defense' or 'information.' Perhaps, if our leaders had to watch those who were tortured – and if they could be somehow made to see the worth of every human being – we would not suffer from such pessimism.

But arguments are not flesh; the law is not the particular suffering of a human being. Without an on-going attention to the immediacy of suffering, and to the price we pay for setting aside questions about dignity, torture will continue. It will be approved and ordered. It will be checked off of boxes on governmental to-do lists. It will be defended as necessary to our safety. Paper convictions are easily destroyed. Without our existential convictions tested on the proving ground of torturous practice, torture at the level of policy will not cease.

Why even seeing suffering and humanity is not enough

Policy makers do not torture. If they did, they might well see that their fearful responses to those they have 'Othered' are neither effective nor justified. Their existential convictions might hold up where paper convictions have not.

But we cannot place all of our hope in the direct experience of torture and its attendant difficulties. This would be naïve, and it would miss part of the nature and reality of torture, as well as the complex relationship human beings have to the suffering of others. People *do* torture, after all. To claim that such people do not empathize with their victims, or that they do not recognize their suffering and their humanity, seems to miss something essential about torture. In some ways, torture *depends* on an appreciation of both the suffering and the subjectivity of the person being tortured. One must be able to empathize with them to the extent that one recognizes what will *cause* suffering. One must be able to *see* the suffering of others to determine if one's torturous techniques are producing the kinds of results one is seeking. And to manipulate an agent's subjectivity against itself – which, as we have seen, is the *modus operandi* of modern torture – requires that one sees the humanity before one.

Those conducting torture, as we have seen, may well maintain their paper convictions. They might regard their actions as against the letter and spirit of the law, or even as deeply immoral, and nevertheless proceed, providing rationalizations when needed by appealing to national security, or higher purposes, or some other thing. Just as likely, though, is the possibility that one's paper convictions will be changed by the conduct of torture: the conviction that torture is deeply immoral will give way to a conviction that it is a necessary evil, or that the victims of torture deserve what they get. And as we have also seen, regardless of one's paper convictions, the initial reluctance to maim and kill (an existential conviction) is systematically deconstructed through training and gradual exposure to the techniques of torture.

Training aims to eliminate whatever moral perception agents bring to their training. Existential convictions are not set aside so much as eliminated, and the effects this has on the torturer himself are often debilitating. Our pessimism here about the prospects of ending torture thus takes a different form: our visceral convictions are things that can be altered by institutional life. Even *seeing* the suffering and humanity of our victims is insufficient when we have been trained to regard such things as *irrelevant*. So long as our policy-makers and intelligence personnel cannot *see* this suffering, they will continue to support institutions that aim to destroy the very *capacity* to recognize the moral worth of human beings in others. In this way, the death of paper convictions on one level can lead to the elimination of existential convictions on another. This division of labor makes the chances of stopping torture on the ground (rather than in the policy room) abysmally small, and perhaps utterly hopeless.

Is there no hope? Pessimism about ending torture

Arguments are not without their place. They are important instruments in what must be a multi-faceted attack on those who defend and carry out torture. When policy-makers and academics choose to play the reason-giving game, we must be prepared to meet them on their own ground, and show them exactly where they err, and what consequences such errors have. But reason alone, as we have seen, is insufficient to end torture. Our paper convictions are simply too flimsy; our moral commitments to flaccid.

Nor are our existential convictions enough to stop torture by those who carry it out – not when they have been trained in such a way as to eliminate the very worth of those they torture. This places us in an incredible precarious position: arguments and law will not convince those who make policy and material decisions not to engage in torture, and they have no occasion (neither have they the will) to witness the practices they prescribe. Those who *can* see the horrendous character of torture, though, have been subjected to institutional pressures that make seeing what they have been ordered to do as a moral failure virtually impossible. If they *do* see the moral failures of the policies they are asked to implement, they can leak information to the press, and they can quit. When they quit, they are replaced by 'better' soldiers or agents. When they leak information to the press, argument and appeal to law come back full-force – but once again to no avail. The cycle continues, and there seems little hope of ending it.

The central obstacle to the elimination of torture is not the use of law, nor is it the use of argument. Both of these avenues are useful only to the extent that they reflect a capacity to experience the worth of the humanity of others. Those who order torture are not confronted with what they are ordering; those who carry out torture have been trained in such a way that actually *seeing* the problems inherent in what they are doing is a sign of failure. To cite the law, or even to offer argument, is in one sense simply not enough. A failure to see the humanity of another is not a failure of *argument*, and hence will not be corrected by criticisms of argument.

Our failure to see the worth of the humanity of those we order tortured is, as we have seen, often unknown to even us. We continue to construct arguments to subvert the law, or to justify our exceptions to it, and ignore the particularity of the suffering we cause. In doing so, we create conditions that destroy the ability of those who act in our name to even *see* the problematic nature of what they are doing. Lurking behind our ratiocination may well be the very darkness we think we have overcome through the power of argument: the will to destroy, no matter the cost.

How can we end torture? Only by seeing the face of our victims for what they are: the flesh of our own humanity, a flesh that has as much worth as our own; only by eliminating those institutions that make seeing the importance and worth of this humanity all but impossible.

I do not know how to do this. I am not even sure it is possible. But this does not mean that we shouldn't *try*. Even if torture cannot be eliminated, we can make every effort to decrease its use, and to prosecute fully those who are complicit in it. While I am deeply pessimistic about ending torture, I cannot help but hold out some hope that we might *diminish* it. We are *homo torquere, homo tormentum* – the animal who tortures and is tortured. That much cannot be denied. But that is not all we are.

We are also the animal that *hopes*.

Notes

1. "Failures of Sight."
2. Let me reiterate that I am not saying my decision, as a 19-year old, was wrong. (I think, in fact that it was the right decision. Had things gone otherwise, I would not have my two children or my wife). The anecdote is meant to spell out how our assertions about what's wrong may have little bearing on our actions. In my view, this points to an important fact about moral life: what matters to us *existentially* is far more important than what matters to us only propositionally.
3. See his *Sources of the Self*.
4. Judith Butler makes this point brilliantly in *Precarious Life*. See 41.
5. "On Torture," in *Are Women Human? and Other International Dialogues*.
6. See his *The Construction of Social Reality*.

Selected Bibliography

Anthologies

Note: Chapters from volumes are cited in chapter endnotes

Anonymous, *Abu Ghraib: The Politics of Torture*, Berkeley: North Atlantic Books, 2004.

Metin Başoğlu (ed.), *Torture and Its Consequences: Current Treatment Approaches*, Cambridge and New York: Cambridge University Press, 1992.

Albert D. Biderman and Herbert Zimmer (eds), *The Manipulation of Human Behavior*, New York and London: John Wiley & Sons, Inc., 1961.

Ronald D. Crelinsten and Alex P. Schmid (eds), *The Politics of Pain: Torturers and Their Masters,* Boulder and San Francisco: Westview Press, 1995.

M. Katherine B. Darmer, Robert M. Baird and Stuart E. Rosenbaum (eds), *Civil Liberties vs. National Security in a Post-9/11 World*, Amherst, NY: Prometheus Books, 2004.

Peggy DesAutels and Margaret Urban Walker (eds), *Moral Psychology: Feminist Ethics and Social Theory*, Lanham, MD: Rowman and Littlefield, 2004.

Bertil Dunér (ed.), *An End to Torture: Strategies for Its Eradication*, New York: St. Martin's Press, 1999.

R. G. Frey and Christopher W. Morris (eds), *Violence, Terrorism, and Justice*, Cambridge: Cambridge University Press, 1991.

Ellen Gerrity, Terrence M. Keane, Farris Tuma (eds), *The Mental Health Consequences of Torture*, Dordrecht: Springer Publishing, 2001.

Mary-Jo Delvecchio Good, Paul E. Brodwin, Byron J. Good, Arthur Kleinman (eds), *Pain as Human Experience: An Anthropological Perspective*, Berkeley: University of California Press, 1994.

Sep Graessner, Norbert Gurris, and Christian Pross (eds), *At the Side of Torture Survivors: Treating a Terrible Assault on Human Dignity*, Baltimore: Johns Hopkins University Press, 2001.

Karen J. Greenberg (ed.), *The Torture Debate in America*, New York: Cambridge University Press, 2006.

Roy Gutman, David Reiff and Anthony Dworkin (eds), *Crimes of War: What the Public Should Know*, New York and London: W.W. Norton and Company, 2007.

Ernest F. Henderson (ed.), *Select Historical Documents of the Middle Ages*, London: George Bell and Sons, 1910.

Thomas Hilde (ed.), *On Torture*, Baltimore: Johns Hopkins University Press, 2008.

Intelligence Science Board, The National Defense Intelligence College (edited), *Educing Information: Terrorism: Science and Art*, Washington, DC: NDIC Press, 2006.

Amaney Jamal and Nadine Naber (eds), *Race and Arab Americans Before and After 9/11: From Invisible Citizens to Visible Subjects*, New York: Syracuse University Press, 2008.

Joshua Knobe and Shaun Nichols (eds), *Experimental Philosophy*, New York and Oxford: Oxford University Press, 2008.

Steven P. Lee (ed.), *Intervention, Terrorism and Torture: Contemporary Challenges to Just War Theory*, Dordrecht: Springer Publications, 2006.

Sanford Levinson, *Torture: A Collection*, New York: Oxford University Press, 2004.

Tara McKelvey (ed.), *One of the Boys: Women As Aggressors and Torturers*, California: Seal Press, 2007.

Jeff Malpas and Norelle Lickiss (eds), *Perspectives on Human Dignity: A Conversation*, Dordrecht: Springer Publications, 2007.

Arthur G. Miller (ed.), *The Social Psychology of Good and Evil*, New York: The Guilford Press, 2005.

Caroline O.N. Moser and Fiona C. Clark (eds), *Victims, Perpetrators or Actors?: Gender, Armed Conflict and Political Violence*, London and New York: Zed Books, 2001.

Mohamed Nimer (ed.), *Islamophobia and Anti-Americanism: Causes and Remedies*, Maryland: Amana Publications, 2007.

Almerindo E. Ojeda (ed.), *The Trauma of Psychological Torture,* Westport, CT: Praeger, 2008.

Kenneth Roth and Minky Worden (eds), *Torture: Does it Make Us Safer? Is It Ever OK? A Human Rights Perspective*, New York: The New Press and Human Rights Watch, 2005.

William F. Schulz (ed.), *The Phenomenon of Torture*, Philadelphia: University of Pennsylvania Press, 2007.

András Szántó (ed.), *What Orwell Didn't Know: Propaganda and the New Face of American Politics,* New York: Public Affairs, 2007, pp. 158–65.

Articles in Journals

Inger Agger, "Sexual Torture of Political Prisoners: An Overview," *Journal of Traumatic Stress,* 1989, Vol. 2, No. 3, pp. 306–17.

Fritz Allhoff, "Terrorism and Torture," *International Journal of Applied Philosophy*, 2003, 17:1, pp. 121–34.

Fritz Allhoff, "A Defense of Torture: Separation of Cases, Ticking Time-bombs, and Moral Justification," *International Journal of Applied Philosophy*, 2005, 19:2, pp. 243–64.

Jose E. Alvarez, "Torturing the Law," *Case Western Reserve Journal of International Law*, 2006, Vol. 37, 2/3, pp. 175–223.

Kristine Amris, Sofie Danneskiold-Samsoe, Soren Torp-Pederson, Inge Genefke, Bente Danneskiold-Samsoe, "Producing Medicolegal Evidence: Documentation of Torture Versus the Saudi Arabian State of Denial," *Torture: Journal on Rehabilitation of Torture Survivors and Prevention of Torture,* 2007, Vol. 17, No. 3, pp. 181–95.

Jean Maria Arrigo, "A Utilitarian Argument against Torture Interrogation of Terrorists," *Science and Engineering Ethics,* 2004, 10, pp. 543–72.

Jean Maria Arrigo and Ray Bennett, "Organizational Supports for Abusive Interrogations in the 'War on Terror'," *Peace and Conflict: Journal of Peace Psychology,* Vol. 13, No. 4 November 2007, pp. 411–21.

Jean Maria Arrigo and Richard V. Wagner, "Psychologists and Military Interrogators Rethink the Psychology of Torture," *Peace and Conflict: Journal of Peace Psychology,* Vol. 13, No. 4, November 2007, pp. 393–8.

S. E. Asch, "Opinions and Social Pressure," *Scientific American,* November 1955, pp. 31–5.

Stephanie Athey, "Rethinking Torture's Dark Chamber," *Peace Review: A Journal of Social Justice,* 2008, 20, pp. 13–21.

Metin Başoğlu, Maria Livanou, Cvetana Crnobarić, "Torture vs Other Cruel, Inhuman, and Degrading Treatment: Is the Distinction Real or Apparent?" *Archives of General Psychiatry* 64: March, 2007, pp. 277–85.

Metin Başoğlu, Isaac M. Marks, and Seda Sengun, "Amitriptyline for PTSD in a Torture Survivor: A Case Study," *Journal of Traumatic Stress,* 1992, Vol. 5, No. 1, pp. 77–83.

C.D. Batson et al., "Failure to Help in a Hurry: Callousness or Conflict?" 1978, *Personality and Social Psychology Bulletin,* 4, pp. 97–101.

P. Bauer, "Statement on interrogation practices to the House Committee on the Armed Services," July 2006, (Online) Retrieved May 28, 2007, from http://www.amnestyusa.org/denounce_torture/statement_on_interrogation.pdf

Jonathan Bean, David Ng, Hakan Demirtas and Patrick Guinan, "Medical Students Attitudes Towards Torture," *Torture: Journal on Rehabilitation of Torture Survivors and Prevention of Torture,* 2008, Vol. 18, No. 2, pp. 99–103.

Kevin Beck, "Balkan Immigrants," *Torture: Journal on Rehabilitation of Torture Survivors and Prevention of Torture,* 2007, Vol. 17, No. 3.

Gilbert Beebe, "Follow-up Studies of World War II and Korean War Prisoners," *American Journal of Epidemiology,* 1970, Vol. 92, No. 2.

Jeannine Bell, "'Behind the Mortal Bone': The (In)Effectiveness of Torture," *Indiana Law Journal,* July 2008, Vol. 83, pp. 1–23.

R. Bennett (pseudonym), "Interrogator's request to professional psychologists," J. M. Arrigo (ed.), *Visible remedies for invisible settings and sources of torture* (American Psychological Association annual convention), 2006, New Orleans.

Ray Bennett (pseudonym), "Endorsement by the Seminar Military Interrogators," *Peace and Conflict: Journal of Peace Psychology,* 2007, Vol. 13, No. 4, November, pp. 391–2.

Jonathan I. Bisson, "Pharmacological Treatment to Prevent and Treat

Post-Traumatic Stress Disorder," *Torture: Journal on Rehabilitation of Torture Survivors and Prevention of Torture*, 2008, Vol. 18, No. 2, pp. 104–6.

Bob Brecher, "Our Obligation to the Dead," *Journal of Applied Philosophy*, 2002, Vol. 19, No. 2.

Vittorio Bufacchi and Jean-Maria Arrigo, "Terrorism and the State: A Refutation of the Ticking–Bomb Argument," *Journal of Applied Philosophy*, 2006, 23:3, pp. 355–73.

Claudia Card, "Ticking Bombs and Interrogations," *Criminal Law and Philosophy*, 2008, 2:1, pp. 1–15.

Clare Chambers, "Torture as an Evil: Response to Claudia Card, 'Ticking Bombs and Interrogation'," *Criminal Law and Philosophy*, 2008, 2, pp. 17–20.

Ronald D. Crelinsten, "The World of Torture: A constructed reality," 2003, *Theoretical Criminology*, Vol. 7(3), 293–318.

Howard J. Curzer, "Admirable Immorality, Dirty Hands, Ticking Bombs, and Torturing Innocents," 2006, *The Southern Journal of Philosophy*, XLIV, pp. 31–56.

J.M. Darley and C.D. Batson, "From Jerusalem to Jericho: A Study of Situational Variables in Helping Behavior," *Journal of Personality and Social Psychology*, 1973, 27, pp. 100–8.

J.M. Darley and B. Latane, "Bystander Intervention in Emergencies: Diffusion of Responsibilities," *Journal of Personality and Social Psychology*, 1968, 8, pp. 377–83.

Michael Davis, "The Moral Justifiability of Torture and other Cruel, Inhuman, or Degrading Treatment," *International Journal of Applied Philosophy*, 2005, 19:2, pp. 161–78.

Laura A. Dickinson, "Torture and Contract," *Case Western Reserve Journal of International Law*, 2006, 37, 2/3, pp. 267–75.

Christopher J. Einolf, "The Fall and Rise of Torture: A Comparative and Historical Analysis," *Sociological Theory*, 25:2, June 2007.

R.D. Emerick, "Politicizing 'Torture': Torturing a Metaphor," unpublished.

Marcello Ferrada-Noli, Marie Asberg and Kari Armstad, "Suicidal Behavior After Severe Trauma, Part 2: The Association Between Methods of Torture and of Suicidal Ideation in Posttraumatic Stress Disorder," *Journal of Traumatic Stress*, 1998, Vol. 11, No. 1, pp. 113–23.

Andrew Fiala, "A Critique of Exceptions: Torture, Terrorism, and the Lesser Evil Argument," *International Journal of Applied Philosophy*, 2006, 20:1, 127–42.

Andrew Fiala, "Waterboarding, Torture, and Violence: Normative Definitions and the Burden of Proof," *Review Journal of Political Philosophy*, 2008, Vol. 6, No. 1, pp. 153–73.

Yael Fischman, "Secondary Trauma in the Legal Professions, a Clinical Perspective," *Torture: Journal on Rehabilitation of Torture Survivors and Prevention of Torture*, 2008, 18, No. 2, pp. 107–15.

R. Fried and L. Berkowitz, "Music Hath Charms. . .and Can Influence Helpfulness," 1979, *Journal of Applied Social Psychology*, 9, pp. 199–208.

Raimond Gaita, "Torture: The Lesser Evil," *Tijdschrift-voor-Filosofie*, 2006, 68:2, pp. 251–78.

Amihud Gilead, "Torture and Singularity," *Public Affairs Quarterly,* July 2005, Vol. 19, No. 3.

Richard Goldstone, "Combating Terrorism: Zero Tolerance for Torture," *Case Western Reserve Journal of International Law,* 2006, 37, 2/3, pp. 343–8.

Lauren Goodsmith, "Beyond Where It Started: A Look at the 'Healing Images' Experience," *Torture: Journal on Rehabilitation of Torture Survivors and Prevention of Torture,* 2007, Vol. 17, No. 3, pp. 222–32.

Michael Gross, "Just and Jewish Warfare—Israeli Soldiers Seem to Disregard Rules of War," *Tikkun,* September 2001.

Jan Ole Haagensen, "The Role of the Istanbul-Protocol in the Uphill Battle for Torture Survivors Being Granted Asylum in Europe and Ensuring the Perpetrators Pay," *Torture: Journal on Rehabilitation of Torture Survivors and Prevention of Torture,* 2007, Vol. 17, No. 3, pp. 326–39.

Ton Haans, "The Proposal for Supervision Training in Palestine/Middle East," *Torture: Journal on Rehabilitation of Torture Survivors and Prevention of Torture,* 2007, Vol. 17, No. 3.

C. Haney, W. C. Banks and P. G. Zimbardo, "Interpersonal dynamics in a simulated prison," *International Journal of Criminology and Penology,* 1973, 1, 69–97.

Liam Harte, "Must Terrorism Be Violent?" *Review Journal of Political Philosophy,* 2008, Vol. 6, No. 1, pp. 102–22.

Liam Harte, "Could New Terrorism Exist? A Philosophical Critique of the 'Expert Analysis'," 2009, unpublished manuscript.

Gordon Hull, "One View of the Dungeon: The Ticking Time Bomb between Governmentality and Sovereignty," *International Philosophical Quarterly,* forthcoming.

A. M. Isen and P. F. Levin, "Effect of Feeling Good on Helping: Cookies and Kindness," *Journal of Personality and Social Psychology,* 1972, 21, pp. 384–8.

Hélène Jaffé, "How To Deal With Torture Victims." *Torture: Journal on Rehabilitation of Torture Survivors and Prevention of Torture,* 2008, Vol. 18, No. 2, pp. 130–8.

Ronnie Janoff-Bulman, "Erroneous Assumptions: Popular Belief in the Effectiveness of Torture Interrogation," *Peace and Conflict: Journal of Peace Psychology,* (13)4, pp. 429–35.

James M. Jaranson and Michael K. Popkin, *Caring for Victims of Torture,* 1998, American Psychiatric Publishing, Inc.

Jehangir Jilani, "Detainees in Saudi Arabia," *Torture: Journal on Rehabilitation of Torture Survivors and Prevention of Torture,* 2008, Vol. 18, No. 2, p. 140.

Michael B. Jones, "Speaking Power to Truth: Female Suicide Bombers and the Gendering of Violence," *Review Journal of Political Philosophy,* 2008, Vol. 6, No. 3, pp. 128–46.

Walter Kälin, "The struggle against torture," *International Review of the Red Cross,* 1998, no. 324, pp. 433–44.

Marianne Kastrup, "Coping with Exposure to Torture," *Contemporary Family Therapy,* Winter 1989, 10(4), pp. 280–7.

Herbert C. Kelman, "The policy context of torture: A social psychological analysis" in *International Review of the Red Cross,* March 2005, Vol. 87, No. 857.

Stephen Kershnar, "Objections to the Systematic Imposition of Punitive Torture," *International Journal of Applied Philosophy,* 1999, 13:1, pp. 47–56.

Stephen Kershnar, "For Interrogational Torture," *International Journal of Applied Philosophy,* 2005, 19:2, pp. 223–41.

Ali Khaji, "Prisoners of War and Torture Need More Attention," *Torture: Journal on Rehabilitation of Torture Survivors and Prevention of Torture,* 2007, Vol. 17, No. 3.

B.M. Klayman, "The Definition of Torture in International Law," *Temple Law Quarterly,* 1978, Vol. 51, 449–517.

Patrick Lenta, "The Purposes of Torture," *South African Journal of Philosophy,* 2006, 25:1, pp. 48–61.

Aaron Lercher, "Torture and Moral Knowledge," *Review Journal of Political Philosophy,* 2008, Vol. 6, No. 1, pp. 67–74.

Sanford Levinson, "Slavery and the Phenomenology of Torture," *Social Research,* Spring 2007, Vol. 74, No. 1, pp. 149–68.

Alexandra Liedl and Christine Knaevelsrud, "Chronic Pain and PTSD: The Perpetual Avoidance Model and its Treatment Implications," *Torture: Journal on Rehabilitation of Torture Victims and Prevention of Torture,* 2008, Vol. 18, No. 2, pp. 69–77.

David Luban, "The War on Terrorism and the End of Human Rights," *Philosophy and Public Policy Quarterly,* 2002, 22:3, pp. 9–14.

Clark McCauley, "Toward a Social Psychology of Professional Military Interrogation", *Peace and Conflict: Journal of Peace Psychology,* November 2007, Vol. 13, No. 4, pp. 399–410.

Nicolas McGinnis, "Phenomenology, Interrogation and Biopower: Merleau-Ponty on 'Human Resources Exploitation'," *Review Journal of Political Philosophy,* forthcoming, 2010.

Clare McGlynn, "Rape as 'Torture'? Catherine MacKinnon and Questions of Feminist Strategy," *Feminist Legal Studies,* 2008, Vol. 16, pp. 71–85.

Tibor R. Machan, "Exploring Extreme Violence (Torture)," *Journal of Social Philosophy,* 1990, Vol. 21, Spring, pp. 92–7.

Jeff McMahan, "Torture, Morality, and Law," *Case Western Reserve Journal of International Law,* 2006, 37, 2/3, pp. 241–8.

Lene Mandel and Lise Worm, "Documentation of Torture Victims, Assessment of the Procedure for Medico-Legal Documentation," *Torture: Journal on Rehabilitation of Torture Survivors and Prevention of Torture,* 2007, Vol. 17, No. 3, pp. 196–202.

Nicole Masmas, Eva Moller, Cæcile Buhmann, Vibeke Bunch, Jean Hald Jensen, Trine Norregård Hansen, Louise Moller Forgensen, Claes Kjær, Maiken Mannstaedt, Annemette Oxholm, Jutta Skau, Lotte Theilade, Lise Worm,

Morten Estrom, "Asylum Seekers in Denmark: A Study of Health Status and Grade of Traumatization of Newly Arrived Asylum Seeker," *Torture: Journal on Rehabilitation of Torture Victims and Prevention of Torture*, 2008, Vol. 18, No. 2, pp. 77–86.

K. E. Matthews and L. K. Cannon, "Environmental Noise Level as a Determinant of Helping Behavior," *Journal of Personality and Social Psychology*, 1975, 32, pp. 571–7.

Larry May, "Torturing Detainees During Interrogation," *International Journal of Applied Philosophy*, 2005, 19:2, pp. 193–208.

Jamie Mayerfeld, "In Defense of the Absolute Prohibition of Torture," *Public Affairs Quarterly*, April 2008, Vol. 22, No. 2.

Steven H. Miles, "Human Rights Abuses, Transparency, Impunity and the Web," *Torture: Journal on Rehabilitation of Torture Survivors and Prevention of Torture*, 2007, Vol. 17, No. 3, pp. 216–21.

Gail H. Miller, "Defining Torture," *Floersheimer Center for Constitutional Democracy, Occasional Paper #3*, 2005.

Seumas Miller, "Is Torture Ever Morally Justifiable?" *International Journal of Applied Philosophy*, 2005, 19:2, pp. 179–92.

Seumas Miller, "Torture and Counterterrorism," *Iyyun*, 2006, 25:1, pp. 62–76.

Benito Morentin, Luis F. Callado and M. Itxaso Idoyaga, "A Follow-Up Study of Allegations of Ill-Treatment/Torture in Incommunicado Detainees in Spain. Failure of International Preventative Mechanisms," *Torture: Journal on Rehabilitation of Torture Survivors and Prevention of Torture*, 2008, Vol. 18, No. 2, pp. 87–98.

Stephen Nathanson, "Terrorism, Supreme Emergency, Noncombatant Immunity: A Critique of Michael Walzer's Ethics of War," *The Jerusalem Philosophical Quarterly*, 2006, Vol. 55, pp. 3–26.

Jay Newman, "Torture and Responsibility," *Journal of Value Inquiry*, 1974, 8:3, pp. 161–74.

Kelly Oliver, "Bodies against the law: Abu Ghraib and the war on terror," *Continental Philosophy Review*, 2009, Vol. 42, pp. 63–80.

Roger Paden, "Surveillance and Torture: Foucault and Orwell on the Methods of Discipline," *Social Theory and Practice*, 1984, 10:3, pp. 261–71.

Erin Louise Palmer, "Reinterpreting Torture: Presidential Signing Statements and the Circumvention of US and International Law," *Human Rights Brief*, 2006, Vol. 14, No. 1.

Victoria Palmer, "[Un]feeling: Embodied Violence and Dismemberment in the Development in Ethical Relations," *Review Journal of Political Philosophy*, 2008, Vol. 6, No. 2, pp. 17–33.

John T. Parry and Welsh S. White, "Interrogating Suspected Terrorists: Should Torture Be an Option?" *The University of Pittsburgh Law Review*, 2002, 63:743, pp. 743–66.

Frederick Piggot, "Justification Doctrine in the Prohibition on Torture, Cruel,

Inhuman or Degrading Treatment," *Torture: Journal on Rehabilitation of Torture Survivors and Prevention of Torture*, 2008, Vol. 18, No. 2, pp. 116–29.

J. Quiroga and J.M. Jaranson, "Politically-motivated torture and its survivors: A desk study review of the literature", *Torture*, 2005, 15 (2–3), pp. 39–45.

Jeffrey Reiman, "Justice, Civilization, and the Death Penalty: Answering Van den Haag," *Philosophy and Public Affairs*, Spring 1985, Vol. 14, No. 2, pp. 115–48.

Hernan Reyes, "The worst scars are in the mind: psychological torture," *International Review of the Red Cross*, September 2007, Vol. 89, No. 867.

Richard L. Rubenstein, "The Bureaucratization of Torture," *Journal of Social Philosophy*, 1982, 13, pp. 31–51.

Nancy Sherman, "Torturers and the Tortured," *South African Journal of Philosophy*, 2006, 25:1, pp. 77–88.

Henry Shue, "Torture in Dreamland: Disposing of the Ticking Bomb," *Case Western Reserve Journal of International Law*, 2006, 37, 2/3, pp. 231–9.

Annemarie J.M. Smith, Wim Chr. Kleijn, R. Wim Trijsburg and Giel J.M. Hutschemaekers, "How Therapists Cope With Clients' Traumatic Experiences," *Torture: Journal on Rehabilitation of Torture Survivors and Prevention of Torture*, 2007, Vol. 17, No. 3, pp. 203–16.

Susan Sontag, "Regarding the Torture of Others," 23 May, 2004, *New York Times Magazine*.

Uwe Steinhoff, "The Case for Dirty Harry and Against Alan Dershowitz," *Journal of Applied Philosophy*, 2006, 23:3, pp. 337–53.

Peter Suedfeld, "Torture, Interrogation, Security, and Psychology: Absolutistic versus Complex Thinking," *Analyses of Social Issues and Public policy*, 2007, Vol. 7, No. 1, pp. 1–9.

Chanterelle Sung, "Torturing the Ticking Bomb Terrorist: An Analysis of Judicially Sanctioned Torture in the Context of Terrorism," *The Boston College Third World Law Journal*, 2003, 23:193, pp. 193–212.

David Sussman, "What's Wrong with Torture?" *Philosophy and Public Affairs*, 2005, 33:1, pp. 1–33.

David Sussman, "Defining Torture," *Case Western Reserve Journal of International Law*, 2006, 37, 2/3, pp. 225–30.

David Sussman, "'Torture Lite': A Response," *Ethics and International Affairs*, 2009, pp. 63–7.

David Thurston, "The Rise and Fall of Judicial Torture: Why It Was Used in Early Modern Europe and the Soviet Union," *Human Rights Review*, July–September 2000, pp. 26–58.

Christopher W. Tindale, "The Logic of Torture: A Critical Examination," *Social Theory and Practice*, 1996, 22:3, pp. 349–74.

Christopher W. Tindale, "Tragic Choices: Reaffirming Absolutes in the Torture Debate," *International Journal of Applied Philosophy*, 2005, 19:2, pp. 209–22.

William Twining, "Bentham on Torture," *Northern Ireland Legal Quarterly,* 1973, 24: 3, pp. 305–57.

William Twining and Barrie Paskins, "Torture and Philosophy," *Aristotelian Society,* 1978, 52, pp. 143–68.

Sumner B. Twiss, "Torture, Justification, and Human Rights: Toward an Absolute Proscription," *Human Rights Quarterly,* 2007, 29, pp. 346–67.

Marcelo N. Viñar, "Civilization and torture: beyond the medical and psychiatric approach," *International Review of the Red Cross,* September 2007, Vol. 89, No. 867, pp. 619–33.

Alan Wertheimer, "What is Consent? And is it Important?" *Buffalo Criminal Law Review,* 2000, 3, pp. 557–83.

Eric Wiland, "The Ethics of Torture and Terrorism," *Review Journal of Political Philosophy,* 2008, Vol. 6, No. 1, pp. 139–52.

J. Jeremy Wisnewski, "A Defense of Cannibalism," *Public Affairs Quarterly*, July 2004, 18:3.

J. Jeremy Wisnewski, "Murder, Cannibalism, and Indirect Suicide: A Philosophical Study of a Recent Case," *Philosophy in the Contemporary World,* Spring, 2007, 14:1.

J. Jeremy Wisnewski, "It's About Time: Defusing the Ticking Bomb Argument," *International Journal of Applied Philosophy,* 2008, 22:1, pp. 103–16.

J. Jeremy Wisnewski, "Unwarranted Torture Warrants: A Critique of the Dershowitz Proposal," *Journal of Social Philosophy,* Summer 2008, Vol. XXXIX, No. 2.

J. Jeremy Wisnewski, "Hearing the Still-Ticking-Bomb: A Reply," *Journal of Applied Philosophy,* 2009, Vol. 26, No. 2.

J. Jeremy Wisnewski, "What we owe the dead," *Journal of Applied Philosophy,* 2009, Vol. 26, No. 1.

J. Jeremy Wisnewski and Henry Jacoby, "Failures of Sight: An Argument for Moral Perception," *American Philosophical Quarterly* (co-authored with Henry Jacoby) 3, July 2007, 44.

Jessica Wolfendale, "Training Torturers: A Critique of the 'Ticking Bomb' Argument," *Social Theory and Practice,* April 2006, 32:2.

Jessica Wolfendale, "Stoic Warriors and Stoic Torturers: The Moral Psychology of Military Torture," *South African Journal of Philosophy,* 2006, 25:1, pp. 62–76.

Jessica Wolfendale, "The Myth of 'Torture Lite'," *Ethics & International Affairs,* 2009, pp. 47–61.

Niels Steenstrup Zeeberg, "Torture—a public health puzzle in Europe," *Torture Supplemental 1,* 1998, pp. 25–44.

Books

Giorgio Agamben, *Homo Sacer: Sovereign Power and Bare Life,* trans. Daniel Heller-Roazen, Stanford: Stanford University Press, 1998.

Giorgio Agamben, *State of Exception,* trans. Kevin Attell, Chicago and London: University of Chicago Press, 2005.

Matthew Alexander, *How To Break A Terrorist: The U.S. Interrogators Who Used Brains, Not Brutality, To Take Down the Deadliest Man In Iraq*, New York and London: Free Press, 2008.

Henri Alleg, *The Question*, Lincoln and London: University of Nebraska Press, 2006.

Fritz Allhoff, *Terrorism, Ticking Time-Bombs, and Torture*, Chicago: University of Chicago Press, forthcoming.

Archdiocese of Sao Paulo, *Torture in Brazil: A Shocking Report on the Pervasive Use of Torture by Brazilian Military Governments, 1964–1979*, New York: Random House, 1986.

Hannah Arendt, *The Origins of Totalitarianism*, New York and London: Harcourt, Inc., 1985.

Hannah Arendt, *The Human Condition,* 2nd edn, Chicago and London: University of Chicago Press, 1998.

Hannah Arendt, *Eichman in Jerusalem,* New York: Penguin Classics, 2006.

Aristotle, *The Complete Works of Aristotle* (two vols), Princeton: Princeton University Press, 1984.

J. L. Austin, *Philosophical Papers*, Oxford and New York: Oxford University Press, 1961.

Mike Bagaric and Julie Clarke, *Torture: When the Unthinkable is Morally Permissable*, Albany: State University of New York Press, 2007.

Robert Bartlett, *Trial by Fire and Water: The Medieval Judicial Ordeal*, Oxford: Oxford University Press, 1986.

Moazzam Begg, *Enemy Combatant: My Imprisonment at Guantanamo, Bagram, and Kandahar*, London: New Press, 2006.

Ahcene Boulesbaa, *The U. N. Convention on Torture and the Prospects for Enforcement (International Studies in Human Rights)*, New York: Springer, 1999.

Bob Brecher, *Torture and the Ticking Bomb,* Malden and Oxford: Blackwell Publishing, 2007.

Susan Brownmiller, *Against our Will*, New York: Fawcett Books, 1975.

Judith Butler, *Precarious Life: The Powers of Mourning and Violence*, London and New York: Verso, 2006.

Judith Butler, *Frames of War: When Is Life Grievable?* London and New York: Verso, 2009.

Antonio Cassese, *Inhuman States: Imprisonment, Detention and Torture in Europe Today*, Boston: Polity Press, 1996.

Gérard Chaliand and Arnaud Blin, *The History of Terrorism: From Antiquity to al Qaeda*, California: University of California Press, 2007.

John Conroy, *Unspeakable Acts, Ordinary People: The Dynamics of Torture*, Berkeley: University of California Press, 2000.

Angela Y. Davis, *Are Prisons Obsolete?,* New York: Seven Stories Press, 2003.

Angela Y. Davis, *Abolition Democracy: Beyond Empire, Prisons, and Torture*, New York: Seven Stories Press, 2005.

Alan M. Dershowitz, *Why Terrorism Works: Understanding the Threat, Responding to the Challenge,* New Haven, CT: Yale University Press, 2002.

John Doris, *Lack of Character: Personality and Moral Behavior*, Cambridge: Cambridge University Press, 2002.

Stephen F. Eisenman, *The Abu Ghraib Effect*, London: Reaktion Books, 2007.

Peter Elsass, *Treating Victims of Torture and Violence: Theoretical, Cross-Cultural, and Clinical Implications*, New York: New York University Press, 1997.

John Hart Ely, *Democracy and Distrust,* Cambridge, MA: Harvard University Press, 1980.

Malcolm D. Evans and Rod Morgan, *Preventing Torture: A Study of the European Convention for the Prevention of Torture and Inhuman or Degrading Treatment or Punishment*, Oxford: Oxford University Press, 1998.

Susan Faludi, *The Terror Dream: Fear and Fantasy in Post 9/11 America*, New York: Metropolitan Books, 2007.

Joel Feinberg, *Harm to Others,* New York and Oxford: Oxford University Press, 1987.

Marguerite Feitlowitz, *A Lexicon of Terror: Argentina and the Legacies of Torture*, Oxford: Oxford University Press, 1999.

John Martin Fischer (ed.), *The Metaphysics of Death,* Stanford: Stanford University Press, 1993.

Michel Foucault, *Discipline and Punish,* New York: Vintage Press, 1977.

Michel Foucault, *Abnormal: Lectures at the College de France, 1974–1975,* New York: Picador Press, 1999.

Raimond Gaita, *Thinking About Torture*, Oxford and New York: Routledge Press, 2007.

Antonio Gallonio, *Torturers and Torments of the Christian Martyrs*, Los Angeles: Feral House, 2004.

Paul Gilbert, *New Terror, New Wars*, Washington, DC: Georgetown University Press, 2003.

Yuval Ginbar, *Why Not Torture Terrorists: Moral, Practical, and Legal Aspects of the 'Ticking Bomb' Justification for Torture*, Oxford and New York: Oxford University Press, 2008.

Jonathan Glover, *Humanity: A Moral History of the 20th century*, New Haven and London: Yale University Press, 1999.

Ariel Glucklich, *Sacred Pain: Hurting the Body for the Sake of the Soul*, New York: Oxford University Press, 2001.

Peter Gottschalk and Gabriel Greenberg, *Islamophobia: Making Muslims the Enemy*, Latham and Boulder: Rowman and Littlefield Publishers, Inc., 2008.

Philip Gourevitch and Errol Morris, *Standard Operating Procedure*, New York: Penguin Press, 2008.

Amos N. Guiora, *Constitutional Limits On Coercive Interrogation*, Oxford and New York: Oxford University Press, 2008.

Michael Haas, *George W. Bush, War Criminal?: The Bush Administration's Liability for 265 War Crimes*, Westport, CT and London: Praeger, 2009.

Jennifer K. Harbury, *Truth, Torture, and the American Way: The History and Consequences of U.S. Involvement in Torture*, Boston: Beacon Press, 2005.

Adolf Hitler, *Mein Kampf*, New York: Stackpole Sons Publishers, 1939.

Martha K. Huggins, Mika Haritos-Fatouros and Philip G. Zimbardo, *Violence Workers: Police Torturers and Murderers Reconstruct Brazilian Atrocities*, Berkeley and Los Angeles: University of California Press, 2002.

Michael Ignatieff, *The Lesser Evil: Political Ethics in an Age of Terror*, Princeton: Princeton University Press, 2004.

Richard Jackson, *Writing the War on Terrorism: Language, Politics and Counter-Terrorism*, Manchester and New York: Manchester University Press, 2005.

Derek Jeffreys, *Spirituality and the Ethics of Torture*, New York: Palgrave MacMillan, 2009.

Paul W. Kahn, *Sacred Violence: Torture, Terror and Sovereignty*, Ann Arbor: University of Michigan Press, 2008.

Immanuel Kant, *Metaphysics of Morals*, Cambridge and New York: Cambridge University Press, 1996.

Immanuel Kant, *Groundwork for the Metaphysics of Morals*, Cambridge and New York: Cambridge University Press, 1997.

Colleen Elizabeth Kelley, *Post-9/11 American Presidential Rhetoric: A Study of Protofacist Discourse*, Lanham and Boulder: Lexington Books, 2007.

Douglas Kellner, *From 9/11 to Terror War: The Dangers of the Bush Legacy*, Lanham and Boulder: Rowman and Littlefield Publishers, Inc., 2003.

Naomi Klein, *The Shock Doctrine: The Rise of Disaster Capitalism*, New York: Picador Press, 2007.

Arthur Koestler, *Darkness At Noon: A Novel*, trans. Daphne Hardy, New York and London: Scribner Press, 1968.

Murat Kurnaz, *Five Years of My Life: An Innocent Man in Guantanamo*, New York: Palgrave MacMillan, 2008.

John H. Langbein, *Torture and the Law of Proof: Europe and England in the Ancien Regime*, Chicago: University of Chicago Press, 2006.

Bibb Latane and J.M. Darley, *The Unresponsive Bystander: Why Doesn't He Help?*, New York: Appleton-Century-Crofts, 1970.

Marnia Lazreg, *Torture and the Twilight of Empire*, Princeton: Princeton University Press, 2008.

Jack Levin, *Sociological Snapshots*, Lanham and Boulder: Lexington Books, 1990.

Robert Jay Lifton, *The Nazi Doctors: Medical Killing and the Psychology of Genocide*, Chicago: Basic Books, 1986.

Bruce Lincoln, *Religion, Empire, and Torture: The Case of Achaemenian Persia, with a Postscript on Abu Ghraib*, Chicago: University of Chicago Press, 2007.

Joseph McCabe, *The History Of Torture: A Study Of Cruelty, The Ugliest Impulse In Man*, New York: Kessinger Publishing, 2007.

Alfred W. McCoy, *A Question of Torture: CIA Interrogation, from the Cold War to the War on Terror*, New York: Owl Books, 2006.

Chris Mackey and Greg Miller, *The Interrogators*, New York: Back Bay Books, 2004.

Catharine A. MacKinnon, *Are Women Human? and Other International Dialogues*, Cambridge, MA and London: The Belknap Press of Harvard University Press, 2006.

Jonathan Mahler, *The Challenge: Hamden v. Rumsfeld and the Fight Over Presidential Power*, New York: Farrar, Straus and Giroux, 2008.

Daniel P. Mannix, *The History of Torture*, Phoenix Mill: Sutton Publishing, 2003.

Joseph Margulies, *Guantánamo and the Abuse of Presidential Power*, New York: Simon and Schuster Paperbacks, 2006.

Richard Matthews, *The Absolute Violation: Why Torture Must Be Prohibited*, Montreal and Kingston: McGill Queen's University Press, 2008.

Larry May, *War Crimes and Just War*, Cambridge: Cambridge University Press, 2007.

Jane Mayer, *The Dark Side*, New York: Doubleday, 2008.

Alec Mellor, *La Torture*, Paris: Horizons litteraires, 1949.

Mitchell B. Merback, *The Thief, the Cross and the Wheel: Pain and the Spectacle of Punishment in Medieval and Renaissance Europe*, Chicago and London: University of Chicago Press, 1998.

Steven H. Miles, *Oath Betrayed: Torture, Medical Complicity, and the War on Terror*, New York: Random House, 2006.

Stanley Milgram, *Obedience to Authority*, New York: Harper Perennial, 1974.

James Miller, *The Passions of Michel Foucault*, New York: Doubleday, 1993.

Kate Millett, *The Politics of Cruelty: An Essay on the Literature of Political Imprisonment*, New York and London: W.W. Norton and Company, 1994.

Richard Mills, *Suspended Animation: Pain, Pleasure, and Punishment in Medieval Culture*, London: Reaktion Press, 2005.

Mark J. Osiel, *Mass Atrocity, Ordinary Evil, and Hannah Arendt: Criminal Consciousness in Argentina's Dirty War*, New Haven: Yale University Press, 2001.

Michael Otterman, *American Torture: From the Cold War to Abu Ghraib and Beyond*, London: Pluto Press, 2007.

John Perry, *Torture: Religious Ethics and National Security*, Maryknoll: Orbis Books, 2005.

Edward Peters, *Torture*, Philadelphia: University of Pennsylvania Press, 1985.

Steven Poole, *Unspeak: How Words Become a Message, How Weapons Become a Message, and How That Message Becomes Reality*, New York: Grove Press, 2006.

Lila Rajiva, *Language of Empire: Abu Ghraib and the American Media*, New York: Monthly Review Press, 2005.

Darius M. Rejali, *Torture and Modernity: Self, Society, and State in Modern Iran*, Boulder, CO: Westview Press, 1984.

Darius M. Rejali, *Torture and Democracy*, Princeton: Princeton University Press, 2007.

David Rodin, *War, Torture and Terrorism: Ethics and War in the 21st Century*, Boston and Oxford: Blackwell Publishing Limited, 2007.

Richard Rorty, *Contingency, Irony, and Solidarity*, New York and Cambridge: Cambridge University Press, 1989.

Malise Ruthven, *Torture: The Grand Conspiracy*, London: Weidenfeld and Nicolson, 1978.

Steven Salaita, *Anti-Arab Racism in the USA: Where It Comes from and What It Means for Politics Today*, London and Ann Arbor, MI: Pluto Press, 2006.

Philippe Sands, *Torture Team: Rumsfeld's Memo and the Betrayal of American Values*, New York: Palgrave MacMillan, 2008.

Elaine Scarry, *The Body in Pain: The Making and Unmaking of the World*, New York: Oxford University Press, 1985.

John Searle, *The Construction of Social Reality*, New York: Free Press, 1997.

Laura J. Shepherd, *Gender, Violence & Security*, London and New York: Zed Books, 2008.

Lisa Silverman, *Tortured Subjects: Pain, Truth, and the Body in Early Modern France*, Chicago and London: University of Chicago Press, 2001.

Peter Singer, *The President of Good and Evil*, New York: Dutton, 2004.

Susan Sontag, *Regarding the Pain of Others*, New York: Picador, 2003.

Ervin Staub, *The Roots of Evil: the Origins of Genocide and Other Group Violence*, Cambridge: Cambridge University Press, 1989.

Uwe Steinhoff, *On the Ethics of War and Terrorism*, Oxford: Oxford University Press, 2007.

Robert D. Stolorow, *Trauma and Human Experience: Autobiographical, Psychoanalytic and Philosophical Reflections*, New York and London: The Analytic Press, 2007.

Peter Suedfeld, *Psychology and Torture*, London: Taylor & Francis, 1990.

Charles Taylor, *Sources of the Self*, Cambridge: Harvard University Press, 1992.

Claude Thomas, *At Hell's Gate: A Soldier's Journey from War to Peace*, Boston: Shambhala Publications, 2004.

Guus Van Der Veer, *Counselling and Therapy with Refugees and Victims of Trauma: Psychological Problems of Victims of War, Torture and Repression*, New York: Wiley, 1999.

Patrick Wall, *Pain: The Science of Suffering*, New York: Columbia University Press, 2000.

Michael Walzer, *Just and Unjust Wars: A Moral Argument with Historical Illustrations*, New York: Basic Books, 1977.

Daniel Wegner, *The Illusion of Conscious Will*, Cambridge, MA: MIT Press, 2002.

Alan Wertheimer, *Consent to Sexual Relations*, Cambridge: Cambridge University Press, 2004.

Lawrence Weschler, *A Miracle, A Universe: Settling Accounts with Torturers,* Chicago: University of Chicago Press, 1990.

Kristian Williams, *American Methods: Torture and the Logic of Domination,* Cambridge, MA: South End Press, 2006.

John P. Wilson, *Broken Spirits: The Treatment of Traumatized Asylum Seekers, Refugees, War and Torture Victims,* London: Routledge, 2004.

J. Jeremy Wisnewski, *Wittgenstein and Ethical Inquiry,* London: Continuum, 2007.

J. Jeremy Wisnewski, *Heidegger: A Beginner's Guide,* One World Press, forthcoming 2011.

J. Jeremy Wisnewski and R.D. Emerick, *The Ethics of Torture,* London: Continuum, 2009.

Ludwig Wittgenstein, *Philosophical Investigations,* Malden and Oxford: Blackwell Publishing, 1953.

Ludwig Wittgenstein, *On Certainty,* ed. G.E.M. Anscombe and G.H. von Wright, trans. Denis Paul and G.E.M. Anscomb, New York: Harper & Row, 1972.

Jessica Wolfendale, *Torture and the Military Profession,* New York: Palgrave Macmillan, 2007.

Robert Wright, *The Moral Animal,* New York: Vintage Press, 1995.

Philip Zimbardo, *The Lucifer Effect: Understanding How Good People Turn Evil,* New York: Random House, 2007.

DVDs

"Beyond Torture: The Gulag of Pitesti, Romania." *Wild Canary Sights and Sounds.*

"Gitmo: The New Rules of War." *ATMO,* 2005.

"The Bush Crimes Commission Hearings." *International Commission of Inquiry on Crimes Against Humanity Committed By the Bush Administration.*

"The Dark Art of Interrogation." *A&E Television Network.* 2005.

"The Road to Guantánamo." *Sony Pictures Home Entertainment.* 2006.

"The Unexplained: Surviving Pain and Torture." *A&E Television Network.* 1997.

Government Documents, Treaties, and Resolutions

P. Bauer, Statement on interrogation practices to the House Committee on the Armed Services, 2006, July 31.(Online) Retrieved May 28, 2007, from http://www.amnestyusa.org/denounce_torture/statement_on_interrogation.pdf

Ian Brownlie and Guy S. Goodwin-Gill, *Basic Documents on Human Rights,* New York: Oxford University Press, 2002.

— *Commentary on the United Nations Convention on the Rights of the Child, Article 37: Prohibition of Torture, Death Penalty, Life Imprisonment and Deprivation of Liberty,* Brill Academic Publishers, 2006.

—*Conclusions and Recommendations of the UN Committee Against Torture: Eleventh to Twenty–Second Sessions (1993–1999)* (Raoul Wallenberg Institute Series of Intergovernmental Human Rights Documentation), Springer, 2000.

—*Essential Handbook for KGB Agents*, London: Industrial Information Index.

—Memorandum for Alberto R. Gonzales, Counsel to the President from US Department of Justice, Office of Legal Counsel," In *Civil Liberties vs. National Security in a Post–9/11 World*. Darmer, M. Katherine B., Robert M. Baird and Stuart E. Rosenbaum (eds), Amherst, NY: Prometheus Books, 2004, pp. 303–16.

—CIA: *Human Resource Exploitation Training Manual*, Government Document. Available through ACLU, 1983.

—CIA: *KUBARK Manual*. Government Document, 1963. Available at http://www.gwu.edu/~nsarchiv/NSAEBB/NSAEBB27/01–01.htm, as well as through the ACLU.

—*ICRC Report on the Treatment of Fourteen 'High Value Detainees' in CIA Custody*, February 2007

—*Landau Commission Report*, in *The Phenomenon of Torture*, ed. William F. Schulz, Philadelphia: University of Pennsylvania Press, 2007, pp. 267–74.

Department of the Army, *U.S. Army Intelligence and Interrogation Handbook: The Official Guide on Prisoner Interrogation*, Guilford, DE: The Lyons Press, 2005.

Karen J. Greenberg, *The Torture Papers: The Road to Abu Ghraib*, Cambridge: Cambridge University Press, 2005.

Jameel Jaffer and Amrit Singh, *Administration of Torture: A Documentary Record from Washington to Abu Ghraib and Beyond*, Irvington, NY: Columbia University Press, 2007.

H.L. Pohlman, *Terrorism and the Constitution: The Post-9/11 Cases*, New York: Rowman and Littlefield, 2008.

W. Michael Reisman and Chris T. Anoniou (eds), *The Laws of War: A Comprehensive Collection of Primary Documents on International Laws Governing Armed Conflict*, New York: Vintage Books, 1994.

Adam Roberts and Richard Guelff, *Documents on the Laws of War*, Oxford: Clarendon Press, 1989.

Christopher H. Smith, *U.S. Policy Towards Victims of Torture: Hearing Before the Committee on International Relations, U.S. House of Representatives*, Darby, PA: Diane Pub Co., 1999.

Supreme Court of the United States, *Rasul v. Bush*, 542 U. S. 466, 2004.

Supreme Court of the United States, *Hamdi v. Rumsfeld*, 542 U. S. 507, 2004.

Supreme Court of the United States, *Hamdan v. Rumsfeld*, 548 U. S. 557, 2006.

Supreme Court of the United States, *Boumediene et al v. Bush*, 553 U. S., 2008.

US Department of Justice, Memoranda. All memoranda are available electronically from the American Civil Liberties Union. http://www.aclu.org/accountability/released.html

News Sources

"Alleged Torture Photos Slated for Destruction" *The Washington Independent*, July 7, 2009, http://washingtonindependent.com/49932/alleged-torture-photos-slated-for-destruction

"Attorney general leaning toward torture inquiry," July 16, 2006, *The Baltimore Sun*, http://www.baltimoresun.com/news/nation-world/bal-te.brief-s120jul12,0,3979540.story

"Cambodia's torture prison survivors testify at tribunal," July 3, 2009, ABC Radio Australia, http://www.radioaustralia.net.au/connectasia/stories/200907/s2615923.htm

"Cops Accused of Torturing Teenager," *Mohave Daily Minor*, Dec. 19, 1986

"Claims Filed for Alleged Torture by 'Stun Guns' Huntington Beach Police Accused of Cruel Tactics," Dec. 26, *Los Angeles Times*.

"Huntington Park Department Leads Southeast in Police Brutality Claims," July 6, 1986, *Los Angeles Times*, Dec. 19, 1986

"Interview with Dick Cheney," *State of the Union with John King*, CNN, March 15, 2009.

"Iran: Detainees Describe Beatings, Pressure to Confess," *Human Rights Watch*, July 8, 2009.

http://www.hrw.org/en/news/2009/07/08/iran-detainees-describe-beatings-pressure-confess

"The Lingering Effects of Torture: After Guantanamo, Scientists and Advocates Study Detainees," ABC News, July 3, 2009www.abcnews.go.com/Technology/story?id=7986990&page=1

"Mexico Accused of Torture in Drug War: Army Using Brutality To Fight Trafficking, Rights Groups Say," *Washington Post*, July 9, 2009 http://www.washingtonpost.com/wp-dyn/content/article/2009/07/08/AR2009070804197.html

"No Torture. No Exceptions." *The Washington Monthly,* January/February/March, 2008.

"Obama on AIG Rage, Recession, Challenges," *60 Minutes*, March 22, 2009.

"Pakistan torture victims plan legal action to force inquiry," *The Guardian*, July 8, 2009,

http://www.guardian.co.uk/politics/2009/jul/08/pakistan-torture-inquiry-mi5-mi6

"Tony Blair knew of secret policy on terror interrogations," *The Guardian*, June 18, 2009, http://www.guardian.co.uk/politics/2009/jun/18/tony-blair-secret-torture-policy

Mark Bowden, "The Dark Art of Interrogation," *The Atlantic Monthly*, October 2003, pp. 51–76.

Stephen Budiansky, "Truth Extraction," *The Atlantic Monthly,* June 2005, pp. 32–5.

David Cole, "The Torture Veto," *The Nation,* March 31, 2008.

John Cooper, "German Racked by torture controversy," *The Guardian,* February 28, 2003.

Mark Danner, "US Torture: Voices from the Black Sites," *The New York Review of Books,* April 9, 2009, Vol. 56, No. 6.

Mark Danner, "The Red Cross Torture Report: What It Means," *The New York Review of Books,* April 30, 2009, Vol. 56, No. 7.

Ariel Dorfman, "The Price we pay for Paradise is Torture," *The Australian*, May 10, 2004.

Dan Eggen and Paul Kane, "On Day 2, Democrats See Change in Mukasey; Nominee Endorses President's Positions," *The Washington Post*, Oct. 19, 2007, pp. A1.

Dan Eggen, "Bush Approved Meetings on Interrogation Techniques; President's Comments to ABC News Prove Top-Level Involvement in Allowing Harsh Coercion," *Washington Post*, April 12, 2008, A3.

James Glanz, "Torture is Often a Temptation and Almost Never Work," *The New York Times*, May 9, 2004.

Tim Golden, "In U.S. Report, Brutal Details of 2 Afghan Inmates' Deaths," *The New York Times*, May 20, 2005, A1.

Adam Hochschild, "What's in a Word? Torture," *The New York Times*, May 23, 2004.

Michael Levin, "The Case for Torture," *Newsweek*, June 7, 1982.

Dahlia Lithwick, "Getting Away with Torture; Legal Maneuvering has shielded those responsible for conditions at Guantanamo Bay," *Newsweek*, New York: May 5, 2008. Vol 151, No. 18.

Steven Lee Myers "Veto of Bill on C.I.A. Tactics Affirms Bush's Legacy," *The New York Times*, March 9, 2008, A1.

Tony Norman, "Making Torture the American Way," *Pittsburgh Post-Gazette*, March 11, 2008, A2.

Dana Priest and Barton Gellam, "US Decries Abuse but Defends Interrogations" *The Washington Post*, December 26, 2002.

Frank Rich, "The Real-life '24' of Summer 2008," *The New York Times*, July 13, 2008, WK 12.

Helen Thomas, "Bush Admits he Approved Torture," *Seattle Post-Intelligencer*, May 2, 2008, B5.

"One-third support torture," BBC News, last accessed on 17 August 2007 http://news.bbc.co.uk/1/hi/in_depth/6063386.stm#table

Reports from Non-Governmental Organizations

2003–2007 Report on Hate Crimes and Discrimination Against Arab Americans, American-Arab Anti-Discrimination Committee Research Institute, 89.

Amnesty International, *Report on Torture*, New York: Farrar, Straus and Giroux, 1975.

Amnesty International, *Torture Worldwide: An Affront to Human Dignity*, New York: Amnesty International, 2000.

Break Them Down, Report by Physicians for Human Rights, Washington, DC, 2005.

Robert B. Edgerton and Keith F. Otterbein, *The Worldwide Practice of Torture: A Preliminary Report*, Lewiston, NY: Edwin Mellen Pr, 2007.

Leif Holmström (ed), *Conclusions and Recommendations of the UN Committee against Torture*, The Hague: Martinus Nijhoff Publishers, 2000.

ICRC Report on the Treatment of Fourteen 'High Value Detainees' in CIA Custody, February 2007.

"Independent Monitoring of Human Rights in Places of Detention in the Middle East and North Africa." *Torture: Journal on Rehabilitation of Torture Victims and Prevention of Torture,* ed. Henrik Marcussen, Vol. 19, Supplement 1, 2009.

Report on Hate Crimes and Discrimination Against Arab Americans: The Post-September 11 Backlash, American-Arab Anti-Discrimination Committee Research Institute, 129.

"Rethinking The Psychology Of Torture: A Preliminary Report from Former Interrogators and Research Psychologists," Psychologists for Social Responsibility, www.psysr.org

Selected Useful Websites

American Civil Liberties Union: Accountability for Torture
http://www.aclu.org/accountability/released.html
A resource for all of the de-classified memos released under the Freedom of Information Act by the Bush administration.

The Avalon Project at Yale Law School
http://www.yale.edu/lawweb/avalon/20th.htm
An excellent resource for full texts of treaties, resolutions, court rulings, and more (including the Geneva Conventions, the UN Convention against Torture, and more).

Berlin Center for the Treatment of Torture Victims [in German]
http://www.folteropfer.de/

Canadian Center for Victims of Torture
http://www.ccvt.org/links.html

Center for Victims f Torture
http://www.cvt.org/

Human Rights First: End Torture Now
http://www.humanrightsfirst.org/us_law/etn/index.asp

International Committee of the Red Cross
http://www.icrc.org/eng
An excellent resource for many facets of torture. See in particular the available articles.

International Rehabilitation Council for Torture Victims
http://www.irct.org/publications/preventing-torture-within-the-fight-against-terror.aspx
The source of the 'Preventing torture in the fight against terror' Newsletter, which is available at no cost at the above site.

Resources for Torture Survivors, Refugees, Detainees, & Asylum-Seekers
http://www.kspope.com/torvic/torture.php
An excellent site containing links to resources for victims of torture.

Survivors International
http://www.survivorsintl.org

World Organization Against Torture
http://www.omct.org

Index